The Handbook of Research in Middle Level Education

edited by

Vincent A. Anfara, Jr.
Temple University

80 Mason Street
Greenwich, Connecticut 06830

Library of Congress Cataloging-in-Publication Data available

Handbook of research in middle level education / edited by Vincent A. Anfara.
p. cm.
Includes bibliographical references and index.
ISBN 1-930608-73-X
1. Middle school education--United States. 2. Middle schools--United States. 3. Educational change--United States. I. Anfara, Vincent A.
LB1623.5 .H36 2001
373.236--dc21
2001004278

Printed in the United States of America

The Handbook of Research in Middle Level Education

Research in Middle Level Education Special Interest Group

The purpose of the SIG is to improve, promote, and disseminate educational research reflecting early adolescence and middle level education.

+++

Officers 2000–2002

PRESIDENT	Barbara Whinery, University of Northern Colorado
PROGRAM CHAIR/ PRESIDENT-ELECT	Vincent A. Anfara, Jr., Temple University
VICE PRESIDENT	Nora Alder, Virginia Commonwealth University
SECRETARY	Kimberly Hartman, University of North Carolina, Charlotte
TREASURER	Nancy Mizelle, Georgia College and State University

+++

Membership Information

Contact:

Nancy Mizelle
Georgia College and State University
School of Education
Milledgeville, GA 31061

or

AERA Subscription Department
1230 17th Street NW
Washington, DC 20036-3078

CONTENTS

INTRODUCTION

SETTING THE STAGE: AN INTRODUCTION TO MIDDLE LEVEL EDUCATION

Vincent A. Anfara, Jr.

Should the developmental needs of the learner dictate the curricular and instructional practices of a school? Should these developmental needs also affect the structure of schools as we know them, necessitating the creation of new programs like advisor-advisee, more flexible daily schedules, alternative policies regarding such things as student assessment, and the like? If you are reading this book, your answers are probably a resounding "Yes!" The middle school movement represents a commitment to base school practices on the developmental characteristics of students who are 10 to 14 years of age.

The 1980s and the 1990s were characterized by an increased recognition of young adolescence as a developmental period and the need for developmentally appropriate educational opportunities. In this Introduction to *The Handbook of Research in Middle Level Education* I trace the historical development of the middle school, assess the rationale for middle schools, and look at some of the recent indictments that have been levied against this reform effort. It is precisely because of these indictments that we must step back and assess what we know, how we know it, and whether or not the theory of middle level reform has had any effect on the real world of middle schools. In short, have our middle schools changed in name only? It is my hope that this introduction will give the novice to middle level educational issues a basis to understand the more complex issues and problems that are discussed in chapters one through nine.

CONSTRUCTING THE MIDDLE SCHOOL: AN HISTORICAL JOURNEY

In 1989 the Carnegie Task Force on Education of Young Adolescents noted that "young adolescents face significant turning points" (p. 8). While *Turning Points* seemed to set the stage for continuing discussion and debate on the nature and character of middle level education, the call for middle level reform was not new. Jackson, the Project Director of the Carnegie Task Force, noted: "Nevertheless, some educators have commented that there is very little new in this report. 'We are already doing that' is a common response to many of the recommendations in *Turning Points* from schools across the nation" (1990, p. 1).

Earlier reports called for the need for something different to happen in the way school in general was organized. Cognizant of this need, the Committee on College Entrance Requirements, commissioned by the National Education Association (1899), wrote that "the most necessary and far-reaching reforms in secondary education must begin in the seventh and eighth grades in our schools" (p. 659). The commission noted that the seventh grade was a "natural turning point in the pupil's life, as the age of adolescence demands new methods and [a] wiser direction" (p. 659).

While much of the debate centered around whether or not to keep eight years of elementary school and four years of secondary schooling (see Gruhn & Douglass, 1956), high dropout rates were blamed on the difficult transition from elementary to high school. The first response to the problematic eight-four organization of schools was the creation of the junior high. Appearing in the first decade of the twentieth century, junior highs were hailed for their ability to prevent dropouts and to prepare students for the job market. The hope was that the curriculum, as well as the students, would be invigorated by the new format.

At the beginning of the 1900s, early psychologists, like G. Stanley Hall (1905), noted that schools needed to address the developmental needs of students. Hall's studies influenced Americans to accept that the field of education should be grounded in psychology and that adolescence should be given scientific study. Van Til, Vars, and Lounsbury (1961) wrote that "the development of the new science of individual differences in the early twentieth century provided another justification for the organization of the junior high" (p. 18). In 1918, the Commission on the Reorganization of Secondary Education recommended the new organization in its annual report:

> We, therefore, recommend a reorganization of the school system whereby the first six years shall be devoted to elementary education designed to meet

> the needs of pupils approximately 6 to 12 years of age, and the second six years to secondary education designed to meet the needs of pupils approximately 12 to 18 years of age. The six years devoted to secondary education may well be divided into two periods which may be designated as the junior and senior periods. (pp. 12–13)

What is important for us to remember from this junior high period is the recognition that schools were to understand and respond to the particular nature of the early adolescent while attempting to continue the influence of the home (see Koos, 1927). According to George and Alexander (1993), "the junior high emerged, originally, as an attempt to satisfy the call for a richer curriculum than the elementary school was able to offer, and a more personal atmosphere than the high school was able to develop" (p. 285). Indeed, the uniqueness of the student provided the foundation upon which debates about the nature of the school program would flourish (see Cuban, 1992, for a more thorough treatment of the development of the junior high).

By the 1960s much of the literature on the junior high noted that such schools had turned into "miniature high schools" (Johnson, Dupuis, Musial, & Hall, 1994). Junior highs had become "pale imitations of senior high schools" (Grooms, 1967). Indeed, the call to reform junior highs was heard as early as the 1920s, within two decades of their founding. While the junior high movement was an effort to separate the early adolescents and to provide programs uniquely designed for them, a knowledge base was not available to sustain the uniqueness of the reform movement; thus, the movement gradually moved toward a subject orientation and more closely imitated what had existed in the past (Lewis, 1992, p. 9). Echoing this assessment, Alexander and George (1981) stated that "unequivocally, many junior high schools became in time almost duplicate copies of their senior high schools in terms of credit and grading systems, methods of teaching, time schedules and student activities, so that sixth graders in June became high school students in September without adequate readiness or maturity" (p. 11). In effect, aided by additional sociological and psychological research during the 1950s and 1960s (see Bossing, 1954; Gruhn & Douglass, 1956; Lounsbury, 1960; Tanner, 1962), educators judged the junior high school organization as inappropriate for young people who are psychologically, socially, mentally, emotionally, and physically at a very different place than adolescents. Noar (1961), a junior high educator and advocate of adolescents, stated, "The junior high schools originally founded to meet the need for education on a level intermediate between elementary school and high school have generally been accused of falling short of helping children for whom they are designed" (p. 10). Eventually, by the 1960s the call to reform the junior high had evolved into a call for the creation of the middle school.

It is precisely the uniqueness of these "in-between" years that led many educators, including Eichhorn (1966), to favor the creation of middle schools to serve students in transition from childhood to adolescence. According to Scales (1991), the uniqueness of this developmental period is characterized by seven needs, including the need for: (1) positive social interaction with adults and peers, (2) structure and clear limits, (3) physical activity, (4) creative expression, (5) competence and achievement, (6) meaningful participation in both family and school, and (7) opportunities for self-definition. Or as Stevenson (1992) stated, "Every child wants to believe in himself or herself as a successful person; every youngster wants to be liked and respected; every youngster wants physical exercise and freedom to move; and youngsters want life to be just" (p. 123).

While middle schools had modest beginnings in the early 1950s and 1960s, their incredible growth in numbers began in the mid- and late-1960s. By the mid-1970s, most of the eastern United States had established programs and facilities which reflected the increased knowledge of the educational needs of young people 10 to 14 years of age. Once again, an altered school district organizational pattern—an elementary unit of grades kindergarten through five, a middle school grouping of grades six through eight, and a high school unit of grades nine through twelve—was initiated. It is interesting to note that some school districts never fully adopted the idea of a middle school and retained many of their junior highs alongside middle schools that were newly created.

In the midst of this debate, the National Education Association (NEA) defined middle school as: "The school which stands academically between elementary and high school, is housed separately (ideally in a building especially designed for this purpose), and offers at least three years of schooling beginning with either grade five or six" (1965, p. 5). In 1995, the National Middle School Association (NMSA) would define the middle schools as "mainly 6–8 schools, but also 5–8, 5–7, and 7–8; based on developmental needs (social and academic) of young adolescents, organized by interdisciplinary teams, with flexible organizational structures, using varied learning and teaching approaches" (p. 1).

SOLIDIFYING THE MIDDLE SCHOOL CONCEPT: THE NEED FOR A CLEAR RATIONALE

In 1969 the Council on the Emerging Adolescent Learner was established by the Association for Supervision and Curriculum Development (ASCD). That council was followed by both formal and informal working groups until 1974 when the Executive Council of ASCD appointed a group and charged them with "developing a paper for the Association identifying the rationale and significance of the American middle school and stressing the kinds of programs appropriate for emerging adolescent learners" (ASCD,

1975, p. v). In 1975, ASCD published *The Middle School We Need* which reasserted the need to develop schools around the needs and characteristics of young adolescents. From this, more and more educators came to realize that the transition from childhood to adolescence required a program of continuous progress education and a broad and flexible curriculum, with appropriate instructional, guidance, and administrative support and implementation.

In 1973, the National Middle School Association (NMSA) was created. In a 1977 report of its Committee on Future Goals and Directions to NMSA, the following set of goals for the middle school was presented and subsequently adopted by the Association:

1. Every student should be well known as a person by at least one adult in the school who accepts responsibility for his/her guidance.
2. Every student should be helped to achieve optimum mastery of the skills of continued learning together with a commitment to their use and improvement.
3. Every student should have ample experiences designed to develop decision-making and problem-solving skills.
4. Every student should acquire a functional body of fundamental knowledge.
5. Every student should have opportunities to explore and develop interests in aesthetics, leisure, career, and other aspects of life. (p. 16)

The Association for Supervision and Curriculum Development (ASCD) in 1975 identified a number of variables that they deemed extremely important organizational considerations for the middle school. They viewed middle schools as "taking full cognizance of the dynamic physical, social, and intellectual changes that are occurring in young people during the 10- to 14-year-old span, and providing a program with the major purpose of creating a facultative climate so that the transescents can understand themselves and the challenges that are occurring within and around them" (p. 6). ASCD suggested that middle schools provide opportunities for innovations and that such innovation might include team teaching, individualized instruction, flexible scheduling, and some form of continuous progress.

Many schools were resistant to implementing the recommendations offered by NMSA or ASCD. In 1975 ASCD revealed that "the available research indicates a significant gap between the main tenets of the theoretical middle school concept proposed by leading middle school authorities and actual educational practices in most middle schools" (p. 3).

In 1982 *This We Believe* was published by the National Middle School Association (later revised in 1992 and 1995). This position paper set forth 10 essential elements or characteristics of a middle school. These included:

1. Educators knowledgeable about and committed to young adolescents,
2. A balanced curriculum based on the needs of young adolescents,
3. A range of organizational arrangements (flexible structures),
4. Varied instructional strategies,
5. A full exploratory program,
6. Comprehensive advising and counseling,
7. Continuous progress for students,
8. Evaluation procedures compatible with the nature of young adolescent needs,
9. Cooperative planning, and
10. Positive school climate. (NMSA, 1995, p.11)

In 1985 the National Association of Secondary School Principals (NASSP) released *An Agenda for Excellence in Middle Level Education* which described the most successful middle schools as being client-oriented. Focusing on 12 areas (i.e., culture and climate, student development, school organization, curriculum, learning and instruction, transition, client-centeredness and connections) this document aimed at building school programs responsive to the needs of students. The dimension entitled "school organization" encourages:

> ...the smooth operation of the academic program, clear communication among teachers and administrators, and maximum teacher and student control over the quality of the learning environment. The organization of the school should contribute to a sense of belonging on the part of the people who work and learn there, and should mitigate against anonymity and alienation from the primary mission of the school. (NASSP, 1985, pp. 10–11)

An Agenda for Excellence documents that in order to achieve academic productivity, middle schools should be organized:

1. so that decisions are made at the lowest possible level in the organization ... by teams of teachers working closely together with students and other school personnel;
2. so that the effects of size are minimized, large schools should be broken into smaller units or "families;"
3. with a class schedule that allows the greatest amount of uninterrupted learning time for teams of teachers working with groups of students; and
4. with advisory groups of teachers and parents participating in important decisions about building goals, budget priorities, and school climate. (pp. 10–11)

In 1989 the Carnegie Task Force on Education of Young Adolescents issued *Turning Points: Preparing American Youth for the 21st Century* which noted that "a volatile mismatch exists between the organization and curriculum of middle grade schools and the intellectual and emotional needs of young adolescents. Caught in a vortex of changing demands, the engagement of many youth in learning diminished, and their rates of alienation, substance abuse, absenteeism, and dropping out of school begin to rise" (pp. 8–9). In short, *Turning Points* challenged middle schools to be places where close, trusting relationships with adults and peers create a climate for personal growth and intellectual development. To accomplish this, middle school were to:

1. create small communities for learning,
2. teach a core academic curriculum,
3. ensure success for all,
4. empower teachers and administrators,
5. staff middle schools with teachers who are expert at teaching adolescents,
6. improve academic performance of students,
7. re-engage families in the educational process, and
8. connect schools with communities. (1989, p. 9)

With this information in hand, some middle schools began changing the structure of their programs, adding such components as interdisciplinary teaming and advisory programs. The middle school movement was grounded in the reality that "the nature and education of young adolescents must be an integrated venture; physical, social, emotional, and intellectual development are each inexorably woven together in the fabric of early adolescent life" (Alexander & McEwin, 1989, p.1).

George, Stevenson, Thomason, and Beane (1992) observed that something was different about *Turning Points* (1989). "Perhaps because of the public prestige associated with the members of the commission, and because of the quality of work previously completed by other Carnegie groups, *Turning Points* has received a great deal more public attention than earlier studies" (p. 12). Additionally, the Carnegie Council offered grants to 27 states which submitted competitive plans for middle school improvement. These grants helped turn the recommendations into reality—bridging the gap between theory and practice. Middle level education was suddenly in the spotlight. Alexander and McEwin (1989) reported that the number of schools organized in a grade six through eight configuration grew from 1,663 schools in 1970–71 to 4,329 in 1986–87—an increase of 160%. According to the *Digest of Education Statistics* (Department of Educational Statistics, 1995), there were 9,573 middle level schools by 1993–94. This amounts to approximately three middle schools for every junior high in existence. The most recent figures (Bradley & Manzo, 2000) document the existence of 16,000 middle schools and only 2,000 junior highs

Following these reports issued by NMSA, ASCD, NASSP, and Carnegie, a myriad of philosophical, ideological, and political arguments were advanced that supported a very consistent collection of ideas about what constituted a "good middle school"—interdisciplinary teaming, small learning communities, flexible scheduling, advisory periods, among others. While it seems common sense to assume that schools would respond to the needs of their students and create developmentally appropriate learning environments, it is evident from the history of middle level reform that schools are slow to change. Capelluti and Stokes (1991) reminded us:

> Although there is considerable knowledge about the characteristics and interests of early adolescents, this information has not at all times been reflected in what and how we teach these students. These differences are, in fact, the foundation upon which the middle school level is based. It is this uniqueness that provides the rationale and justification for creating a middle level school as a distinct entity within a school system. (p. iii)

With an understanding of the rationale for creating the middle school and some knowledge of its essential characteristics, let's turn our attention from "construction" to "deconstruction." Have the policy statements issued by ASCD, NMSA, NASSP, or Carnegie had any effect on what happening in America's middle schools? Do middle schools measure up to the standards that have been set for them? Have structures been institutionalized in our middle schools that are more symbolic in nature than effective in practice? Are developmentally appropriate middle schools more fiction than fact?

DECONSTRUCTING THE MIDDLE SCHOOL

While there seems to be general agreement as to what middle schools should look like (i.e., advisories, exploratory/integrative curriculum, interdisciplinary teaming), we are acutely aware that translating these structures into reality has been slow. Offering insight into this problem, Manning (1993) wrote: "while developmental psychologists have offered insightful theories about physical, psychosocial and cognitive development, the process of translating them into practice has been somewhat slow, especially beyond the elementary school years" (p. iii). In a similar analysis, Jackson, project director for *Turning Points*, noted that "recent studies show that few of the recommended actions, though frequently proposed, are actually practiced in schools" (1990, p. 1).

Manning (1993) cited several factors that have contributed to an increased emphasis on developmentally responsive middle schools. These include: (1) early adolescence being accepted as a legitimate developmental period, (2) the move of the middle school beyond its infancy to a period where reform is possible, (3) the existence of studies and reports that look at the responsiveness of schools to young adolescents, and (4) the existence of professional organizations that are committed to young adolescents and their education (p. iii).

But there are several obstacles in the way. Many middle schools continue to operate as "transitional schools" (Manning, 1993)—merely housing students between elementary and high school. Additionally, while many of our middle schools place a major emphasis on school organization, what remains lacking are appropriate educational environments and curricula. As the research so keenly demonstrates we cannot pick and choose the parts of middle level reform we want to implement. For significant positive effects on student achievement, varying combinations of middle school structures must be implemented (Felner, Jackson, Kasak, Mulhall, Brand, & Flowers, 1997).

We have more compelling evidence for the reform of middle schools than for many of the other educational reforms we have embraced. When, then, will the call for appropriate middle level educational organization be heard? When will our middle schools respond to the needs of young adolescents? Continuing the task of "deconstruction," let's turn now to some of the indictments that have been levied against America's middle schools and their students.

The Reform Pendulum Swings Again

Middle schools are on the defensive. Recent articles dealing with middle level education have been replete with accounts of what is happening in grades 6–8, especially regarding curriculum. The Southern Regional Education Board in March 1998 concluded that middle schools are a "weak link" in the K–12 education chain. *Education Week* published two articles attacking middle schools; one was titled "A Crack in the Middle" (March 1998) and the other was "Muddle in the Middle" (April 1998). Tucker and Codding (cited in Bradley, 1998) referred to middle schools as "the wasteland of our primary and secondary landscape." In short, middle schools are being accused of falling short of helping the student for whom they were designed. As Bradley (1998) noted, "...the middle school model has come under attack for supplanting academic rigor with a focus on students' social, emotional, and physical needs" (p. 38).

Most of the recent articles that attack our middle schools cite evidence that is mounting from studies like the Third International Math and Science Study (TIMSS). TIMSS is the largest international comparative study of educational achievement to date—with data on approximately 500,000 students from 41 countries. Students from three distinct target populations are assessed: (1) nine-year-olds (typically grades three or four), (2) thirteen-year-olds (in grades seven and eight), and (3) students enrolled in the final year of secondary schooling. Focusing on the thirteen-year-old population, the international comparison suggests a general improvement in U.S. science scores from a 1991 assessment that placed American middle school students below average. But middle school performance in math remains below the international average. In mathematics, 20 countries outperformed the United States, 13 performed similarly, and 7 scored below the U.S. In science, 9 countries outperformed the United States, 16 performed similarly, and 15 scored below.

Among the findings drawn from the Third International Mathematics and Science Study (TIMSS) are the following:

1. eighth-grade mathematics classes in the U.S. are not as advanced and not as focused as those in Japan and Germany;
2. topics taught in U.S. eighth-grade mathematics classrooms are at a seventh-grade level by international standards;
3. the content of U.S. mathematics classes requires less high-level thought than classes in Germany and Japan; and
4. U.S. mathematics teachers' typical goal is to teach students how to do something, while Japanese teachers' goal is to help their students understand mathematical concepts. (from *A Sourcebook of 8th-Grade Findings: TIMSS,* 1997, p. 6)

Curriculum in both math and science have been characterized as "a mile wide and an inch deep." More topics are included in the curriculum at each middle grade than are found in the curricula of most other countries. Coupled with more topics is instruction that is not oriented toward understanding and intellectual challenge. According to Silver (1998), "U.S. teachers tend to use tasks that engage students with low-level cognitive activity, such as memorizing and recalling, rather than high-level thinking, such as reasoning and problem solving" (p. 3).

In his review of the TIMSS results, Silver (1998) found "...a pervasive and intolerable mediocrity in mathematics teaching and learning in the middle grades..." (p. 1). Whitmire (1998), voicing a similar opinion, writes: "...U.S. students stagnate in seventh and eighth grades, leaving them unprepared and unmotivated for the stiff high school ... classes looming ahead" (A-1).

Johnston and Williamson (1998) investigated four communities to identify the concerns and issues of parents regarding middle schools. The analysis of 1,900 surveys, 400 interviews, and 350 exit interviews revealed that parents were concerned with: (1) the pervasive anonymity in middle schools, (2) the format and content of the curriculum, (3) the lack of rigor and challenge of the curriculum, and (4) poor instructional techniques. In reference to anonymity, parents felt that it was easy for their children to "get lost in the crowd" because of the larger student populations found in middle than in elementary schools. "Only 39 percent felt that 'there is an adult in this school who knows my child well and can offer advice and assistance'"

(p. 47). Curriculum was characterized by parents as "trivial," "disjointed," and "lacking rigor." Johnston and Williamson wrote, "Partly because the curriculum is not always clear, many parents lament the lack of "rigor" in the middle level program, citing low expectations for student work, trivial assignments, or vast quantities of mindless exercises in lieu of demanding, engaging work" (p. 48). Lastly, instruction was viewed by a significant number of parents as "dull and boring." "Among the parents interviewed in this study, parents noted that their children often complained of being bored, and that instruction consisted largely of teacher lecture, student seatwork, and pencil-and-paper testing" (Johnston & Williamson, p. 50).

Responses to this recent attack on middle schools have been varied. Some critics blame the current condition of our middle schools on the lack of middle level teacher preparation programs. Bradley (1998) wrote, "A majority of middle-grades teachers, meanwhile, were prepared either to teach elementary or high school. Most were licensed to teach elementary school, leaving them unprepared to handle more complex academic content" (p. 40). Others point the finger at the textbooks we are using. An article in a local newspaper in Pennsylvania was titled "Books blamed for U.S. 8th-graders' low test scores." In essence, national textbook publishing companies are blamed for contributing to a middle school curriculum that is "a mile wide and an inch deep." There is also the underlying assumption that middle school curriculum would be more rigorous if it were established at the state or local level rather than a national level by publishing houses. Lastly, there are those who blame the middle school structure itself and are returning to a K–8 and 9–12 configuration in their school systems. As noted by Bradley (1998), "At least one district is throwing in the towel. The Cincinnati school system is phasing out middle schools entirely, in favor of K–8 schools" (p. 40).

Johnston and Williamson (1998) acknowledged that "regardless of the reasons for their place in the spotlight of many districts, middle level schools clearly receive a lot of attention, invite careful and often critical scrutiny, and engender strong public opinions about what they do and how they do it" (p. 44). Wherever the blame is placed, the fact remains that the reform pendulum is swinging again. Concerned citizens, parents, and academics are quick to blame the problems faced by middle schools on the focus on the affective—the psychosocial needs of young adolescents. How far will we allow the pendulum to swing in the movement between student-centered and subject-centered approaches to schooling? Will developmentally appropriate middle schools survive the current attacks? Have middle schools cosmetically adopted only the "face-lift" part of the reforms and left the "developmentally appropriate" middle school to be more fiction than fact?

Middle schools are at a crossroads. We must step back and evaluate where we have and are focusing our energies. We need to strive for higher levels of implementation of middle level reform so that middle schools are more than just a name above the school door. It is my hope that readers of

The Handbook of Research in Middle Level Education will find insights and solutions for these issues and problems in the chapters that follow.

ORGANIZATION OF THE HANDBOOK

This book is organized into two parts. Part I contains five chapters that focus on current research on the status of the middle school concept. Chapter authors look critically at some of the essential components of the middle school philosophy: advisory programs, teaming, effective middle level teaching, curriculum, and flexible scheduling. In addition to providing the reader with a comprehensive review of the literature on each topic, many of the authors in Part I of *The Handbook of Research in Middle Level Education* have offered the reader empirical data and insights from recent studies they have conducted.

Part Two provides the framework for moving middle level reform forward into the 21st century. The preparation of teachers and administrators to effectively work in middle schools and to implement middle level reform has not been given serious enough attention. As in many educational reform initiatives, there were expectations that practitioners in the field would know how to implement the reform and that almost magically advisories, transition programs, teaming, and interdisciplinary curriculum would result. The four chapters in Part 2 deal with issues related to middle school staffing, teacher preparation, the middle school principalship, and directions for the future from *Turning Points 2000* (Jackson & Davis, 2000).

ACKNOWLEDGMENTS

Assuming the responsibilities of series editor for *The Handbook of Research in Middle Level Education* was a challenge. But this challenge was a pleasant one due to the researchers who contributed to the first volume in this series. I have had the privilege of working with most of these authors over the past five years. There is no doubt that we all share a love for middle level education and have dedicated our professional careers toward improving schools for young adolescents.

Special thanks are extended to the Research in Middle Level Education Special Interest Group of the American Educational Research Association (AERA). The SIG officially endorses this book series and members of this group serve as the Editorial Advisory Board. I am indebted to members of the Editorial Advisory Board for the contributions they have made and the expertise they have offered.

I would also like to thank George Johnson, Publisher, from Information Age Publishing for the encouragement he has given to me in the conceptualization and preparation of the book manuscript. Lastly, I would like to thank Dan Weinles and Christopher Weiler, doctoral students and graduate assistants in the Department of Educational Leadership and Policy Studies at Temple University, for their invaluable assistance.

REFERENCES

Alexander, W., & George, P. (1981). *The exemplary middle school.* New York: Holt, Reinhart, and Winston.

Alexander, W., & McEwin, C. (1989). *Schools in the middle: Progress 1968–1988. NASSP schools in the middle: A report on trends and practices.* Reston, VA: National Association of Secondary School Principals.

Association for Supervision and Curriculum Development. (1975). *The middle school we need.* Washington, DC: Author.

Bossing, N. (1954). A junior high designed for tomorrow. *The Clearing House, 9,* 3–7.

Bradley, J. (1998, April 15). Muddle in the middle. *Education Week, 17*(31), 38–42.

Bradley, A., & Manzo, K. (2000, October 4). The weak link. *Education Week* (supplement), 3–8.

Capelluti, J., & Stokes, D. (1991). *Middle Level education programs, policies, and practices.* Reston, VA: National Association of Secondary School Principals.

Carnegie Task Force on Education of Young Adolescents. (1989). *Turning Points: Preparing American youth for the 21st century.* Washington, DC: Carnegie Council on Adolescent Development.

Commission on the Reorganization of Secondary Education. (1918). *Cardinal principles of secondary education.* Washington, DC: Department of the Interior, Bureau of Education.

Cuban, L. (1992). What happens to reforms that last? The case of the junior high school. *American Educational Research Journal, 29*(1), 227–251.

Department of Education Statistics. (1995). *Digest of Education Statistics.* Washington, DC: National Center for Education Statistics.

Eichhorn, D. (1966). *The middle school.* New York: Center for Applied Research in Education.

Felner, R., Jackson, A., Kasak, D., Mulhall, P., Brand, S., & Flowers, N. (1997). The impact of school reform for the middle years: Longitudinal study of a network engaged in *Turning Points-based* comprehensive school transformation. *Phi Delta Kappan, 78*(7), 528–532, 541–550.

George, P., & Alexander, W. (1993). *The exemplary middle school* (2nd edition). New York: Holt, Reinhart, and Winston.

George, P., Stevenson, C., Thomason, J., & Beane, J. (1992). *The middle school: And beyond.* Alexandria, VA: Association for Supervision and Curriculum Development.

Grooms, M. (1967). *Perspectives on the middle school.* Cincinnati, OH: Merrill.

Gruhn, W., & Douglass, H. (1956). *The modern junior high school* (2nd edition). New York: Ronald Press.

Hall, G. (1905). *Adolescence: Its psychology and its relations to physiology, anthropology, sociology, sex, crime, religion and education* (Vol. II). New York: Appleton & Co.

Jackson, A. (1990). From knowledge to practice: Implementing the recommendations of *Turning Points. Middle School Journal, 21*(3), 1–3.

Jackson, A., & Davis, G. (2000). *Turning points 2000: Educating adolescents in the 21st century.* New York: Teachers College Press.

Johnson, J., Dupuis, V., Musial, D., & Hall, G. (1994). *Introduction to the foundations of American education.* Needham Heights, MA: Allyn and Bacon.

Johnston, J., & Williamson, R. (1998). Listening to four communities: Parent and public concerns about middle level schools. *NASSP Bulletin, 82*(597), 44–52.

Koos, L. (1927). *The junior high school.* Boston, MA: Ginn and Company.

Lewis, A. (1992). Middle schools come to age. *Education Digest, 58*(2), 4–7.

Lounsbury, J. (1960). How the junior high school came to be. *Educational Leadership, 18,* 145–147.

Manning, M.L. (1993). *Developmentally appropriate middle level schools.* Wheaton, MD: Association for Childhood Education International.

Mid-Atlantic Eisenhower Consortium for Mathematics and Science Education. (1997). *Asourcebook of 8th-grade findings: TIMSS.* Philadelphia, PA: Research for Better Schools.

National Association of Secondary School Principals Council on Middle Level Education. (1985). *An agenda for excellence at the middle level.* Reston, VA: Author.

National Education Association. (1899). *Journal of proceedings and addresses.* Denver, CO; Author.

National Education Association. (1965). *Middle schools.* Washington, DC: Author.

National Middle School Association. (1977). Report of the NMSA committee on future goals and directions. *Middle School Journal, 8,* 16.

National Middle School Association. (1982/1992/1995). *This we believe.* Columbus, OH: Author.

National Middle School Association. (1995). *NMSA research summary #3: Numbers of middle schools and students.* (On-line, NMSA website, www.nmsa.org/ressum3.html).

Noar, G. (1961). *Junior high school: Today and tomorrow.* Englewood Cliffs, NJ: Prentice Hall.

Scales, P. (1991). *A portrait of young adolescents in the 1990s: Implications for promoting healthy growth and development.* Minneapolis, MN: Search Institute/Center for Early Adolescence.

Silver, E. (1998). *Improving mathematics in middle school: Lessons from TIMMS and related research.* Washington, DC: U.S. Department of Education, Office of Educational Research and Improvement.

Stevenson, C. (1992). *Teaching ten to fourteen year olds.* White Plains, NY: Longman.

Tanner, J. (1962). *Growth at adolescence.* Oxford: Blackwell Scientific Publications.

Van Til, W., Vars, G., & Lounsbury, J. (1961). *Modern education for the junior high school years.* Indianapolis: Bobbs-Merill Company, Inc.

Whitmire, R. (1998, March). Middle schools targeted as weak link in education chain. *The Reporter,* pp. A1, A4.

PART I

CURRENT RESEARCH ON THE STATUS OF THE MIDDLE SCHOOL CONCEPT: A CRITICAL LOOK AT MIDDLE LEVEL REFORM FROM THE 1980s TO THE PRESENT

CHAPTER 1

ADVISOR-ADVISEE PROGRAMS

Community Building in a State of Affective Disorder?

Vincent A. Anfara, Jr. and Kathleen M. Brown

ABSTRACT

This chapter focuses on one of the components of middle level reform, the advisor-advisee program. While recent research point to positive results of advisory programs, it remains one of the most difficult components of middle level reform to implement in schools. In addition to providing a comprehensive review of the literature, the authors present their readers with a qualitative case study conducted in six middle schools. Data were collected utilizing interviews and observations. Since relationships are the essence of advisory programs, the concepts of community and care were used as the conceptual framework for this study. Findings are organized around the following themes: Caring is Woman's Work, Fear of the Affective Domain, Battle Lines: Administrative Support versus Teacher Resistance Student Mingling or Teacher Meddling, and From Attention Provider to Detention Giver. Practical suggestions are offered to middle level practitioners interested in successfully implementing advisory programs in schools.

...the school is in the best position of all U.S. institutions to initiate and strengthen links that support children and adolescents...
—Brofenbrenner (1988, p. 54)

The quality of the relationship between teachers and students is the single most important aspect of middle level education.
—Van Hoose (1991, p. 7)

INTRODUCTION

Reports calling for reform of middle level schooling first appeared in the mid-1970s. While it is commonsense to assume that schools would respond to the needs of their students and create developmentally appropriate learning environments, it is evident from the history of middle level reform that schools are slow to change. In their 1989 report, *Turning Points: Preparing American Youth for the 21st Century,* the Carnegie Task Force claimed that "a volatile mismatch exists between the organization and curriculum of middle grade schools and the intellectual and emotional needs of young adolescents. Caught in a vortex of changing demands, the engagement of many youth in learning diminishes, and their rates of alienation, substance abuse, absenteeism, and dropping out of school begin to rise" (pp. 8–9). Jackson (1990), Project Director for *Turning Points* also noted that "recent studies show that few of the recommended actions, though frequently proposed, are actually practiced in schools" (p. 1) (also see Alexander & McEwin, 1989; Cawelti, 1988; and Mc Iver, 1990 for a similar analysis). These middle-level reform efforts include teaming, flexible-scheduling, exploratory curriculum, and advisory programs. This chapter focuses on one component of middle level reform, the advisor-advisee program. Beane and Lipka (1987) presented the following description of advisory programs:

> Advisory programs are designed to deal directly with the affective needs of transescents. Activities may range from non-formal interactions to use of systematically developed units whose organizing center are drawn from the common problems, needs, interests, or concerns of transescents, such as "getting along with peers," "living in the school," or "developing self-concept." In the best of these programs, transescents have an opportunity to get to know one adult really well, to find a point of security in the institution, and to learn about what it means to be a healthy human being. (p. 40)

While recent research points to positive results of advisory programs (Connors, 1991; Mac Iver, 1990; Putbrese, 1989; Vars, 1989), it remains one of the most difficult of the middle level concepts to implement (Anfara & Brown, 2000; Fenwick, 1992; Lounsbury & Clark, 1990). Many advisory programs are not functioning as they were initially intended and have simply taken the place of homeroom. Because of the tremendous potential of the middle school concept to contribute to the improvement of schools, we feel it most important to investigate the current status, strengths as well as shortcomings, of advisory programs. To this end, this chapter is focused.

REVIEW OF LITERATURE

While there is still a need for considerably more research about the effectiveness of advisory programs (Clark & Clark, 1994), some of the most frequently mentioned purposes of advisories include:

1. Promoting opportunities for social development,
2. Assisting students with academic problems,
3. Facilitating positive involvement between teachers and administrators and students,
4. Providing an adult advocate for each student in the school,
5. Promoting positive school climate. (Clark & Clark, 1994, pp. 135–136)

Regarding the effectiveness of such programs, Mac Iver (1990) found that when teacher advisories focused on social and academic support activities that a strong relationship existed to the reduction of dropouts. Connors (1986) found evidence that advisory programs helped students grow emotionally and socially, contributed to a positive school climate, helped students learn about school and get along with their classmates, and enhanced teacher-student relationships. George and Oldaker (1985) suggested that when advisory programs are combined with other components of the middle school concept, student self-concept improves, dropout rates decrease, and school climate becomes more positive.

While these studies all point to the possible positive effects of advisory programs, we are warned that schools have a very difficult time both implementing and sustaining this component of middle school reform (Fenwick, 1992; Lounsbury & Clark, 1990). A number of studies (Batsell, 1995; Bunte, 1995; Dale, 1993; Lee, 1995; Mosidi, 1994) addressed the issue of implementation of advisory programs. Findings from these research projects note that successful implementation must address issues related to staff capacity, technical/administrative support, limiting the number of students (15–20) in each advisory, differing expectations on the part of teachers and administrators, the allotment of time to advisory periods as well as to teacher planning, a well-defined advisory curriculum, a feedback/maintenance loop for program review and revision, the transformation of the school's cultural norms, and the management of organizational politics.

Some researchers provided their readers with sample program development time lines (Ayres, 1994) or a listing of the "Ten Steps to a Successful Advisory Program" (Hertzog, 1992). Others suggested what the critical program features are (see Table 1) and how best to prepare teachers for their role in the program (Gill & Read, 1990; James, 1986).

Table 1. Components of Successful Advisor-Advisee Programs: Rationale, Design and Emphasis

Rationale for Advisor-Advisee Programs

- Promote small, caring communities of learners
- Promote mutually respectful and meaningful relationships
- Provide individual attention to students
- Provide each student with an opportunity to "belong"
- Allow teachers to be actively involved in the affective development of students
- Emphasize the social and emotional development of every young adolescent
- Assist students with interpersonal communication skills development

Design of Advisor-Advisee programs

- Need careful organizing, planning, preparing, implementing and monitoring
- Need guidance department, administration, and district level support
- Need teacher, parent, student input and active involvement
- Need teachers/advisors trained and committed to teaching young adolescents
- Need relevant, ongoing professional development opportunities
- Number of Meetings per Week—scheduled daily, regularly
- Length of Advisory Meetings—20 to 40 minutes, uninterrupted
- Time of Day Advisories Scheduled—morning, flexible
- Number of Students Assigned to Advisory Groups—10 to 20 students
- Assigning Students—see advisor during the course of the day

Emphasis of Advisor-Advisee Programs

- Based on teacher and student input
- Based on the affective domain
- Address needs of specific school and community
- Social/Communication/Positive Interpersonal Relationships
- Respect for Self and Others/Good Citizen
- Accepting Responsibility for Education and Actions
- Develop Group, team, and School Spirit
- Academic Monitoring/Assistance/Motivation
- Study, Test-taking, and Note-taking Skills Instruction
- Self-Esteem Activities/Self-Awareness Growth
- Appreciating Talents, Health, and Potential
- Understanding and Making Commitments

Table 1. Components of Successful Advisor-Advisee Programs: Rationale, Design and Emphasis (Cont.)

Decision Making/Coping Skills/Problem Solving
Career Education/Guidance/Future Planning
Setting and Obtaining Goals/Organizing Time
Intramural Activities/Community Service Projects
School Issues and Concerns/Adjustments
Substance Abuse/Current Adolescent Issues

Despite an expanding amount of literature on advisory programs, few researchers have systematically probed the subjective experiences of participants in advisory programs as disclosed by both students and teachers. This chapter is dedicated to making the voices of both students and teachers heard in regard to their advisory experiences. Sardo-Brown and Shetlar (1994) acknowledged that "more investigations of both teacher and student perceptions of the advisor-advisee period need to be done in a variety of different types of schools" (p. 23). The research methodology employed in this study was developed especially to ensure that an emic perspective would result. However, before we turn to the design, let us now look briefly at the conceptual framework that drives the analysis of the data—the ethic of caring and the importance of community.

THEORETICAL/CONCEPTUAL FRAMEWORK FOR ANALYSIS

According to Van Hoose (1991) relationships are the essence of advisory programs. These relationships connect teachers and students, as well as students and students, in a "warm, caring, friendly environment" (Carnegie Task Force, 1989). We are reminded by the scholarship of Mayeroff (1971) and Gaylin (1976) that we as human beings are ontologically relational and that caring interactions are a natural expression of that fact. Communities are created around these relationships. Buber (1958) acknowledged that we can experience what it means "to be" only through our participation in caring relationships. Let us look, then, at the conceptual framework that guides this research—the concepts of community and caring.

Community

According to Sergiovanni (1996), communities "create social structure that bond people together in a oneness, and that bind them to a set of shared values and ideas" (p. 47). Sergiovanni continued by arguing that this bonding and binding is tight enough to transform them from a collection of "I's" into a collective "we." Communities are characterized by qualities such as purpose, trust, respect, commitment, unconditional acceptance and belonging, safe-haven, and shared responsibility.

Exploring the conditions and qualities of communities, Tonnies (1887/1957) made the distinction between *gemeinschaft* and *gesellschaft*. While these are two "ideal forms" that do not exist in the real world, the distinction between them is important for our discussion. *Gemeinschaft* refers to community while *gesellschaft* translates to society. As we moved away from a traditional community concept to a societal ideal, community qualities were replaced with contractual ones. Relationships became very formal with job descriptions and role expectations. The qualities of a community (mentioned above) were lost. Sergiovanni (1994), following the work of Tonnies, noted that "gemeinschaft enterprises ... strive to go beyond calculated to committed involvement" (p. 50).

In his discussion of community, Mitchell (1990) suggested that modern culture has disabled virtually everyone due to "rapid and repeated episodes of loss" (p. 22). Loss includes disrupted families, poverty, as well as other experiences that destroy one's sense of security and well-being. To regain this sense of security, we seek membership in groups or communities that support "consistent and continuous nurturance of belonging" (p. 39). Mitchell challenged educational leaders to create such communities in our schools.

Caring

Beck (1994) recognized that "young people in our schools speak poignantly of their longing to be cared for and the perceived lack of care that characterizes not only our schools but society at large" (p. ix) (see also Anfara & Miron, 1996). Braddock and McPartland (1992) acknowledged that "students must also be attached to their schools in human terms and on a personal level, with the perception that their teachers care about them..." (p. 160).

Caring has been explored from the perspective of many fields—social policy (Watson, 1980), social work (Imre, 1982), and family studies (Hobbs, Dokecki, Hoover-Dempsey, Moroney, Shayne, & Weeks, 1984) to name only a few. Hobbs et al. call on scholars and practitioners to move toward "the creation and support of a competent and caring society" (p. 4). In the field of education Gilligan (1982), Barth (1990), Noddings (1992), Sergiovanni (1992, 1994) and Beck (1994) have all called upon us to practice a caring ethic. Beck (1994) is so strong in her conviction that she wrote:

> Furthermore, I believe that a conceptual framework that emphasizes personal development, the cultivation of community, and an ethic of caring, offers the *only* valid starting point from which academicians and practitioners can hammer out organizational and instructional theories and methodologies that can adequately meet the challenges facing education in the 1990s and beyond. (p. 2, emphasis added)

Noddings (1984) acknowledged that the term "caring" does not easily lend itself to an operational definition. Echoing the ideas of Buber, Noddings wrote that "the relational mode seems to be essential to living fully as a person" (p. 35). But she also emphasizes that "vulnerability is potentially increased when I care, for I can be hurt through the other as well as through myself" (p. 33).

In *On Caring* (1971) Mayeroff acknowledged that "to care for another person, in the most significant sense, is to help him grow and actualize himself" (p. 1). For Gaylin (1976), true caring happens when people relate to each other in ways that promote the healthy unfolding of all types of development. In short, people are relational and caring acts are an appropriate expression of this human quality. Communities, then, become the context in which care can be exhibited. Hobbs et al. (1984) proposed that community is essential to the creation of caring relationships.

In her discussion of caring, Beck (1994) noted that caring involves three activities: (1) receiving another person's perspective, (2) responding appropriately to the other's perception, and (3) remaining committed to the relationship. She writes:

> Caring is ... distinguished by the fact that there is commitment between people who care. This commitment shifts caring from being a conditional act dependent on merit or whim, and moves it toward being an unconditional act marked by acceptance, nurturance, and grace. (p. 20)

In conclusion, as Beck purported, "A caring educational ethic would support the idea that schools should promote maximum individual and community growth and development..." (p. 65).

Why this discussion of community and caring? Basically because the link between caring and learning is very strong. Students, according to Noddings (1992) will "do things for people they like and trust. ... They listen to people who matter to them, and to whom they matter. As we are reminded by Palmer (1983), "But what scholars now say—and what good teachers have always known—is that real learning does not happen until students are brought into relationship with the teacher, with each other, and with the subject. We cannot learn deeply and well until a community of learning is created in the classroom" (p. xvi).

DESIGN

All empirical studies have an implicit, if not explicit, research design. Yin (1994) discussed design as "an action plan for getting from here to there" (p. 19). This study was designed to understand and describe the nature of advisory programs as they contribute to a sense of community and caring in the context of middle school reform. This study is theoretically driven and descriptive, stressing the importance of context, setting, and the subject's frame of reference (an emic perspective).

The major questions to be answered by this research project are: (1) How do advisory programs help or hinder the creation a sense of community and caring for students and teachers? (2) How do the structural/procedural components of an advisory program enhance or hinder the creation of this sense of community?, and (3) What do teachers and students say is the most important effect of advisory programs on school?

This study employs a qualitative case study methodology (Merriam, 1988) to gain a richer understanding of the unit of analysis. Specifically, a multiple-case (holistic) design is employed (Yin, 1994). We are reminded by Herriott and Firestone (1983) that the evidence from multiple cases is often more compelling and the overall study can be regarded as more robust, without sacrificing within-site understanding. Additionally, a multiple case holistic design increases the potential for generalizing findings beyond a particular case (see Merriam, 1988).

Sites

Data for this study were collected from six middle schools (see Appendix A for portraits of these six schools) located in two large metropolitan areas—the Greater Philadelphia Region and the Greater New Orleans Area. The three schools in the Greater New Orleans Area adopted the middle school concept and started their advisory programs approximately three years ago as part of a Goals 2000 subgrant awarded by the State of Louisiana. All three of these schools are part of a school district that services approximately 54,576 students in 83 schools. Approximately 65% of the students in this school district receive free or reduced-priced lunch.

Schools implementing advisory programs were harder to locate in the Greater Philadelphia Region. A wide variety of programs exist that are labeled advisory programs—from exemplary programs that are a central part of the school day to those that are informally conducted with a limited number of teachers and students. Because of this problem, we looked to neighboring counties. Four suburban counties surround Philadelphia, the fifth largest school system in the nation. The Philadelphia School District services approximately 213,000 students in 257 schools. Finally, one middle school was selected from the Philadelphia School District and two were selected from a northwestern county bordering Philadelphia.

Procedures

At each of these six schools, a minimum of three teachers and three students were interviewed (see Appendix B for interview questions). The names of the schools as well as the names of teachers and students have been changed and pseudonyms have been used. Using a type of nonprobability sampling or purposive sampling, principals, assistant principals, or counselors were asked to select teachers and students for these interviews. No criteria were required for selection of informants other than the teachers or students had to be officially involved in an advisory program for at least one school year. The 36 semi-structured interviews were recorded and later transcribed for purposes of analysis. To enhance design validity participant language or verbatim accounts are presented in the analysis of this paper. Observations were conducted at the 6 sites and documents (i.e., examples of advisory activities, agendas from planning sessions, newsletters to parents) were collected to help in the triangulation of the data. Additionally, a questionnaire (see Appendix B) concerning procedural matters was designed and administered to the teachers in Louisiana. It was thought that interview time would be limited because of the necessity to travel to the site from Philadelphia and that time could best be spent talking about more substantive (relational) than procedural issues.

The two researchers involved in this project equally divided responsibilities regarding interviews and observations. Using multiple researchers also helped in establishing design validity. Analysis was begun by reading and rereading the transcripts and the development of initial codes and themes. At this point in the analysis, the two researchers met to debate the interpretation that has been presented in this research. Wasser and Bresler (1996) referred to this as the "interpretive zone"—"the place where multiple viewpoints are held in dynamic tension" (p. 6). The results of these procedures lead to the presentation of a cross-case analysis (Yin, 1994).

To help establish the trustworthiness of this research, the "debated" interpretation was presented to some of the initial informants for participant review. To help in minimizing researcher bias, a field log was maintained in which decisions were recorded relative to the emerging design and data validity. Additionally, all dates, times, places, persons, and activities to obtain access to informants, as well as researcher impressions, were recorded.

ANALYSIS

Confronted with a mountain of impressions, documents, transcribed interviews, and field notes, the qualitative researcher faces the difficult task of making sense of what has been learned. Van Maanen (1988) discussed this process as telling the "tales of the field." It is our hope that this analysis will take the reader into the center of the advisory experiences being described from an emic perspective. The use of two researchers proved invaluable in this process of making sense of the data. Before we proceed, though, we must revisit the central questions that this research hopes to answer. The three questions include: (1) How do advisory programs help or hinder the creation of a sense of community and caring for students and teachers?, (2) How do the structural/ procedural components of an advisory program help or hinder the creation of this sense of community?, and (3) What do teachers and students say is the most significant effect of advisory programs on school? To begin our "tales" let us now turn to the first question.

Question # 1: A Sense of Community and Care

While the rationale for middle school advisory programs is multifaceted, a common theme that is found in most programs is the importance of an adult who cares for an adolescent who is experiencing an important developmental period in life. Galassi, Gulledge and Cox (1997) wrote that "the extent to which AA is perceived to contribute to and affect the degree of caring in the school seems to be an important subjective outcome that cuts across virtually all AA programs" (p. 326). As the interviews progressed in this research, two major themes revolving around care and community emerged. First, we were surprised when we began to hear that "caring is woman's work." We were less surprised by the second major theme—fear of the affective domain.

Caring is Woman's Work

That the analysis relative to caring and community would involve gender issues was truly not expected by either researcher. Let us listen to some of the salient statements from teachers about this issue:

> **Female Teacher**: The advisory program is pretty much woman run. People that are not advisors are men. I think there are only two men in the building that have an advisory and the women have complained about that a lot. He [the principal—a male] says that women

are better nurturers and make better advisors. And I've got to agree with him on that. I think they [women] do make better advisors. They have a completely different attitude toward the advisory program, toward being in a close-knit group, toward the family thing, toward letting the kids get to know you. In the very beginning, the very first year, there were a lot of men and then all of the people that were removed have all been men.

Female Teacher: His [the principal's] first priority is what is good for the kids. I think the women do a better job in the advisory program with the children, and that's his first priority.

Female Teacher: In the sixth grade there is only one man—and this is his first year. So we'll see what happens next year. He is a nurturing kind of guy, though.

Male Teacher: And not everybody participates. There are quite a few men on the faculty who do not want anything to do with this program. They are not sold on the idea of getting to know the students on a more personal basis.

Male Teacher: It was mainly the men who voiced some opposition. They just did not want to be involved in this kind of thing. I guess they thought the women should do it. They didn't complain too much, but the counselor got the picture quickly that she had better not use them if she expected some degree of success with the project. She tried to find other things for them to do—like coordinate some intramural games among the advisories and things like that.

In her 1989 publication Charol Shakeshaft noted that "...women and men manage in markedly different ways" (p. 166). She continues by acknowledging that there are differences in "...the way they spend their time, in their day-to-day interactions, in the priorities that guide their actions, ... and in the satisfaction they derive from their work" (p. 170). The end result is that the work environment is different for men and women. In discussing this difference, Shakeshaft (1989) claimed that women use language that encourages community building, respect their audience through listening and responding in a nonantagonistic manner while men do not.

All of this points once again to the role of gender in not only organizational (school) effectiveness, but program (advisor-advisee) effectiveness.

Fear of the Affective Domain: For Some Yes and for Some No

Most teachers (especially those who are certified for secondary education) will recall their college days and acknowledge that they were well prepare to teach their subject matter. Many can probably remember studying Bloom's (1956) *Taxonomy of Educational Objectives: Cognitive Domain.* But fewer are probably familiar with Krathwohl's (1964) *Taxonomy of Educational Objectives: Affective Domain.*

Many of the teachers interviewed for this study were vocal about the role of guidance in the educational process. We are reminded by Brewer (1937) and Jones and Hand (1938) that guidance and education were so interwoven in the 1920s and 1930s that the classroom teacher was viewed as the perfect person to deliver guidance. In fact, desired changes in behavior, not subject mastery, were promoted as the goal of the teaching process. Mastery of subject matter was secondary to the acquisition of necessary life skills. Van Til, Vars and Lounsbury (1961), as well as Jenkins (1977), also remind us guidance is everyone's responsibility, not just that of the school's counselor. But some of the teachers who were interviewed have a different opinion on this matter. First, let's turn to their comments to hear the perspective of those who feared the affective domain:

Teacher: The faculty's primary argument for not wanting an advisory program is that we need academics more!

Teacher: Advisors are uncomfortable with the topics and do not do it daily.

Teacher: I think there is always a mixed reaction whenever you start any new program. Because the reaction is, oh well, I'm not comfortable with all that touchy-feely type of stuff.

Teacher: I could remember the man that I taught with saying, you know, I don't want to be their friend. You know, I want to be their teacher, I don't want to be their friend. I don't want to know their business and I don't like them knowing anything about me. And you just can't have, you know—the kids like to know what you did on the weekend, and if you have kids, how many kids do you have and where do you go on vacation and stuff. And if you're not willing to share that kind of thing—you know, because you don't want to take academic time to do that kind of stuff. But, I remember that comment distinctly, that has stuck in my mind. And I remember another—and these were both males—the other male says, you know, I'm no psychologist and I guess they have the wrong idea.

Teacher: Teachers' complaints about not wanting to do the advisory program included just not being comfortable with the affective domain—feeling uncomfortable with sitting and talking with students. And you have to be very careful what you get into in the advisory—but just not wanting that role entirely.

Teacher: The teachers are uncomfortable with the topics that need to be covered. They feel that the school counselors should deal with these issues.

Teacher: Teachers are not prepared to deal with students on this level. They are prepared to teach some subject matter.

Ornstein and Hunkins (1988) reminded their readers that "some educators, and many parents, view the taxonomy (affective domain) with concern. They feel that the school is responsible for the cognitive dimensions of learning, but has little responsibility in the affective or values domain" (p. 156). But Combs (1962), an effective spokesman for affective education, commented, "Education must be concerned with the values, beliefs, convictions, and doubts of students. These realities ... are just as important, if not more so, as the so-called ... facts" (p. 200). Let's now turn to those who felt comfortable dealing in this domain:

Teacher: Staff members act like more of a coach. It is an opportunity for us to get to know the children so that if there are problems somewhere along the line, we can help them. Our role is to make school easier for the children.

Teacher: During our advisory time we work on interpersonal relationships, peer skills—dealing with peers. I'll also approach this and find out about any social or academic problems they are having.

Student: We sort of play games to get to know each other better. It's sort of like a working together game. We also sometimes, last year we got in a circle once every three advisories and we would just talk about any problems that we had.

Teacher: I'd like to think that it makes a difference. I'd like to hope that it does—that we are helping them to be kinder and gentler to each other.

Teacher: I don't see it so much as value training. I see it more as just a family-like type of atmosphere where there's somebody that you can go to if you're having a problem and you're struggling. And just a more relaxed setting ... for the students to get to know each other a little better other than just academics.

A Sense of Community and Care: A Summary

As noted, advisory programs provide mutual benefits for students as well as teachers. One of these benefits is the sense of community and care that changes the school climate. As one of the principals noted, "Yes, you can actually feel the climate. Some schools where there is not a formed relationship between the teachers and the kids, there is not that supportive feeling" (administrator interview, September 29, 1997). But, the work of making these changes seems to fall on both the female teachers and those who are comfortable with the affective domain. We are reminded of a quote from Trubowitz (1994):

> In the best of all educational worlds, advisories might not even be necessary. With small classes and with teacher recognition that the affective and cognitive are inextricably interrelated, what occurs in advisory programs can be made commonplace in regular classrooms. In the interim advisor-advisory programs can do much to enrich the school lives of young adolescents. (p. 5)

We are left, though, asking the bewildering questions: When will these changes become commonplace? When will middle schools respond to the needs of their students and create developmentally appropriate learning environments?

Question # 2: The Structural/Procedural Components and the Sense of Community

One of the things that struck both researchers was the tremendous diversity in how advisory programs were structured. At some of the schools advisory periods were scheduled every day as an integral part of the school day. At one of the schools students and teachers met when and if they could find the time—at lunch or after school. In most of the schools students and teachers met two or three times a week for advisory. With such a vast array of programs called advisory, we were interested in the degree to which the structure and procedural components actually affected the sense of community and care at the school. In looking at this question, two themes emerged from the data: (1) Battle lines: Administrative support versus teacher resistance and (2) Student mingling or teacher meddling?

Once again, let us turn to the voices of both students and teachers to support these themes.

Battle Lines: Administrative Support Vs. Teacher Resistance

Discussing advisory programs Mc Ewin (1981) stated that "The understanding and support of the principal is the key determiner of success or failure" (p. 345). Indeed, not only teachers (Lounsbury, 1991) and counselors, but middle school principals have a responsibility in keeping their advisory programs working successfully. Galassi et al. (1997) wrote that "there is a theory that the top-down effect of a principal's lack of enthusiasm for advisory time will influence teachers and undermine the program" (p. 317). Let's turn now to what teachers think about this issue of administrative support. These teachers are from three of the schools that are experiencing some problems with their advisory programs:

> **Teacher**: At first, the faculty was receptive to the advisory program. It failed after two years ... no administrative backing, no accountability.

> **Teacher**: At first the faculty seemed to be enthusiastic and willing to try the program, but as the program progressed and the administration didn't live up to its promises, enthusiasm turned to resentment.

> **Teacher**: The administration gave no support to advisors. ... Complaints to the administration were not welcomed and the people presenting them were criticized and considered uncooperative.

In contrast, the following quotes are from teachers who have very supportive principals. These advisory programs are getting stronger and better as each school year passes.

> **Teacher**: I think that it's very well organized. I think (the principal) has really put into place an advisory program that is very workable. We put the time into our schedules.

> **Teacher**: I think the most positive aspect is that it's well organized around a common theme and that you can stay focused on your goal or your purposes for that particular year.

With little administrative support it is easy to see how teachers' attitudes toward advisory programs may be affected. While the reasons for program success or failure may be complex, we feel that an essential component that must be in place is the support of the principal. This support must not only be there in the implementation stages, but must continue for program maintenance and development.

Existing opposite administrative support is the reality of teacher resistance to program implementation. Cole (1994) acknowledged that "if teachers in a school do not embrace the program, it will fail" (p.3). In support of this theme of teacher resistance we offer the reader the following teacher and administrator quotes:

Teacher: When the advisory activity was scheduled, those days grew to be dreaded. Joyful comments floated around the building on days when the activity had to be canceled for a specific reason.

Teacher: It is no longer in existence, primarily because of faculty dissatisfaction.

Teacher: The group's argument was that it increased their workload. They had to prepare for another class.

Teacher: The advisors' attitudes concerning the program were the most negative aspects of the program. Negative attitudes concerning the (advisory) meetings were discouraging.

Administrator: There was a little bit of grumbling. Major detriment against it, teachers will tell you how much can you have us do? We're teaching our subjects, doing 100 other little things, now on top of it you want me to establish relationships with my 33 students. That's pretty hard to do. Major way to object—prep time is my time.

In contrast, at one of the schools where the advisory program was very successful a teacher commented, "If I would have seen resistance, then it probably would not have worked. You have to have people who are receptive, if you don't then it's not going to work."

Student Mingling or Teacher Meddling?

The second theme to emerge from looking at the structural components of an advisory program dealt with the issue of student mingling versus teacher meddling. The data will demonstrate that while some students loved the ability to "mingle" with other students and teachers, there were students who felt that their right to privacy was or could possibly be violated. If they wanted to talk with someone, they would—but don't force the issue. Note these positions in the following accounts. First, we will hear from those who think the advisory process leads to mingling:

Student: I think it's a really good program just because it's not like a stressful subject. You got to just sort let go and just be yourself during the day and just talk to your teachers and get to know them better and have them get to know you.

Student: I get to know them (fellow advisees), I get to know how they feel, I really get to know what they're like and how they interact—so I can work with them better.

Teacher: She was very open telling me what was going on. Very easy to talk to and I think she was relieved that she had somebody she could safely let it out.

Teacher: Some students look at it as a chance to get to know other people better, even another faculty member better.

On the other hand, let us now turn to those who think this whole process leads to meddling and an invasion of a student's right to privacy.

Teacher: The children only wanted to play games ... they did not seem to derive much satisfaction from contact with the adults.

Teacher: The most negative aspect of the program was that students were reluctant to share.

Teacher: Some faculty complained about students being committed to not sharing their thoughts and feelings on different issues discussed.

Student: Like some things I like about it and some things I dislike—like having to tell them what I'm thinking or feeling about things—that's my business, not theirs. It's (the advisory program) just OK.

One of the key recommendations in *Turning Points* (Carnegie Task Force, 1989) is the need to establish "small communities for learning, where stable, close, mutually respectful relationships with adults and peers are considered fundamental..." (p.9). An important word that seems to have gotten misplaced in some advisory programs is "respectful." From the data collected for this study it has become clearer to us that teachers need to be sensitive to students' needs (Manning, 1993) and must respect their students' right to privacy (Cole, 1992). These elements are essential if trust is to be developed between teacher and student—an essential component to the educational process (Anfara & Miron, 1996).

Structural Components and Community: A Summary

In our second research question we asked if the structural components of an advisory program affected the creation of a sense of community. In one word, then, the answer to our question would be "yes." School administrators need to be cognizant of the fact that there are many structural elements (i.e., scheduling, staff development, staff support services, faculty and student input while creating the program, awareness of the needs of the students) that can make or break a successful advisory program. Instead of a sense of community (your intended consequence), you can be left with dissatisfied teachers and students (unintended consequences). Your faculty can become polarized over the project and students and teachers can grow to resent advisory sessions. As one teacher responded, "This advisor-advisee project has destroyed any sense of collegiality in this faculty. We are now in two opposing camps. The school has really suffered trying to deal with this."

Question # 3: The Effect of Advisory on Teachers and Students

The last question looks at what teachers and students consider to be the most important effects of advisory programs on their schools. Two themes emerged from the data regarding this issue. The first is called "From Attention Provider to Detention Giver," and the second theme deals with the fact that everyone seems to be able to point to "something good." Let's look at what teachers and students had to say about these themes.

From Attention Provider to Detention Giver

The Carnegie Task Force (1989) cited as one of the key elements of learning communities the fact that "small group advisories ... ensure that every student is known well by at least one adult" (p. 9). It is hoped that this individual attention will result in improved student attitudes toward school, increased academic achievement, increased self-esteem, and a reduction in behavioral problems (Andrews & Stern, 1992). Our findings are mixed on this issue. We found reference to discipline problems as well as mention of the attention that students get as a result of advisory sessions. Let's turn to the data to hear what teacher and students have to say about this theme—"attention provider to detention giver."

Student accounts that supported the idea of an adult providing attention and some degree of improvement in academics or behavior include:

Student: Like if I am in trouble, he'll (teacher) talk with me about it so that I can control what I do. Yeah! I've gotten in a lot less trouble. I used to get suspended a lot.

Student: I like it cause she would talk to me about doing better. I got better in, like my behavior and uhm ... yeah, I am much better now.

Student: Uhm, hum. Like, Uhm, cause last year I had a bad year and like Mr. M was my adopted buddy (advisor) and if I got problems, I go to him.

One teacher commented, "She was disruptive in class and in my homeroom. I was able to talk to her mentor (advisor) about some issues and I've seen some changes with a couple of kids I had problems with."

But in contrast to these statements we must listen to the following teachers who experienced student disciplinary problems which added to a sense of uneasiness relative to participation in advisory activities.

Teacher: The administration gave no support to advisors on the handling of disruptive students. Advisors had to make-do as best they could, which frequently meant that the time spent in the activity was unproductive because of one or more disruptive students. Advisors would have to give additional time to hold detentions, give written work, call parents, or whatever needed to be done.

Teacher: It's a much looser situation than the regular classroom and some students use that time to act out and show off to their friends, have a hard time getting on task because it is a looser situation. I deal with it like any other class procedure where you can give warnings and do whatever you want with that but if it's not getting any better you can use a time out, demerit, detention, phone the parents.

Sardo-Brown and Shetlar (1994) discussed the removal of disruptive students from the advisory period. This was not an issue that was anticipated by either researcher. So much of the literature dealing with the effects of advisory is focused on the improvement of student satisfaction with school, the establishment of relationships, and the reduction of behavioral problems. The data from this study point to the necessity of dealing with the issue of disruptive students in a straightforward manner.

No Matter What Happens, Something Good Seems to Result!

The second theme to emerge from our last research question points to the positive effects of this component of the middle school concept. No matter how terrible things seemed, no matter how disorganized the program was, no matter how disruptive students were, teachers and students had positive comments.

> **Teacher**: The most positive aspect is teachers and students getting together in a non-teaching atmosphere.
>
> **Teacher**: A chance for students to get individual help.
>
> **Teacher**: The students benefitted from having another adult with whom they could communicate with on a regular basis.
>
> **Student**: Yeah! I mean it (the advisory program) makes me feel better about coming to school. Just like to know I always have someone to talk to if I need to.
>
> **Teacher**: It gives them a chance to interact with an adult in a positive way, a nonthreatening way, a non-authoritative way.
>
> **Student**: I don't like going to school, but it made it easier for me. I knew there would be someone there to help me if I was struggling, like now.

Discussing the positive effects of advisory, one of the school principals noted, "That you will, as one of my colleagues here put it, save lives. At times, especially with today's kids, things reach crisis level and we literally save a life. It is certainly a long term thing—but maybe a kid will have a brighter future because of the relationship they formed with somebody."

Effects on Teacher and Students: A Summary

As we previously mentioned, the rationale for middle school advisory programs is multifaceted. While there are disciplinary problems that need to be addressed, the mutual benefits to both teachers and students, not to mention school climate, are great. This notion of mutual benefit is supported by the scholarship of Stevenson (1992). In summary, though, Alexander and George (1981) offer some important thoughts to ponder:

> Teachers need this type of involvement no less than students do. Since most teachers really do seem to have a deep felt need to make a significantly posi-

> tive difference in the lives of their students, and the daily demands of the classroom often seem to make this difficult or impossible, the advisor-advisee program provides the teacher with an opportunity to get to know some manageable number of students in a meaningful way. (p. 90)

SOME PRACTICAL SUGGESTIONS

Now that the "tales of the field" have been told, we turn to some practical suggestions for educators who are thinking about implementing advisory programs in their schools. These lessons, learned from the field, will hopefully help in the avoidance of some of the most common pitfalls. We, then, offer the following considerations.

A successful advisory program should:

1. develop both short and long range goals,
2. be cognizant of students', teachers', and parents' needs,
3. provide for initial and ongoing staff training and development,
4. provide an orientation for students, teachers, and parents,
5. honor small student-teacher ratios,
6. be structured in the daily schedule of the school,
7. be very aware of school climate/culture,
8. involve students, parents, and faculty in the planning phase, and
9. respect teachers' and students' rights to privacy.

While many of these suggestions have been offered by others (Cole, 1992; George & Lawrence, 1982; Phillips, 1986; Schurr, 1992), what we find striking about these recommendations is that they came from teachers, students, and administrators who are hard at work in our middle schools. There is, indeed, much to still be learned about the development, implementation, and survival of advisory programs in America's middle schools.

REFERENCES

Alexander, W., & George, P. (1981). *The exemplary middle school.* New York: Holt, Reinhart, and Winston.

Alexander, W., & McEwin, C. (1989). Schools in the middle: Progress 1968–1988. *NASSP schools in the middle: A report on trends and practices.* Reston, VA: National Association of Secondary School Principals.

Andrews, B, & Stern, J. (1992). An advisory program—A little can mean a lot! *Middle School Journal, 24*(1), 39–41.

Anfara, V. , & Brown, K. (2000). Advisory programs and the feminization of teaching: An unintended consequence of a middle school reform. *Middle School Journal, 31*(3), 26–31.

Anfara, V., & Miron, L. (1996). Beyond caring: A look at practical intersubjectivity as a new paradigm to govern educational reform. *Journal for a Just and Caring Education, 2*(3), 304–330.

Ayres, L. (1994). Middle school advisory programs: Findings from the field. *Middle SchoolJournal, 25*(3), 8–14.

Barth, R. (1990). *Improving schools from within: Teachers, parents, and principals can make the difference.* San Francisco, CA: Jossey-Bass.

Batsell, G. (1995). *Progress toward implementation of developmentally responsive practice in Arizona middle level schools, 1989–1994.* Unpublished doctoral dissertation, University of Arizona.

Beane, J., & Lipka, R. (1987). *When kids come first: Enhancing self-esteem.* Columbus, OH: National Middle School Association.

Beck, L. (1994). *Reclaiming educational administration as a caring profession.* New York: Teachers College Press.

Bloom, B. (1956). *Taxonomy of educational objectives, handbook I: Cognitive domain.* New York: McKay.

Braddock, J., & McPartland, J. (1992). Education of early adolescents. *Review of Research in Education, 19,* 135–170.

Brewer, J. (1937). *Education as guidance.* New York: Macmillan.

Brofenbrenner, U. (1988). Alienation and the four worlds of childhood. In L.H. Golubchick & B. Persky (Eds.), *Urban, social, and educational issues* (pp.52–58). Garden City, NY: Avery.

Buber, M. (1958). *Between man and man.* New York: Macmillan.

Bunte, A. (1995). *Success factors in the implementation of advisory programs in selected Illinois middle schools.* Unpublished doctoral dissertation, Southern Illinois University at Carbondale.

Carnegie Task Force on Education of Young Adolescents. (1989). *Turning points: Preparing American youth for the 21st century.* Washington, D.C.: Carnegie Council on Adolescent Development.

Cawelti, G. (1988). Middle schools, a better match with early adolescent needs, ASCD survey finds. *ASCD Curriculum update.* Alexandria, VA.: Association for Supervision and Curriculum Development.

Clark, S., & Clark, D. (1994). *Restructuring the middle level school: Implications for school leaders.* Albany, NY: State University of New York Press.

Cole, C. (1992). *Nurturing a teacher advisory program.* Columbus, OH: National Middle School Association.

Cole, C. (1994). Teachers' attitudes before beginning a teacher advisory program. *Middle School Journal, 25*(5), 3–7.

Combs, A. (Ed.). (1962). *Perceiving, behaving, becoming: A new focus for education.* Washington, D.C.: Association for Supervision and Curriculum Development.

Connors, N. (1986). *A case study to determine the essential components and effects of an advisor/advisee program in an exemplary middle school.* Unpublished doctoral dissertation. Florida State University, Tallahassee, FL.

Connors, N. (1991). Teacher advisory: The fourth r. In J.L. Irvin (Ed.), *Transforming middle level education: Perspectives and possibilities* (pp.162–178). Needham Heights, MA: Allyn and Bacon.

Dale, P. (1993). *Leadership, development, and organization of an advisor/advisee program: A comparative case study of two middle schools.* Unpublished doctoral dissertation, Fordham University, New York.

Fenwick, J. (1992). *Managing middle grade reform—An "American 2000" agenda.* San Diego, CA: Fenwick and Associates, Inc.

Galassi, J., Gulledge, S., & Cox, N. (1997). Middle school advisories: Retrospect and prospect. *Review of Educational Research, 67*(3), 301–338.

Gaylin, W. (1976). *Caring.* New York: Knopf.

George, P., & Lawrence, G. (1982). *Handbook for middle school teaching.* Glenview, IL: Scott, Foresman and Company.

George, P., & Oldaker, L. (1985). *Evidence for the middle school.* Columbus, OH: National Middle School Association.

Gill, J., & Read, E. (1990). The experts comment on advisor-advisee programs. *Middle School Journal, 21*(5), 31–33.

Gilligan, C. (1982). *In a different voice: Psychological theory and women's development.* Cambridge, MA: Harvard University Press.

Herriott, R., & Firestone, W. (1983). Multisite qualitative policy research: Optimizing description and generalizability. *Educational Researcher, 12,* 14–19.

Hertzog, C. (1992). Middle level advisory programs: From the ground up. *Schools in the Middle, 2*(1), 23–27.

Hobbs, N., Dokecki, P., Hoover-Dempsey, K., Moroney, R., Shayne, M., & Weeks, K. (1984). *Strengthening families.* San Francisco, CA: Jossey-Bass.

Imre, R. (1982). *Knowing and caring: Philosophical issues in social work.* New York: University Press of America.

Jackson, A. (1990). From knowledge to practice: Implementing the recommendations of *Turning Points. Middle School Journal, 21*(3), 1–3.

James, M. (1986). *Adviser-advisee programs: Why, what, and how.* Columbus, OH: National Middle School Association.

Jenkins, J. (1977). The teacher-adviser: An old solution looking for a problem. *NASSP Bulletin, 61,* 29–34.

Jones, A., & Hand, H. (1938). Guidance and purposive living. In G. Whipple (Ed.), *The thirty-seventh yearbook of the National Society for the Study of Education: Part I. Guidance in educational institutions* (pp. 3–29). Bloomington, IL: Public School Publishing Company.

Krathwohl, D. (1964). *Taxonomy of educational objectives, handbook II: Affective domain.* New York: McKay.

Lee, S. (1995). *Implementing the teacher advisory program at the middle school: A case study of technical, normative and political perspectives of change.* Unpublished doctoral dissertation, University of California, Los Angeles.

Lounsbury, J. (1991). *As I see it.* Columbus, OH: National Middle School Association.

Lounsbury, J., & Clark, D. (1990). *Inside grade eight: From apathy to excitement.* Reston, VA: National Association of Secondary School Principals.

Mac Iver, D. (1990). Meeting the needs of young adolescents: Advisory groups, interdisciplinary teaching teams, and school transition programs. *Phi Delta Kappan, 71*(6), 458–464.

Manning, M. (1993). Cultural and gender differences in young adolescents. *Middle School Journal, 25*(1), 13–17.

Mayeroff, M. (1971). *On caring.* New York: Harper & Row.

McEwin, C. (1981). Establishing teacher-advisory programs in middle level schools. *Journal of Early Adolescence, 1,* 337–348.

Merriam, S. (1988). *Case study research in education: A qualitative approach.* San Francisco, CA: Jossey-Bass Publishers.

Mitchell, B. (1990). Loss, belonging, and becoming: Social policy themes for children and schools. In B. Mitchell and L. Cunningham (Eds.), *Educational leadership and changing contexts of families, communities, and schools: Eighty-ninth yearbook of the National Society for the Study of Education* (pp.19–51). Chicago: University of Chicago Press.

Mosidi, M. (1994). *A qualitative study of the process of implementing the advisor-advisee program in a school setting.* Unpublished doctoral dissertation. The University of Toledo.

Noddings, N. (1984). *Caring: A feminine approach to ethics and moral education.* Berkeley: University of California Press.

Noddings, N. (1992). *The challenge to care in schools: Alternative approaches to education.* New York: Teachers College Press.

Ornstein, A., & Hunkins, F. (1988). *Curriculum: Foundations, principles, and issues.* Boston: Allyn and Bacon.

Palmer, P. (1983). *To know as we are known: Education as a spiritual journey.* New York: HarperCollins.

The Philadelphia Inquirer. (1997, September 14). Report card on the schools. L1–L20.

Phillips, R. (1986). *Making advisory programs work.* Tampa, FL: Wiles, Bondi Associates.

Putbrese, L. (1989). Advisory programs at the middle level—The students' response. *NASSP Bulletin, 73*(514), 111–115.

Sardo-Brown, D., & Shetlar, J. (1994). Listening to students and teachers to revise a rural advisory program. *Middle School Journal, 26*(1), 23–25.

Sergiovanni, T. (1992). *Moral leadership: Getting to the heart of school improvement.* San Francisco, CA: Jossey-Bass.

Sergiovanni, T. (1994). *Building community in schools.* San Francisco:, CA: Jossey-Bass.

Sergiovanni, T. (1996). *Leadership for the schoolhouse.* San Francisco, CA: Jossey-Bass Publishers.

Schurr, S. (1992). *How to evaluate your middle school.* Columbus, OH: National Middle School Association.

Shakeshaft, C. (1989). *Women in educational administration.* Newbury Park, CA: Corwin Press, Inc.

Stevenson, C. (1992) *Teaching ten to fourteen year olds.* New York: Longman.

Tonnies, F. (1957). *Community and Society.* (C.P. Loomis, ed. and Trans.). New York: HarperCollins.

Trubowitz, S. (1994, Winter). The quest for the good advisor-advisee program. *Middle Ground,* 3–5.
Van Hoose, J. (1991). The ultimate goal: A/A across the day. *Midpoints, 2*(1), 1–7.
Van Maanen, J. (1988). *Tales of the field: On writing ethnography.* Chicago: The University of Chicago Press.
Van Til, W., Vars, G., & Lounsbury, J. (1961). *Modern education for the junior high school years.* Indianapolis: Bobbs-Merrill Company, Inc.
Vars, G. (1989). A new/old look at the needs of transescents. *Transescence, 9*(2), 15.
Wasser, J., & Bresler, L. (1996). Working in the interpretive zone: Conceptualizing collaboration in qualitative research teams. *Educational Researcher, 25*(5), 5–15.
Watson, D. (1980). *Caring for strangers.* London: Routledge & Kegan Paul.
Yin, R. (1994). *Case study research: Design and methods* (second edition). Thousand Oaks, CA: Sage Publications.

APPENDIX A

PORTRAITS OF THE SIX SCHOOLS

Greater Philadelphia Region

Adams Middle School: Adams is located in Jefferson Township, Grant County which is on the Northwest border of Philadelphia. It is a diverse multi-cultural community that values a high quality education. Recognized in 1996 by *Money* magazine as one of the nation's top 100 school districts, Jefferson Township School District consists of seven schools serving approximately 4700 students. Adams is the district's only middle school (grades 7 and 8). Of the 850 students, 30% are African-American, 60% are White, 8% are Asian, and 2% Hispanic. Only 4% of the students at this middle school qualify as part of low-income families. A staff of 75 teachers seek to "nurture young adolescents at a time when they are trying to make sense of themselves and the world around them" (interview with vice principal, October 15, 1997). The advisory program is known by the acronym SWAP—Students with Academic Potential. Participation is voluntary and approximately 15 teachers out of 60 participate. Teachers typically have one or two advisees. There is no formally scheduled time for students and teachers to meet within the daily schedule. Many participants report that they meet after school or at lunch.

Buchanan Middle School: Buchanan Middle serves Hoover Township, Grant County, which has a total student population of 2,050.The school district is comprised of four schools—two elementary, one middle school, and one high school which are all located within walking distance of each other. The surrounding neighborhood is typical suburbia with large, single-family homes, sidewalks, and plenty of trees. Ethnically, the student population is 96% White, 2% African-American, 1% Asian and 1% Hispanic. Approximately 7% of the students qualify as low-income. The middle school houses grades 5–7 and has received acclaim for its exemplary advisory program, team teaching, and emphasis on technology in the classroom. While the exterior is large, three-story brick building sprawled over a massive campus of playing fields, athletic courts, and open ground, the interior is very warm and cozy. Numerous displays of student artwork and academic achievement decorate the halls and corridors. The students move about comfortably and seem to be very much "at home" in their environment. The advisory program was instituted by the principal who is very much an advocate of the middle school concept. For the 1997–98 school year the school is divided into 38 authors (last year it was tribes) around which activities are planned. In a typical 6 day rotation schedule of 9 periods a day, students and faculty meet in advisories for 2 periods. Each of these periods last for 41 minutes. The Advisor-Advisee ratio is approximately 1 to 14.

Calhoun Middle School: Calhoun Middle School is a racially balanced magnet school nestled in the Port Richmond section of Philadelphia. It houses 900 5th, 6th, 7th, and 8th graders pooled from the surrounding Jackson area. Located at the corner of Lincoln and Johnson, Calhoun structurally is a large four-story brick building defaced with graffiti. The school encompasses a city-wide block with a fenced yard in the rear. The surrounding homes are inner city row houses where a predominately lower socioeconomic working class lives. The neighborhood is ethnically mixed. The streets are somewhat safe during daylight hours but are plagued with drugs and violence after dark. Security guards man the only unlocked entrance to the school. Most of the students who attend Calhoun walk to school, attend regularly, behave properly, and work hard on their studies. They are academically gifted but economically deprived. The administration and staff are warm, welcoming, and caring. Small learning communities have been formed and team teaching occurs. There is a nice "feel" to Calhoun—the students move about freely and seem very much at ease. They view education as important and see it as their vehicle to advance in life. All of the students and teachers at Calhoun participate in the advisory program; the Advisor-Advisee ratio is 1 to 33. The program is scheduled for the first 22 minutes of every day. In connection with this, one additional "Guidance" period, another 22 minutes, is conducted during the course of the week.

Greater New Orleans Area

Dwight Middle School: Dwight Middle School is located on the West Bank of Madison Parish, Louisiana in a suburban setting. A large, two-story brown-brick building built in the early 1980s, the school is clean and decorated with art work done by one of the teachers. The suburban setting is deceptive. The Parish is divided by the Mississippi River and the river separates a predominantly minority population (West Bank) from a predominantly White population (East Bank). Dwight Middle serves a students population from grades 6–8 that is 67.1% African American, 23.8% White, 4.2% Hispanic, 4.6% Asian American, and .3% American Indian. Approximately 80% of the students come from low-income families. Many of the problems faced by students and faculty are similar to those found in urban schools. Most of the parents work in semi-skilled or unskilled jobs and receive some form of government assistance. For most parents a high school education is the extent of their schooling. The school has a population of 1140 students who are taught by approximately 60 teachers who are predominantly White and travel from the East Bank to teach. The advisory program was started three years ago through funding that came from a Goals 2000 subgrant. A change in administration has proven detrimental to the implementation of the middle school concept at this school.

Eisenhower Junior High School: Also located on the West Bank of Madison Parish, this school services 728 students in grades 7–9. Approximately 50.3% of the students are African American, 37.9% White, 2.5% Hispanic, 9% Asian American, and .3% American Indian. Forty-three percent of the students receive free or reduced lunch. The school, three single-story blond-brick buildings (built in the 1970s), is located in a suburban setting with a high fence surrounding the property. The subdivisions that surround the school are racially segregated. The school is in the midst of an African American neighborhood, but there are White and Asian American subdivisions that are in close proximity. Many of the classrooms have murals that were painted by one of the teachers. The school is clean and orderly. Students move around the halls according to established "traffic" pattern, but tend to be quite loud. Hall monitors check for tardy and disruptive students. Most of the 50 faculty members travel from the East Bank to teach at this school. The advisory program was started three years ago as part of a Goals 2000 subgrant.

Franklin Middle School: Located on the East Bank of the Mississippi River, Franklin Middle School is located in buildings that once housed the vocational school for this school system. The wooden buildings have recently been painted blue and red, the school's colors. The facility is well kept, but clearly not of the quality of other school facilities in the school system. Of the 533 students in grades 6–8 approximately 89.1% are African American, 8.1% White, 2% Hispanic, .1% Asian American, and .3% American Indian. Seventy-six percent of the students come from low-income families. This school is the only school on the East Bank with such a high percentage of minority students. Most of the teachers live on the East Bank and are White. The advisory program was started three years ago as part of a Goals 2000 subgrant.

Adams Middle School (Jefferson Township—Grant County)

Enrollment: 5,000 students in the district, 850 students in the school
Racial Composition: 30% Black, 60% White, 2% Hispanic, 8% Asian
Special Education: 6%
Gifted and Talented: 14%
Average Class Size: 23 students
Low-Income Students: 8%
High Reading Scores: 36%
High Math Scores: 41%
Median Teacher Salary: $76,000
5+ Years Teaching Experience: 85%
Spending Per Pupil: $9,800

Calhoun Middle School (Washington Cluster—Philadelphia City District)

Enrollment: 214,000 students in the district, 11,700 students in the cluster, 900 students in the school
Racial Composition: 35% Black, 33% White, 30% Hispanic, 2% Asian
Special Education: 11%
Gifted and Talented: 3%
Average Class Size: 27 students
Low-Income Students: 80%
High Reading Scores: 26%
High Math Scores: 23%
Median Teacher Salary: $50,000
5+ Years Teaching Experience: 78%
Spending Per Pupil: $7,000

Buchanan Middle School
(Hoover Township—Grant County)

Enrollment: 2,050 students in the district, 500 students in the school
Racial Composition: 2% Black, 96% White, 1% Hispanic, 1% Asian
Special Education: 13%

Gifted and Talented: 12%
Average Class Size: 22 students
Low-Income Students: 7%
High Reading Scores: 42%
High Math Scores: 37%
Median teacher Salary: $64,000
5+ Years Teaching Experience: 90%
Spending Per Pupil: $10,500

Source: Taken from *The Philadelphia Inquirer*, Report Card on Schools (1997)

Dwight Middle School
(Madison Parish School System)

Enrollment: 54,568 students in the district, 1140 students in the school
Racial Composition: 67.1% Black, 23.8% White, 4.2% Hispanic, 4.6% Asian American, .3% American Indian
Special Education: 16%
Gifted and Talented: .5%
Average Class Size: 30 students
Low-Income Students: 80%
Median Teacher Salary: $28,651
Spending Per Pupil: $4,870
% Passing Exit Test in Language Arts: 84%, Math: 70%

Franklin Middle School
(Madison Parish School System)

Enrollment: 54,568 students in district, 533 students in school
Racial Composition: 89.1% Black, 8.1% White, 2.0% Hispanic, .1% Asian American, .3% American Indian
Special Education: 20%
Gifted and Talented: .3%
Average Class Size: 26 students
Low-Income Students: 76%
Median Teacher Salary: $28,651
Spending Per Pupil: $4,870
% passing Exit Test in Language Arts: 86%, Math: 68%

Eisenhower Middle School (Madison Parish School System)

Enrollment: 54,568 students in district, 728 students in school
Racial Composition: 50.3% Black, 37.9% White, 2.5% Hispanic, 9% Asian American, .3% American Indian
Special Education: 10%
Gifted and Talented: .3%
Average Class Size: 28 students
Low-Income Students: 43%
Median Teacher Salary: $28,651
Spending Per Pupil: $4,870
% Passing Exit test in Language Arts: 74%, Math: 64%

Source: Taken from Madison Parish District Composite Report (1997)

APPENDIX B

INTERVIEW QUESTIONS

Teacher Interview/Questionnaire

The teacher questions are divided into two parts. Part One is composed of structural/procedural questions that were sent in the form of a questionnaire to the teachers in the Louisiana schools. These questions became part of the semi-structured interview for teachers in the Philadelphia Region. Part Two are relational questions that deal with the teacher/student and student/student relationships typically found in advisory programs.

PART ONE

1. How long have you been involved in the adviser-advisee program at your school?
2. Please explain how the program is organized?
   a. Were the students allowed to choose their adviser? Explain.
   b. How many advisees per adviser?
   c. When do you meet? How often? Where do you meet?
   d. What types of activities do you do in the time allotted? If you can, please attach a sample activity or describe one. Do you monitor student academic progress as part of your adviser duties? Discipline problems? Family/Social problems?
   e. Where did the idea initiate to start an adviser-advisee program in your school? Were you given any training in how to run an advisory group? If yes, please describe.

f. Was the faculty receptive to the program?
g. Was there a group of faculty who were vocal about not wanting to engage in this activity? If you answer *yes* to this, then please try to describe these faculty to me. How long have they been teaching? Do they tend to be male or female? What was this group's primary argument for *not* wanting an advisory program in your school?

3. What do you see as the most positive aspect of the advisory program?
4. What is the most negative aspect of the program?
5. If you could change the program in any way, what would you do differently?
6. Do you feel differently about going to school on days that you meet with your advisees?
7. Has your school developed a resource guide to help in the selection of activities for your advisory group? How are the activities selected?
8. Who is responsible for the advisory program at your school? If there are problems, where do you go for help?

PART TWO

9. Have you gotten to know the students in your advisory group really well?
10. Can your advisory students talk to you whenever they need to? Are you willing to listen to them and assist them in finding solutions to their problems?
11. Do your advisory students look up to you? Are you a role model for them?
12. Has the advisory program helped change your attitude toward or about school? Has the advisory program helped change the students' attitudes toward teachers?
13. As a result of the advisory program, do you get along better with your students? Do students seem to get along better with other students as a result of advisory?
14. Do you feel that the advisory program has helped teachers work more collaboratively?

Student Interview Questions

1. Tell me about your experiences in the advisory program.
2. Have you gotten to know at least one adult really well as a result of advisory periods?
3. Has an adult gotten to know you really well?
4. Can you talk to your advisor whenever you need to?
   Are they willing to listen to you and assist with finding solutions to your problems?
   Can you talk to them about your problems without having to worry about issues of confidence?
5. Do you look up to your advisor? Is he/she a role model for you?
   Do you have the option of changing your advisor if you want?
6. Do you participate in cooperative and group projects that help make you familiar with the school, with other students and adults, and with appropriate school behavior?
   Have you participated in any volunteer youth service activities as part of the advisory program?
7. Do you have more pride in your school as a result of the advisory program?
   Do you think that the advisory program has changed your attitude toward school?
   Has it helped change your attitude toward others? Who?
   Has the advisory program changed your attitude toward yourself?
8. As a result of the advisory program, do you get along better with your classmates?
   Do you get along better with your teachers and other adults at school?
   Do you get along better with your parents?
9. Do you talk to your parents about the advisory program?
10. What has the advisory program taught you?

CHAPTER 2

GET THE BIG PICTURE OF TEAMING

Eliminate Isolation and Competition Through Focus, Leadership and Professional Development

Kathleen M. Brown

ABSTRACT

Reflecting the admonitions of John Dewey that "the school must itself be a community life" (1966, p. 358), middle school reformers advocate interdisciplinary teaming as a wise practice in creating a "small community of learning" (Carnegie Task Force, 1989). This multi-site qualitative case study was conducted to understand and describe the nature and structural organization of interdisciplinary teaming as it either contributes to or hinders the creation of a sense of community and care for students and teachers. *Get the Big Picture: Eliminate Isolation and Competition Through Focus, Leadership and Professional Development* emphasizes the necessity of a team mission that is not vague, not ambiguous, and not fuzzy, but rather clear, understood, and able to be implemented. In an effort to avoid the negatives (isolation, loss of objectivity, competition), a proactive leader stressing proper training is vital!

INTRODUCTION

According to Muth and Alverman (1992), "Interdisciplinary teams create a sense of community among teachers and students" (p. 153). Given this fact and the admonitions of John Dewey that "The school must itself be a community life" (1966, p. 358), middle school reformers advocate interdisciplinary teaming in creating a "small community of learning" (Carnegie Task Force, 1989). *Turning Points 2000* (Jackson & Davis, 2000) declares that "teams offer students the most direct path for forging stable relationships with teachers and peers" (p. 125). This study reviews the literature regarding the rationale, structure, advantages and disadvantages of this essential middle school component. The current—status, strengths as well as shortcomings, of the interdisciplinary nature of team teaching is investigated. In addition, the reader is presented with an outline of the theoretical/conceptual framework serving as the lens through which the data were analyzed—care and community. The design of this multi-site qualitative case study, including sites, sample, and procedures, is also recounted, along with the data analysis procedures and findings.

Because of the tremendous potential of the middle school concept to contribute to the improvement of all schools, regardless of grade level, it is important to explore the "real" day-to-day experiences of team structuring. The factors that help mold a team, that keep them together, the joys, trials and tribulations of belonging, of building relationships, and of establishing a sense of care and community need to be explored. The available research indicates a significant gap between the main tenets of the theoretical middle school concept proposed by leading middle school authorities (National Middle School Association and Carnegie Council on Adolescent Development) and actual educational practices in most middle schools.

LITERATURE REVIEW

Rationale for Interdisciplinary Teaming

One of Sizer's (1992) nine common principles for members of The Coalition of Essential Schools, to be used as a basis for restructuring schools to meet their local needs and situations, is the principle of personalization. Sizer holds that "Teaching and learning should be personalized to the maximum extent feasible. To that end, a goal of no more than eighty students per teacher should be vigorously pursued" (p. 24). According to Alexander and George (1981), "anonymity, amorphousness and anomie seem to characterize contemporary society, and because the schools are in many ways a mirror of the society, these maladies infect the school as well"

(p. 134). The interdisciplinary team organization is a proposed solution to limiting the effects these forces have on middle schools. Teaming addresses the crucial need to help adolescents, ages 10 to 15 years, "acquire durable self-esteem, flexible and inquiring habits of mind, reliable and relatively close human relationships, a sense of belonging in a valued group, and a sense of usefulness in some way beyond the self" (Carnegie Task Force, 1989, p. 12). The Carnegie Task Force reminds us that "many young adolescents attend massive, impersonal schools, learn from unconnected and seemingly irrelevant curricula, know well and trust few adults in school, and lack access to health care, counseling, and the guidance needed to become healthy, thoughtful, and productive adults" (p. 13). Interdisciplinary teaming environments have been shown to benefit middle level learners in a variety of positive ways. "A team provides a valued group that young adolescents need to support their intellectual and interpersonal development. Teams provide a psychological home within the school that helps reduce the stress of isolation and anonymity (Jackson & Davis, 2000, p. 125). The National Middle School Association (NMSA) has taken a firm position on interdisciplinary team organization, suggesting that it is central to the middle level school concept (Vars, 1987).

According to Capelluti and Stokes (1991), the rationale for interdisciplinary teaching teams is that "they provide a manageable, philosophically defensible approach to delivering instruction and guidance to this age group" (p. 8). In theory, staff members can be more responsive to students because they know them more intimately and can, therefore, teach them more effectively because of the small group size and common planning periods. Capelluti and Stokes further explained that students are not the only ones who benefit from interdisciplinary teaming. Teaming provides opportunities for groups to work together toward academic and personal goals and to solve problems before they reach a crisis stage. Teachers report that classroom discipline problems are dramatically reduced through teaming. This middle level approach also "emphasizes collaboration, respect for the knowledge base of the professional staff, equalization of power and responsibility in the school, and participation by all" (Capelluti & Stokes, p. 8). Teacher empowerment, school-based management, and restructuring all contribute to the ideas of ownership and commitment. They promoted the concept that decisions should be made at the level closest to the implementation of the decisions. To this end, schools-within-schools, houses, teams, or learning communities are organizational designs that support the idea that teachers who have more input and whose efforts are acknowledged will be more invested. Three convictions provide the foundations for these adult organizational arrangements. They are:

1. People need a structure that allows for flexibility, creativity, accountability.
2. Professionals need control over their destiny.
3. Working together rather than in isolation leads to greater productivity. (Capelluti & Stokes, 1991, p. 9)

Structure of Interdisciplinary Teaming

Research suggests that middle level schools with a high commitment to interdisciplinary teaming have significantly stronger academic programs (Epstein & Mac Iver, 1990). Studies of successful teams have revealed a number of common organizational features, beliefs, and practices (Erb & Doda, 1989; Erb & Stevenson, 1999; George & Stevenson, 1989). Researchers (Clark & Clark, 1987; Hargreaves, Earl & Ryan, 1996) agree that effective interdisciplinary teaming involves efficient planning and organization, realizable goal-setting and community-building, and collaborative systems of identity and governance formation.

There are a variety of ways of organizing teachers, students, subjects, and time in an interdisciplinary fashion. There are also many variables of staff abilities and interests, certifications, student population, staff personalities, as well as other factors that need to be considered. A number of acceptable models vary in team size from two teachers and 50 to 75 students to six teachers with 150 to 190 students. Optimal teacher to student ratio is 1:20–25. These teachers teach the same students different subjects, share a common schedule and planning period, deliver a curriculum based on integrated themes, and share an adjacent space whenever possible. Characteristics of successful teams include:

1. Heterogeneous grouping of students;
2. Balance in terms of teachers' expertise, age, sex and race;
3. Formal team leaders with specific responsibilities;
4. Team organization for effective decision-making (e.g., goals, grouping, scheduling, homework, discipline);
5. Team sessions for systematic assessment of student strengths and weaknesses;
6. Development of team identity. (Arnold, 1991, excerpted from pp. 20–25)

George, Stevenson, Thomason, and Beane (1992) stated that teaming optimizes the potential for all team members to become acquainted with each other: "The team constitutes an extended family of sorts within which students can form primary social affiliations" (George et al., p. 59). Team identity is a big issue which can be enhanced by a team name, colors, logo, motto, mascot, rules, awards, rituals, and traditions. Team meetings have the potential to engender a sense of belonging and become forums for learning democratic processes. Team themes, projects, plays, shows, service projects, awards, and celebrations all convey the message that the team as a community is important, nurturing, and supportive of its members. "At its best, the team serves as a positive answer for students' need to belong to a sanctioned and defined social group" (George et al., p. 59). At its worse, as described in the "Disadvantages" section, team identity can undermine the ability for the whole faculty to attend to the business of the whole school (Kruse & Louis, 1997).

During the period from 1981 through 1991, George and Alexander (1993) assembled the collective wisdom of hundreds of experienced middle school educators into what they described as the "ten commandments of interdisciplinary team organization at its very best." They are:

1. Interpersonal Compatibility—arranging teams so that members are comfortable with one another is crucial—must be constantly nurtured.
2. Balance—subject strengths, personality style, ethnic background, sex, age, certification—in terms of teachers and students.
3. Planning Time—at least one common planning time per day.
4. Team Leadership—skilled team leader able to work with both teachers and administrators.
5. Personal Characteristics of Members—individual members must like teaching at this level and enjoy their role as team member. They must be optimistic and mature in terms of patience and tolerance.
6. Attitudes Toward Students—pro-student attitude committed to student success. Explore every alternative to improve and motivate.
7. Attitudes Toward Teammates—"diverse but unified." Accept differences, listen respectfully, willing to compromise, agree with school philosophy, show appreciation, and welcome new members.
8. Relative Autonomy—reasonable room for teams to create their own policies, schedules, activities, curriculum plans, systems for monitoring student behavior and academic performance, and for ensuring parent involvement.
9. Principal Involvement—"keep a tight grip on loose reins." Attend team meetings, observe, consult, listen, model and encourage.
10. Continuing Education—in-service sessions support the refinement and extension of teamwork. Training in interpersonal communications skills, conducting effective meetings, and the nature of middle school students. (George & Alexander, excerpted from pp. 292–294)

As a further note, Doda (1977) added the following four central ingredients of "what really makes a team work": (1) total team spirit, fostered by regular spirit-building activities like projects, field trips, honor rolls and special gatherings; (2) constant and effective team communication and conferences between and among teachers; (3) a team approach to discipline; and (4) when possible, a measure of totally teamed instruction (p. 9).

Team Leaders

A major leap forward in team effectiveness can occur when certain practices are instituted regarding team leadership. "They include writing a job description of the team leader, selecting team leaders who have the potential for quality leadership, and providing team-leadership training" (Rottier, 2000, p. 215). *Turning Points* (Carnegie Task Force, 1989) stated that each school-within-school, house, or team organization needs a leader who is directly responsible for:

> ...creating an environment conducive to team teaching. This person is the lead teacher, a person who works with teams of teachers to develop ideas for curriculum, obtains needed resources for instruction, helps teams to solve problems involving individual students, and offers advice when additional support services are needed. (p. 56)

The importance of team leaders is confirmed by Mac Iver (1990) who reported that teams with leaders, whether elected, appointed, or rotated, appear to function better than those without leaders. He found that teams with leaders spent significantly more of their common planning time on team activities. In addition, principals reported more frequent benefits from interdisciplinary teams in schools where there were team leaders. These leaders need to be teachers who understand and know how to apply the skills of collaborative leadership. Glatthorn and Spencer (1986) suggested:

> Typically such leaders do not have access to three important sources of power: They cannot reward; they cannot punish; and they have little formal authority. In such a situation, the research suggests that they need to rely on other power sources: Their expert knowledge; their control of information; and their attractiveness as individuals. They will need to be trained for this sensitive use of power. (p. 156)

In most middle schools, team leaders are formally identified. While often chosen and relied upon, most of these team leaders serve out of a sense of professional duty, not for any rewards gained from occupying the position. In fact, most team leaders work longer and harder than even they believed possible. They enjoy the challenge of extra responsibility and view it as an opportunity for personal and professional growth. The good leader is "well-liked, trusted, efficient, and task-oriented" (George & Alexander, 1993, p. 293). A clearly written definition of their duties usually includes:

1. Function as the liaison between the administration and the team; individually, teachers are encouraged, however, to keep open com-

munication lines with the principal, avoiding any unnecessary hierarchical elevation of the team leader to something in-between teacher and administrator.

2. Program coordination within the team: this is, of course, a task of consuming proportions, including a role in every activity of the team. (George & Alexander, 1993, p. 278)

C. Lipka (1977) agreed that team leadership is a very important component of the whole teaming concept. Her multidimensional task list for team leaders in the middle school can be organized into five categories: team relations, organizational relationships, instructional coordination and development, management activities, and public relations. Six teachers at Lincoln Middle School in Gainesville, Florida, most of whom have been successful team leaders for more than a decade, expand upon Lipka's dimensions in a discussion held in November 1990, describing good and ineffective team leaders:

> Good team leaders have a number of important qualities. They are, first and foremost, good at organization and time management. They also possess excellent communication and interpersonal skills, since most of their power comes from the ability to influence and persuade their peers. They are able to keep their focus on the mission of the school and the team. They are skilled delegators, and also able to build and maintain the morale and cohesiveness of the team.
>
> Ineffective team leaders share a number of weaknesses. They are unable to represent the feelings of their team members in important school problem-solving discussions when the team's feelings are different from their own. They may feel, alternately, that "I have to do everything" or they are a "buck passer." Too often, the ineffective team leader "brings a negative approach to the table." They may not look for opportunities to build leadership skills in other members of their team. They may, lamentably, be unwilling or unable to invest "what it takes" to do the job. (Bell, 1990, excerpted from pp. 82–96)

Role and Responsibilities of Team Members

Just as each school, each team, and each interdisciplinary model is unique, so too are the roles and responsibilities held by the different team members. Exactly what teams do and how they do it varies from middle school to middle school. There are a number of important functions though that successful interdisciplinary teams hold in common.

Team planning is one that must be a priority as more team planning time appears to positively affect team effectiveness (Mac Iver, 1990). A certain degree of structure and goal setting are equally important to effectively functioning teams. Merenbloom (1991) suggested that weekly, quarterly, and yearly goals help to direct the work of the team and provide structure for planning. Merenbloom stated: "Teams should be goal oriented; they should identify needs of students on that team and then work to meet those needs" (p. 29). While establishing team goals and weekly agendas are important organizational functions, it is equally important that teams establish procedures and guidelines for team operation. These guidelines should address the following items:

1. Establish common and/or compatible classroom management and team management procedures. The expectancies for appropriate student behavior should be consistent among the team members.
2. Develop policies and practices for flexible student grouping within the team. Tracking should be avoided; flexible grouping for a variety of instructional experiences should be established.
3. Develop a variety of schedule alternatives (within the block of time scheduled for the team) and establish assignments that will provide equal opportunity for flexibility of time, group size, and teaching load for each teacher on the team.
4. Identify areas appropriate for large group instruction, places where the entire team can get together for films, guest speakers, and other team activities.
5. Examine course content and establish systematic procedures to begin the integration of subject matter.
6. Establish compatible and appropriate procedures for evaluating student work and awarding grades. (Clark & Clark, 1994, pp. 133–134)

George and Alexander (1993) summarized the decisions for which members of middle school teams are responsible into ten categories: (1) Teaching responsibilities; (2) Arranging the physical environment; (3) Structuring academic class time; (4) Grouping students; (5) Scheduling students; (6) Selecting and distributing texts and other materials; (7) Teamed instruction; (8) Other student matters; (9) Relating to other staff members, and (10) Team planning (pp. 266–278). As is evident from this list and the guidelines above, a great amount of time is required for planning, reflection, and integration. It is important to remember that while some teacher responsibilities are more important than others, few decisions can be made without taking the whole school into account.

Advantages of Interdisciplinary Teaming

The advantages of interdisciplinary teaming are numerous. The teaming of teachers facilitates strong support systems for both middle level students and their teachers. Likewise, it increases the flexibility of learning time, provides a better vehicle for instruction, and creates opportunities to make connections across the various subject areas (Alexander & George, 1981; Clark & Clark, 1987, 1992; George & Oldaker, 1985; Mac Iver, 1990). Muth and Alverman (1992) categorized the advantages of interdisciplinary teaming according to four areas. First, because all teachers on a team teach the same students, the needs of each individual student can be met more easily. Secondly, interdisciplinary teams of teachers who plan together can design lessons and units that help students see connections among various disciplines. Next, because the teachers on a team all teach the same group of students, the opportunities are increased for improving interpersonal relationships among the students and between the teachers and students. Lastly, in addition to the advantages they provide students, interdisciplinary teams also offer support to the teachers on the team.

Interdisciplinary teaming environments have been shown to benefit middle level learners in a variety of positive ways. Positive climates and smaller focus groups, facilitated by interdisciplinary teams, have been shown to directly influence psychosocial development and to indirectly influence achievement (Epstein, 1981). Other benefits drawn from research confirm the strong linkage of interdisciplinary teaming organizations to developmentally appropriate practices for young adolescents (Arhar, 1992; Clark & Clark, 1992; Epstein, 1981; Fenwick, 1992; George & Oldaker, 1985; Mac Iver, 1990; Mitman & Lambert, 1992; Rutter, Maughan, Mortimore, Houston, & Smith, 1979).

Numerous advantages for teachers are also found in interdisciplinary teaming organizations. Collaboration with other teachers facilitates communication, enhances satisfaction, and increases opportunities for professional development (Arhar, Johnston, & Markle, 1989). Other benefits, as previously stated, also include a support system among teachers that encourages innovation and the provision for professional autonomy and decision making about instructional and organizational issues (Clark & Clark, 1987).

Clark and Clark (1994) actually separated and described in detail the benefits of interdisciplinary teaming to both students and teachers. When properly implemented, interdisciplinary team organizations:

1. Provide a more comfortable transition from elementary to middle school by creating environments that are conducive to learning and by reducing feelings of anonymity and isolation.
2. Allow teachers to focus collectively on the individual needs of their students and provide greater opportunities for recognition and support.
3. Enable the creation of positive, nurturing environments for learning.

4. Enhance school environments that facilitate the development of positive student attitudes toward teachers, a greater interest in subject matter, a sense of personal freedom, and a sense of self-reliance.
5. Promote a climate that fosters more positive relations among culturally diverse students.
6. Provide an atmosphere of support that influences students to behave in more positive ways, resulting in less inappropriate behavior, truancy, and tardiness.
7. Contribute to successful efforts to reduce dropouts.
8. Promote student insight into the logical relationships between the branches of knowledge.
9. Facilitate increased opportunities for communication between teachers and teachers, students and teachers, and students and students, often creating strong feelings of affiliation.
10. Provide better and more comprehensive communication between the home and school. (pp. 124–125)

The following listing of additional benefits of interdisciplinary teaming for teachers reflects research and practice (Arhar, 1992; Clark & Clark, 1992; Fenwick, 1992; Mitman & Lambert, 1992). Interdisciplinary teaming organizations:

1. Reduce the sense of teacher isolation found in most schools. Team organizations establish the necessary frameworks that allow teachers to work together in solving common instructional problems and to jointly focus on the needs of their students.
2. Create a positive climate in the school by increasing teachers' sense of efficacy and renewing enthusiasm for teaching.
3. Empower teachers to work collaboratively, giving them the autonomy to make instructional decisions based upon the individual needs of their students.
4. Promote major changes in instructional practice. Collaborative planning of instruction which focuses on early adolescent needs and characteristics is likely to result in teachers seeking out and using more developmentally responsive teacher strategies such as cooperative learning and peer tutoring.
5. Enhance positive communication with parents. (Clark & Clark, 1994, p. 126)

George and Alexander (1993) differentiated similar advantages along different lines. They categorized the benefits of interdisciplinary teaming organizations as instructional advantages and affective and behavioral advantages. Instructionally, the advantages include:

1. Team's comprehensive knowledge of student needs and power to plan,
2. Increased intellectual stimulation for teachers which results in interaction with other professionals and support,
3. The group's ability to plan and evaluate instructional programs,
4. More balanced but comprehensive evaluation of individual student progress,
5. Fits well and works synergistically with other middle school reform efforts (ex. advisory programs). (pp. 282–289)

The affective and behavioral advantages of interdisciplinary teaming include:

1. Development of a sense of community,
2. Balance between curriculum and personal knowledge,
3. Parent-team conferences,
4. Teacher cooperation and understanding,
5. Improved standard of student behavior,
6. Reduction in movement of students,
7. Rational, well-planned and consistent set of student behavior rules,
8. Students know they are cared about and have an opportunity to succeed,
9. Team teachers model effective group behavior and working cooperatively,
10. Professional autonomy. (pp. 282–289)

As can be seen from the literature, the concept of interdisciplinary teams in middle grades has several advantages. Teams are helpful because "within well-functioning groups, members can use their personal talents and the complimentary talents of others—a possibility that gives groups an advantage over solitary decision makers" (Lalik & Niles, 1990, p. 320). Teaming helps build a positive school climate where students and teachers are known well, respected as valuable members of a community of learners, and are supported in their efforts to grow, mature and succeed. Interdisciplinary teaming organizations provide for better use of faculty, better frameworks for the use of a variety of educational alternatives, and better opportunities for creating personalized instructional programs (Clark & Clark, 1987).

Disadvantages of Interdisciplinary Teaming

While there are many benefits that occur when interdisciplinary teaming organizations become a part of the school, middle level leaders need to be cognizant of some of the potential problems. Clark and Clark (1994) remind us that although the advantages far outweigh the problems, middle school reformers need to actively address the following problems if they are to be successful in creating effective teams:

1. Teaming is a social enterprise. Successful teams are built around teachers who are skilled in human relations, planning, and decision making. When these skills are not present, the effectiveness of the team may be greatly limited.
2. Effective interdisciplinary teams are built around teachers who like each other, work well together, and share like "beliefs" about the instruction of young adolescents. One of the major reasons teams fail is the lack of compatibility of team members.
3. Interdisciplinary teaming programs involve change, and some teachers will resist change. Some teachers prize their individual classroom autonomy and will resist attempts to involve them in collaborative efforts with other teachers. Teachers who see themselves as rigorous content specialists may resist efforts to integrate their content area with other content areas. Resistance may also come from teachers who do not have good social, planning, or decision-making skills.
4. Interdisciplinary teaming takes more teacher planning time. Team members who are still responsible for the instructional planning and management of their own classrooms must also allocate additional time for team planning. While some teachers will initially view this new time requirement as a burden, they soon come to value this shared time with their colleagues. (Clark & Clark, 1994, pp. 126–127)

According to George and Alexander (1993), common difficulties encountered by middle school personnel implementing interdisciplinary teaming usually revolve around the issues of balance, time, place, autonomy, and interpersonal planning and communication skills. "Balanced teacher and student populations, so that each team is a microcosm of the school at large, are crucial: teachers balanced according to complementing strengths, personal styles, instructional expertise and experience, as well as race, sex and age; students balanced according to sex, achievement, race, exceptionalities and age" (George & Alexander, p. 290). Schools that have imbalanced teams usually find the inequity difficult to manage.

Physical identity and team time are vital components of effective teaming. Teams that are not housed together, that do not have a distinctive and separate territory to call their own, do not develop the closeness necessary for bonding. Just as important, a team planning room, other than the faculty lounge, and time together are essential. Interdisciplinary team organization and thematic unit planning does take more teacher time; without it, teams flounder. Lack of sufficient common planning time is one of the most frequently cited difficulties encountered by disappointed and disenfranchised team teachers.

As mentioned earlier, teams need autonomy to function well. Administrators who are reluctant to loosen the reins and allow teachers to assume more control over the process necessary to remake the educational enterprise, will be unsuccessful in their efforts to implement change. Exemplary middle schools and their leaders find it essential to involve teams in participatory decision making. The Carnegie Report, *Turning Points* (Carnegie Task Force, 1989), called for empowering teachers to make decisions and share the responsibility for school leadership. Teachers, who work with the students daily, must be trusted to do what is best for them. The Carnegie Council on Adolescent Development stated that:

> Teachers on teams should exercise creative control over how curricular goals are to be reached for their team. Teachers should collectively allocate budget and space for their team, choose instructional methods and materials for classroom use, identify and develop interdisciplinary curricular themes, schedule classes, select field experiences including youth service opportunities, and evaluate students' performances in light of school-wide objectives. Teachers on teams should also have a significant voice in recruiting new teachers for the team or with the house. (1989, p. 55)

"Given balance, time, place and autonomy most teams move forward. Without the proper skills and attitudes, however, forward movement will be minimal" (George & Alexander, 1993, p.291). Without good planning skills and well developed interpersonal communication skills, teams have little chance of accomplishing their work-oriented tasks. Middle level leaders are advised to use a variety of methods available to enhance and support team formation, cohesiveness, and collaboration.

Another problem emerged from Hargreaves, Earl and Ryan's (1996) evaluation of schools endeavoring to establish core groupings of students into mini-schools or teams. The criticisms came from the students themselves who became tired of the same old faces. Mixed ability groups of students followed a common curriculum with a small team of teachers. Hargreaves et al. (1996) reported that teachers tended to like this reform because: "It reduced the number of students with whom they were in contact. It enabled them to know their students better, care for them more effectively, plan their work more appropriately, and assess and report on their progress more meaningfully and extensively" (p. 76). As we now know, these findings fit the existing literature very well. However, most students saw things rather differently. They felt denied the opportunities for greater challenge and wider choices, and they minded not being able to meet new people. They got tired of the people with whom they traveled and wanted to broaden their horizons with other, new students (Hargreaves et al., 1996, p. 76). These responses point to the fact that it is important to involve students early in any innovation. They can resist change just as much as teachers can. Middle level leaders need to continue to work hard to find the balance between community and monotony.

The challenge that remains here is to create an experience for the early adolescents that is sufficiently common, caring and inclusive so as to counter the traditional problems of fragmentation and impersonality of secondary schooling, while incorporating enough elements of choice and diversity, and enough changes and challenges in the program and the strategies of teaching and learning, to convey to students a substantial sense of progression from the upper elementary years (Hargreaves et al., 1996, pp. 76–77).

Another interesting study conducted by Kruse and Louis (1997) revealed findings suggesting that "the development of interdisciplinary teaming and a school-based community is not necessarily fully compatible, although they have similar positive results" (p. 266). The team requires a focus on smaller work groups, whereas the schoolwide professional community demands broader ties between staff members than teaming can provide. Teachers in this study, as they spoke about their teamed relationships, suggested that despite their advantages, "teams also undermined the ability for the whole faculty to attend to the business of the whole school. They spoke of five dilemmas in their struggle to balance the demands of being team members within the demands of membership in the larger school community:

1. Time for teams versus time for the school.
2. Focusing on present needs of the team's students versus focusing on students' careers in school.
3. Teacher Development: Time for organizing versus time for reflective dialogue.
4. Team autonomy versus all-school standards.
5. "Keeping the peace" versus critical reflection on practice. (Kruse & Louis, 1997, excerpted from pp. 272–279)

While Kruse and Louis (1997) acknowledged the many benefits of interdisciplinary teaming, they also reported that:

> ...too little time may be devoted to the discussion of important issues for the school as a whole, such as the development of programs for students that articulate across teams and grades, the reinforcement of schoolwide standards and goals, creative challenge and sharing across teams, and the ability of the school to confront and resolve tensions that emerge from reform efforts. The "dailyness of family life" in teams inhibits the evolution of broader reform agendas across the school. (p. 281)

In conjunction with Kruse and Louis's (1997) findings that teachers in interdisciplinary teams tended to cite those groups as their primary form of identification within the larger school community (See Table 1), Powell (1993) discovered similar results among the students themselves. Powell interviewed several seventh-grade students regarding their perspectives of their interdisciplinary team and developed the emergent categories into three themes: (1) feeling like a school family, (2) students' social connections, and (3) expectations of teaching and learning (p.52). Powell specifically asked whether the students saw themselves more as part of a team or more as part of the school. More than 57% of the students responded with team identity, 29% said school, and 14% choose both team and school. These remarkable findings support Kruse and Louis's concern regarding the need to find a happy medium between the development of community at the team level and the development of community at the larger, schoolwide level.

Table 1. Dilemmas for Team and Schoolwide Community

Focus on Team Community	*Focus on School Community*
Time for teams	Time for school
Developing programs for the team's students	Developing programs for the school's students
Organizing the team	Schoolwide reflection
Team autonomy	Schoolwide standards
"Keeping the peace" within teams	Peer challenge and critique across teams (Kruse & Louis, 1997, p.272)

In their book *Changing Middle Schools* (1994), Ames and Miller told the stories of four urban middle schools that have undergone deep transformation, including the implementation of interdisciplinary teaming. The authors reported that one "flip side of the teaming story is that, all too often, extraordinarily fine teams—or individual teachers—who serve as pioneers expose the limitations of others" (p. 132). The very fact that they are different and that they begin to attract praise and attention can create envy and resentment among their peers. A respected social studies teacher at Decatur Middle School acknowledged the problem:

> My perception is that what 8C does should be done by everyone—equipping children with the tools they need to be successful as students and as members of society. But I don't know if there are that many people in this building, or any building for that matter, that are talented enough, patient enough, or caring enough to do what they do. (Ames & Miller, p. 132)

Ames and Miller (1994) warned that with interdisciplinary teaming, a very competitive atmosphere can develop. They described an interesting, what they label "natural" evolution of teaming: (1) the first stage generally involves widespread resentment of the concept of teaming, (2) the second stage is competitive, and (3) the final stage is cooperative (1994, p.133). It takes time and patience for teams to move beyond the jealousy, unwillingness to share, unwillingness to recognize accomplishments phase. Team pride can sometimes actually get in the way of community building, collaboration and cooperation. Middle school leaders are encouraged by Ames and Miller (1994) to "take great pains to praise all the teams, give recognition to the teachers and students alike, and to schedule grade-level meetings on a regular basis to reduce the insularity of individual teams and encourage schoolwide cooperation" (p. 133). This recommendation coincides nicely with the findings of Kruse and Louis (1997) described above.

Maeroff (1993) in Team Building for School Change: Equipping Teachers for New Roles, highlighted time as one of the most persistent barriers to effective interdisciplinary teaming. In addition to this, Maeroff outlined pressures from outside the school which might make the work of teams, however highly dedicated, to be exceedingly problematic. He claimed that "even if all the internal difficulties attendant to team building are conquered, teams may fail because of impediments that originate outside the school" (p. 134). Throughout the chapter on "Obstacles to Teams," Maeroff defined and described the following six areas in which teams most often confront barriers:

1. Societal factors—drugs, poverty, crime, teenage pregnancies, violence.
2. Budgets—lack of funding for in-service, training, staff development.
3. Unions—concerned about implications for teachers.
4. Teacher knowledge and dedication—more needed than usual.
5. Team function—weakened by unclear roles and purpose in the school.
6. Continuity—reduction in staffing and departures of team members (exerpted from pp.134–145).

After providing a definition for team organization, a research-based rationale for the practice, and numerous suggestions for making the most of the opportunities that teaming offers, Erb and Doda (1989) summarized the disadvantages and/or precautions necessary for implementing a teaming approach in the middle school. Many of their recommendations concur with those of the authors' findings described above. Erb and Doda identified "eleven traps that have made team organization difficult, if not impossible, for those educators who inadvertently fell into them" (p. 116). Anticipating and avoiding these problems can lead to a much more satisfying experience with teaming:

1. Failing to recognize the team organization is fundamentally different from traditional departmentalized or self-contained arrangements.
2. Attempting to team without adequate staff development in such aspects as team skills (communication, group decision making, and organization of effective meetings) and team practices (goal setting, record keeping, evaluation).
3. Failing to place team organization at the top of the list of the scheduling priority list so that all else revolves around it—and not the other way around.
4. Failing to understand that new teams will need time and practice in order to develop into fully functioning teams.
5. Failing to consider personalities and interpersonal variables when staffing teaching teams and planning for staff development.
6. Attempting to team without choosing somebody to be responsible for the ongoing monitoring and support of teaming, which must include regular communication between teamed teachers and administration.
7. Failing to organize teams so that they are comprised of teachers with a common planning period who teach different core subjects to a common group of students in some common area of the building.
8. Failing to understand the significance of team identity and the power of symbols, ritual, and ceremony in the life of the team.
9. Failing to integrate team organization with the rest of the school program.
10. Failing to nurture faculty espirit de corps, and failing to nurture academic departments, which retain some important functions.
11. Failing to set goals for the growth and development of teams. (excerpted from pp. 116–122)

CONCLUSION

"Interdisciplinary teaming is perhaps *the* critical element of a transformational middle-level school" (Raebeck, 1992, p.60). Scholars and practitioners from exemplary middle schools agree with Raebeck that the most desirable approach for organizing teachers for middle level education is interdisciplinary teaming (Arhar, 1992; Carnegie Task Force, 1989; George & Alexander, 1993; George & Oldaker, 1985). Some of the most frequently mentioned advantages of interdisciplinary teaming fall into the areas of instruction, affect, and behavior. They include:

1. Helps build a sense of community, collaboration and communication between teachers, students and parents.
2. Nurtures a positive school climate and more balanced approach to knowledge, instruction and evaluation.
3. Fosters professional autonomy, shared commitment, more relevant curriculum, and well-defined student/teacher expectations and standards.

In order to be optimally effective the structure and nature of interdisciplinary teaming should include: (1) ample time and space to plan, bond and make decisions, (2) flexibility in scheduling, grouping and instructional methods, and (3) training in interpersonal skills, effective organizing, and specific preparation to teach young adolescents.

While numerous studies all point to the positive effects and structural components necessary for effective interdisciplinary teaming, we are warned by a few authors that implementing and sustaining a viable program may not be that easy. Sufficient time and space, shared-decision making, well developed interpersonal relationships, variety and change, as we know from human nature, do not necessarily come naturally. Middle level leaders need to be aware of team competitiveness, team identity versus school identity, and team monotony. They also need to realize that organizational changes alone will not alter dramatically the educational experiences of middle grade students. As Lounsbury and Clark (1990) wrote:

> Developmental responsiveness carries with it major implications for school restructuring. It demands that middle level educators move beyond the "mere" form of middle level programs, such as interdisciplinary teaming and teacher advisories, and becomes increasingly concerned with the substance of these programs. (p. 134)

METHODOLOGY

All empirical studies have an implicit, if not explicit, research design. This multi-site qualitative case study was part of a larger research project designed to understand and describe the practice of interdisciplinary teaming as it contributes to a sense of community and caring in the context of middle school reform. Recognizing that "the development of strong teams requires sustained attention to both the quality of key structural elements and the quality of interaction among team members" (Jackson & Davis, 2000, p. 135), the major research question to be answered by this research was: How do the structural/ procedural components of interdisciplinary teaming help or hinder the creation of a sense of community for middle level students and teachers?

Sites and Sample

Data for this study were collected from three very diverse middle schools (See Appendix A for school portraits) located in the large metropolitan area of the Greater Philadelphia Region. Criteria for selection consisted of schools using components of the middle school concept, specifically interdisciplinary teaming. Care was taken to include middle schools which varied according to grade configuration and which ran the gamut of diversity in terms of size, geographical location, racial/ethnic make-up, economic status, and student population.

As structurally diverse as the three middle schools are, there likewise existed a variety of programs labeled interdisciplinary teaming. On one hand, one of the schools visited reported ample time and space for teachers to plan, bond and make decisions. There appeared to be flexibility in scheduling, student grouping, and instructional methods. On the other hand, another of the teaming schools initially revealed frustration due to a lack of time, cohesion, and proper interpersonal communication skills. Specific preparation in effective organizing, working as a team, and teaching young adolescents also varied greatly from site to site. Some schools identified team leaders and detailed roles and responsibilities for members, while others did not.

The only criteria for inclusion in this case study was that the subjects chosen had some involvement in the day to day implementation of interdisciplinary teaming for at least one full school year. A total of 12 teachers and 3 administrators were interviewed to obtain data. The teachers and administrators involved in this study varied with regard to gender, ethnicity and experience. Using a type of nonprobability sampling, the three school administrators were asked to randomly recruit teachers for the interviews (minimum of four teachers from each school). The names of the schools as well as the names of the teachers and principals were changed and a number coding system was created for purposes of anonymity (see Appendix B).

Data Collection Strategies

Semi-structured interviews were the primary data gathering source used to help construct the participants' perspectives of teaming. The interview served as a "conversation with a purpose," yet allowed for individuals to define their world in unique ways (Merriam, 1988, p.71). Keeping the theoretical conception of care and community in mind, the interview questions were divided into two parts. Part one was composed of structural/procedural questions that dealt with the design, composition and philosophy underlying the organization of interdisciplinary teaming. Part two were relational questions that dealt with the teacher/teacher, teacher/student, and student/student relationships typically found in such programs. All of the interviews were tape-recorded and later transcribed for purposes of analysis.

Other sources of data included documents, field notes, and a reflexive journal. Examples of teaming activities, agendas for planning sessions, newsletters to parents, and team schedules were collected and analyzed. As a supplement to interviews, the use of these documents provided contextual richness and grounded the inquiry in a "real-world context" (Merriam, 1988, p. 109). Field notes were written and reviewed after each interview and site visit. A field log was maintained in which decisions relative to the emerging design and data validity were recorded. A reflexive journal was also maintained throughout this study. According to Lincoln and Guba (1985), reflexive journals mirror the "...investigator's mind processes, philosophical position, and bases of decisions about the inquiry" (p. 327). This quiet time set aside to reflect on what was happening, on what was being learned, and on what was being communicated added volume to the descriptive reporting of the data (see Kvale, 1996).

Data Analysis Procedures

Confronted with a mountain of impressions, documents, transcribed interviews, and field notes, the qualitative researcher faces the difficult task of making sense of what has been learned. Van Maanen (1988) discusses this process as telling the "tales of the field." Generating categories, themes, and patterns requires an intense awareness of, and focused attention to, the data, as well as an openness to the subtle, tacit undercurrents of the site's social life. Analysis was conducted across three middle schools and included a search for statements about relationships among the categories of data (Yin, 1994).

As data were coded, the responses were compared within categories and between categories. This technique, described in detail in the work of Glaser and Strauss (1967), is referred to as constant comparative analysis. Utilized in this study, this process aided in identifying patterns, coding data, and categorizing findings. The words and phrases generated from the formulated patterns served as the coding categories.

Conceptual Framework: Care and Community

The need for a school-based community is the center of much discussion in the educational administration literature (Bryk, Lee, & Holland, 1993; Louis, Kruse, & Associates, 1995; Sergiovanni, 1994a). As an image of school reform, community is often seen as a wise practice, an antidote to bureaucracy, which may be efficient but depersonalizes the important developmental processes and ethical or moral dimensions of organizational life (Victor & Cullen, 1988). Formal language is "the language of bureaucracy, of distance; humor, familiar imagery and metaphor, personalized messages are the language of caring" (Starratt, 1994, p. 53). Mitchell (1990) challenged educational leaders to create such communities in our schools, to shift the paradigm of schools from bureaucratic organizations to communities characterized by a context of difference and a commitment of collaboration. Sergiovanni asserted that this concept of community covers notions of family and neighborhood, of commitment and caring, of collaboration and collegiality, and "of felt interdependencies, mutual obligations, and other emotional and normative ties" (1994b, p. 7). The Carnegie Task Force (1989) called for middle schools that:

> Create small communities for learning where stable, close, mutually respectful relationships with adults and peers are considered fundamental for intellectual development and personal growth. The key elements of these communities are schools-within-schools or houses, students and teachers grouped together as teams, and small group advisories that ensure that every student is known well by at least one adult. (p. 9)

Consequently, community can be viewed as a vehicle for revitalizing the work life of teachers and for creating closer connections between students and schools.

Effective middle level schools create environments of "pervasive caring" (George & Oldaker, 1985; Johnston & Markle, 1986). "Interdependence" is the term selected by Gilligan (1982, p. 149) to describe this relational quality. She wrote that, when interdependence exists between people, they are motivated "to act responsively toward self and others and thus to sustain connectivity ... [and an] ethic of care" (p.149). Beck (1994) purported that "a caring educational ethic would support the idea that schools should promote maximum individual and community growth and development..." (p. 65). Such an ethic focuses on the demands of relationships, not from a contractual or legalistic standpoint, but from a standpoint of absolute regard. "An ethics of caring requires fidelity to persons, a willingness to acknowledge their right to be who they are, an openness to encountering them in their authentic individuality, a loyalty to the relationship" (Starratt, 1994, p. 52).

Why this discussion of community and caring? Basically because the link between caring and learning is very strong. Students, according to Noddings (1992) will do things for people they like and trust ... They listen to people who matter to them, and to whom they matter. Palmer (1983) revealed that "what scholars now say—and what good teachers have always known—is that real learning does not happen until students are brought into relationship with the teacher, with each other, and with the subject. We cannot learn deeply and well until a community of learning is created in the classroom" (p. xvi). A closer look at the conceptual framework that guides this research, the wise concepts of community and caring, gives credence to the fact that we need to experience shared values and a sense of kinship. After all, Mitchell (1990) emphasized that a sense of belonging is a prerequisite for "healthy human development" (p. 19).

Methods of Verification

The results of this study were analyzed within the parameters of the methodology chosen. Qualitative studies can be used to obtain in-depth, "thick" description of a setting (Geertz, 1973), a process, a social group, or some pattern of interaction. Multiple methods and sources of evidence, an established chain of evidence, pattern-matching, replication logic in multiple-case studies, use of proper case study protocol, and a developed case study data base are all wise practices that add to the validity and reliability of this study.

DATA ANALYSIS

Structural Components and Community: An Introduction

While one can argue that there has been general agreement as to what structures or components should be operating in middle schools, we are acutely aware that translating these structures into reality has been slow. Supporting this point, Manning (1993) writes: "While developmental psychologists have offered insightful theories about physical, psychosocial and cognitive development, the process of translating them into practice has been somewhat slow, especially beyond the elementary school years" (p. iii). Stevenson and Erb (1998) remind us that a small learning community does not exist if just the structural elements such as common planning time, block scheduling, shared students, and common team areas are provided in a building.

Although these structural elements are *necessary* to create a small community for learning, they are not *sufficient* to define it. Not only must the opportunity be provided, but teachers have to believe in it and choose to do it. Further, they must have the professional development and skills to make it happen. The climate of the school must be supportive of teaming, and teachers must actually engage in teaming practices (Stevenson & Erb, 1998, p. 50).

Successful teaming is defined by the culture of schooling that it creates and sustains. Understanding culture is a more complex task than mastering mechanics. Given this fact, the following questions remain. To what extent have our middle schools really embraced these calls for reform? Have structures been institutionalized in our middle schools that are more symbolic in nature than effective in practice? Have our middle schools cosmetically adopted only the "face-lift" part of the reforms and left the "developmentally appropriate middle school" to be more fiction than fact? The analysis of the data from this study surfaced a major theme which addresses the structural/ procedural elements of interdisciplinary teaming and the creation of a caring community atmosphere. *Get the Big Picture: Eliminate Isolation and Competition Through Focus, Leadership and Professional Development* emphasizes the necessity of a team mission that is not vague, not ambiguous, and not fuzzy, but rather clear, understood, and able to be implemented. In an effort to avoid the negatives (isolation, loss of objectivity, competition), a proactive leader stressing proper training is vital!

GET THE BIG PICTURE: ELIMINATE ISOLATION AND COMPETITION THROUGH FOCUS, LEADERSHIP AND PROFESSIONAL DEVELOPMENT

While there are many benefits that occur when interdisciplinary teaming organizations become a part of the school, middle level leaders need to be cognizant of some of the potential problems. In some instances, the structural and procedural components can actually hinder the creation of a sense of community. The analysis of the data from this study revealed three obstacles to continued growth that teams need to be aware of, need to address and, need to overcome in their efforts to create closer, caring connections. Isolating themselves as a team, losing sight of their objectivity, and competing with other teams in their school obviously do not aid in the overall community building process. The interpersonal relationships among team members need to reflect and reinforce a commitment to "mutual growth and development" rather than "survival and self-interest" (Mitchell, 1990, p. 42). Teachers need to be aware of the "big picture."

Unfortunately, this does not always occur. In fact, Jones (1997) reports that "mature teams often isolate themselves and the result is a membership that rarely extends beyond core teachers" (p.221). Teams can tend to get so comfortable with one another that they actually become opposed to "outsiders" and their input. When asked about principal involvement in team matters, one teacher responded, "very seldom, um very seldom does she come to our grade level team meetings. We kind of don't like her to come because it gets us off track. Yea, we need to stay focused and get our business taken care of" (3T13-FW8-07ES). When asked about larger school issues, another teacher responded in an unsure manner, stating, "well, you know, my territory is my territory, I only know about my grade" (2T07-FW8-20S).

In "The Influence of Middle Level Interdisciplinary Teaming on Teacher Isolation," Mills, Powell, and Pollack (1992) reported a year-long study conducted at a Junior High School in Nevada that involved sixth, seventh, and eighth grade teachers at the school. Researchers reported that teamed teachers did not feel personally isolated, but some felt like "islands in the stream" as the school flowed around their particular team. Some teachers felt isolated within their grade level, others reported isolation from other teachers in their subject area, and some team teachers perceived an isolation from support personnel and other non-teamed staff and students. Whether the teachers interviewed for this particular "Creating Community in Middle Schools" study are consciously aware of their team isolation or not is debatable. What is certain is the fact that some administrators recognize the inappropriate behaviors, label them as a real concern of teaming, and are anxious to take the necessary steps in overcoming and correcting the behaviors.

> **A**: "Well, the caution is that all you see in the school and the halls are the kids you have. All you want to do is close the door and be in your classroom and say this is mine, the rest isn't mine. And kids are involved in not only that SLC, but the bigger community also. You cannot just have a conversation among your people, but you need to meet your colleagues at school so you can see the bigger picture." (1A05-MW5/8-31S)

A: "They lose their communication. What I have found out is that they create a sterile environment by creating grade level teams. Because the schedule is so unforgiving, a 6th grade teacher whose only on the first floor rarely ever gets an opportunity to collaborate or even discuss things with a 7th or 8th grade teacher located on the second floor. This is where vertical teaming, as opposed to our horizontal teaming, would at least force feed the interaction between the grade levels. Obviously it would aid the instructional program because people would know where people were coming from, what materials are used, and what expectations are held. That's been a hard sell here though." (2A10-MW5/8-30S)

A: "Other than the fact that teaming does separate, it's like an island nation, I give the analogy of the Bahamas, you know, we're the Greek city-state. The state becomes so autonomous that from time to time the invisible curriculum takes over." (2A10-MW5/8-30S)

Connected to this notion of team isolation is the idea of loss of objectivity. In an effort to bond and form close relationships, sometimes team members can consciously or unconsciously form unhealthy biases in the process. Once again, they lose sight of the big picture. The goal of fostering small, authentic communities of learners becomes overshadowed by personal complacency with their students and their fellow teachers.

A: "Sometimes you can lose your objectivity because you are so close to the kids. And then you can form, what you want—an emotional bond with the kids, but you lose in your objectivity." (1A05-MW5/8-31S)

T: "I think it's just like a marriage, absolutely. Exactly, apathy sets in—you get real comfortable with people and sometimes you overlook some of the things. And it can consciously be overlooked, right, I guess that's what happens." (2T09-FW6-04E)

T: "Well, I'll tell you what, I worked with a couple of different teams and once you get comfortable, and I'm very comfortable with this team, if any little thing goes wrong, you want to let it just pass by and smooth it over. I mean it's just uncomfortable to rock the boat." (2T08-MW6-30E)

A: "It's a sympathetic fallacy ... And I tend to think that that's the real interrelatedness virus that comes. I'm going to do what my colleagues do, what they are saying. And it's a shame..." (2A10-MW5/8-30S)

The need for a school-based community is the center of much discussion in the educational administration literature (Bryk, Lee, & Holland,

1993; Louis, Kruse, & Associates, 1995; Sergiovanni, 1994b). However, driven by a value system oriented toward individuality, competition, and material success, much of our culture teaches us not the skills of community building but rather of self-absorption and negativity. This stress on competition and individuality narrows and undermines the impulse to care and nourish. Unfortunately, the schools visited and the teachers interviewed for this study are not immune to these realities. Ames and Miller (1994) warn that with interdisciplinary teaming, a very competitive atmosphere can develop. Friendly competition can be enjoyable and productive for some, but it can easily become excessive and get out of hand. Competition can become destructive to a team's spirit of community. It can cause faculty and student morale to suffer greatly. The following comments verify the fact that jealousy, an unwillingness to share, and an unwillingness to recognize others' accomplishments do indeed exist both among and within some teams:

> **T**: "And I have seen people sabotage one another, with that 'Oh, poor baby is Mrs. P. picking on you?' kind of attitude. And they totally sabotage the other person." (1T04-MW8-17S)

> **T**: "We had a big fight because they almost did not give us the 8th grade that we asked for next year. Because we always had the little babies and we're the little cutsie 5th grade teachers (originally). But the people that are teaching 8th grade right now are bombing, so why not? They are always saying what a strong team we are, so give us a chance." (1T03-FW7-07E)

> **A**: "Um, hum yea, there are other pitfalls. For instance, there is some unconscious competition from certain teams. We have some teams who do some very unique creative activities with youngsters that the other teams choose not to do or can't do because of the individual expertise of one or more of the team members. So therefore, the teams themselves have a particular autonomy or individuality which is always compared to what other teams do or don't do. So what I have requested teams to do is to temper their decision for specific activities so that whatever they do other teams can replicate if they wanted to." (2A10-MW5/8-30S)

> **T**: "I don't think it's anything the kids sense, I don't think the kids feel it and I don't think the parents are aware of it. It's just among ourselves ... Okay, we are uh, the four of us tend to be much more laid back as compared to the 8th grade team. Um, the 8th grade team is very, how should I say this, I don't know, they are much more focused on academics and we are focused on academics as well but

we have a more tender side sort of, you know. Yea, well there is competition among the teams. There really is competition and you know what it depends on the administrator because when we first started we had an administrator that favored the 8th grade team. Clearly, blatantly favored the 8th grade team. Now we have a new administrator and a complete flip-flop. I feel that she favors our team. We just shake our heads when three years ago we were the underdogs you know and now, we are like, he-he, you know." (3T11-FW7-09S)

T: "You know, I'll tell you what, the 8th grade team is the power team. We are the disciplinarians, we are the organized ones, we show the most leadership. Um, we are very appropriately placed with the 8th grade students who are in need of what we give them. Um, much more academically challenging to the students, much more demanding, we hold very high standards." (3T13-FW8-07ES)

Recent discussions of community have emphasized the importance of creating schools in which all members share an understanding of a mission and educational vision (Bryk et al., 1993; Louis, 1994; Meier, 1995; Senge, 1990). As a result, Kruse and Louis (1997) state that "teachers and principals are faced with a demand to create both cohesive, often interdisciplinary units that are typically focused on a subset of the school's pupils and the development of a strong school culture that transcends the team" (p. 262). In theory, instruction will be more effective in schools that use interdisciplinary teaming because the teachers on a team can plan thematic units that enable students to make connections between ideas in different disciplines. In practice, as we have already seen and continue to hear, this does not always occur.

T: "I think the opportunities to dovetail the many subjects are there. I think that the opportunity is really fantastic. We don't really have specific interdisciplinary units that we do though, but whenever there is a need, we pick up on it." (2T07-FW8-20S)

A: "Well, the kids at this age level, I mean when you look at them developmentally, they shouldn't be learning facts and data and shouldn't be acquiring knowledge in a vacuum. What they need to see is a synthesis of information and how subjects interplay with one another. Sad to say, this doesn't happen too often." (2A10-MW5/8-30S)

T: "Another problem is that, and I know it's known around the school, is the interdisciplinary units and the cross curricular activities. And I'm telling you, it's just not happening. We don't have things that are lined in this curriculum thread, and this thread ... We try to make

> those kinds of connections but we don't have the time and our curriculum at this point is not ... there is no connection that we can make." (3T13-FW8-07ES)

According to Miller (1987), it is generally agreed by those who study team efforts that there are four major reasons that teams fail.

1. Members do not understand the function, purpose, or goals of the team's effort.
2. Members do not know what roles to play or what tasks are their responsibility.
3. Members do not understand how to complete their tasks or how to work as part of a team.
4. Members do not "buy into" the function, purpose, or goals of the team's effort or they reject their roles or responsibilities.

As evidenced by the dysfunctional behaviors described above, healthy, productive teams need a clear focus, strong leadership, and well-defined professional development in order to properly combat team isolation, complacency, and competition. Teams should not be left to invent themselves without external guidance. A team vision is needed for teams to define their ideals, to articulate the purposes and directions that guide them in their day-to-day functioning, to provide some coherence between values and educational activities. Being mission driven in Dickinson and Erb's (1997) opinion means "having a singular focus on young adolescents. It means working with colleagues with an eye on the needs of youth and not on petty conflicts, personal disagreements, potential slights, or imagined hurts. It means compromise, real listening, openly resolving and confronting problems so that the team can best devote its energies to accomplishing its stated mission" (p. 6). As one teacher so poignantly put it, "I think another advantage to teaming is that we can do projects together. We can share the grading and experience the growth together. I mean we can do a lot of interdisciplinary things" (2T09-FW6-04E). To others it means finding the common ground of shared purpose and direction and reaching some type of consensus, appreciation and deeper cognition:

> **A**: "Teaming allows the teachers to know what they are teaching, what each of them is teaching and to have some interrelatedness." (3A15-FW5/8-25ES)

> **T**: "We teach common ideas, one may have the thread of an idea and somebody will add something to that and get different perspectives. And I think that you begin to see the interconnectedness of the subjects because I think too often, if you just teach one subject, you

forget that the others are connected to it. Well, they have a lot to do with one another." (2T06-MW7-28S)

Teams are often highly motivated at the beginning of their teaming experience, but they require constant guidance, training, and support from leaders. Arnold and Stevenson (1998) believe that no individual has more potential for positive influence on the promise of teaming than the principal. "Teachers look to their leaders for moral direction and support as well as for considerations of time, space, and materials, and budgetary provisions. Clearly the path to successful teaming is made infinitely smoother by informed, trusting, supportive leaders" (Arnold & Stevenson, 1998, p. xiv). Because principals play such a pivotal role in the development and implementation of teaming, Rottier (1996) adds that "they must have a thorough understanding of and a belief in the interdisciplinary organization" (p. 50). As earlier stated, the administrator's role in teaming involves selecting and placing teachers on teams, monitoring and assisting teams, and solving team problems. Effective principals are responsible for helping teams make sound decisions, establish challenging and developmentally responsive programs, and define expectations that reflect the school's overall philosophy. Rottier believes, and the following comments attest to the fact that the attitudes and actions of the principal can either enhance or hinder the operation of teams.

T: "The administration really doesn't get involved in the teams at all. They don't encourage or discourage who you are with. They don't know. I don't think they involve themselves at all. It's not thought about." (1T03-FW7-07E)

T: "No, the Principal is not involved in team matters at all. He is involved in our interactions with the children. But he is not involved with our interaction with each other." (1T04-MW8-17S)

T: "The other thing too, I think I would be more, if I was an administrator, I'd be strong about moving people around. I would pull people; they don't do that because they don't want to make people angry and I think that in some cases they should." (1T02-FW7-06E)

In addition to strong leadership, staff development is another essential element in the successful implementation of the team process. "As teams evolve, their professional development needs are likely to vary over time—typically, teams begin with a focus on relationship building and management issues and then progress to a focus on collaborative teaching and curriculum integration (Pounder, 1998, pp. 77–78). According to Mac Iver (1990), one of the most commonly agreed-on problems is that teachers are insufficiently trained in the team approach. While the administrators interviewed in this study were unaware of any specific training in interpersonal communication skills, in conducting effective meetings, or in the nature of middle school students, the teachers recognized the lack of professional development in these areas as a real detriment to their growth as teachers.

> **A**: "Training in interpersonal communications or conducting effective meeting? "No, I am not aware. I don't know, nothing that we have done as far as professional development." (1A05-MW5/8-31S)

> **A**: "Probably not, no specific middle school training in those days. What they did was they acquired a number of skills because of the philosophy which wrote the design on this building, the instructional program." (2A10-MW5/8-30S)

> **T**: "No training in interpersonal communication skills, in conducting effective meetings, or in the nature of middle school students. This was our first placement. I think it (professional development) might have been helpful when we first started but at this point ... I think we found out the hard way." (1T04-MW8-17S)

> **T**: "No, those are the things that lack in my training." (2T07-FW8-20S)

> **T**: "No, not really, I mean in college we had classes but they've been... There is definitely things lacking here." (3T11-FW7-09S)

CONCLUDING DISCUSSION

Middle level reform—indeed, all school reform—is a developmental process. One teacher states, "Our first year was hard. It was hell, it was awful. It just takes time" (3T13-FW8-07ES). According to Stevenson and Erb (1998),

> It begins by teachers believing and wanting to change. This is accompanied by creating opportunities for change and learning the skills necessary to support it. With a supportive environment and changes in practice, reforms get established. As these reforms are established, they change the way a school works and the way teachers and students experience school. Then, and only then can we expect to see real improvement in student performance and behavior. (p. 52)

The AIMS study, while ongoing, has assisted middle level educators in answering the question "Does it work?" The preliminary results indicate that implementing only a piece of the *Turning Points* (1989) recommendations does not have a positive impact on student outcomes (achievement, health, behavior) but that implementing a number of the recommendations simultaneously, properly sequenced, and properly supported does have a positive impact. We are further reminded by the work of Felner, Jackson, Kasak, Mulhall, Brand, and Flowers (1997), that when practices such as interdisciplinary team organization and advisory groups are implemented together and in proper sequence, with leadership support and with adequate staff development, gains in student achievement and other outcomes are likely to be positive. Planning and developing viable teams are, of course, not as simple as following principles and guidelines. This analysis of the data regarding the structural/procedural components of interdisciplinary teaming concurs with this point. For teams to be successful, time is of the essence. Teams need time to mesh and to meet, time to communicate and to commit, time to establish goals, to set agendas, and to actually become a vital strategy for engaging young adolescents in a developmentally responsive manner. However, time alone is not the only ingredient necessary. A good leader is needed; one who inspires action on plans and facilitates real changes. One who addresses the importance of planning, the development of team procedures, the creation of a team identity, and the necessity for communication, accountability, and interpersonal relationships. Teams need a leader who nurtures and inspires vision. One who realizes that vision, embedded in values, hopes and dreams, becomes reality only through time-consuming and often challenging improvement efforts. It grows out of teamwork and empowerment. Principals need to provide teachers with that vision, the dynamic focus, leadership, and professional development so vital in eliminating team isolation, loss of objectivity, and competition. Administrators need to communicate, to collaborate, to motivate, and to support collegiality for student learning and professional growth and improvement. They need to provide their teachers with specific training, experience in human relationships, and the security of knowing that a strong support system surrounds them.

Jones (1997) reports that successful teams share certain benchmarks of achievement, are treated as professionals whose expertise is both respected and valued, and are supported by the administration, the student body, and the surrounding community. "They take care of one another just as they do their students, for that sense of caring and giving are simply a part of who and what they are" (p. 227). Interdisciplinary teaming has the potential to encourage and enable such community building to occur. It enables positive collegial relationships to form and gives value to each person in the school; it nurtures open communication and collaboration and helps all involved to ask help from one another, offer help to one another, and solve problems together instead of in isolation (Donaldson & Sanderson, 1996).

REFERENCES

Alexander, W., & George, P. (1981). *The exemplary middle school.* New York: Holt, Reinhart, and Winston.

Ames, N., & Miller, E. (1994). *Changing middle schools: How to make schools work for young adolescents.* San Francisco: Jossey-Bass.

Arhar, J. (1992). Interdisciplinary teaming and the social bonding of middle level students. In J.L. Irvin (Ed.), *Transforming middle level education: Perspectives and possibilities* (pp. 139–161). Needham Heights, MA: Allyn and Bacon.

Arhar, J., Johnston, J., & Markle, G. (1989). The effects of teaming on students. *Middle School Journal, 20*(3), 24–27.

Arnold, J. (1991). The revolution in middle school organization. *Momentum, 22*(2), 20–25.

Arnold, J., & Stevenson, C. (1998). *Teachers' teaming handbook: A middle level planning guide.* Fort Worth, TX: Harcourt Brace College Publishers.

Beck, L. (1994). *Reclaiming educational administration as a caring profession.* New York: Teachers College Press.

Bell, N. (1990). *A case study of the implementation of interdisciplinary team organization in a large school district.* Doctoral dissertation, University of Florida.

Bryk, A., Lee, V., & Holland, P. (1993). *Catholic schools and the common good.* Cambridge, MA: Harvard University Press.

Capelluti, J., & Stokes, D. (Eds.). (1991). *Middle level education: Programs, policies, & practices.* Reston, VA: National Association of Secondary School Principals.

Carnegie Task Force on Education of Young Adolescents. (1989). *Turning points: Preparing American youth for the 21st century.* Washington, D.C.: Carnegie Council on Adolescent Development.

Clark, S., & Clark, D. (1987). Interdisciplinary teaming programs: Organization, rationale, and implementation. *Schools in the middle: A report on trends and practices.* Reston, VA: National Association of Secondary School Principals.

Clark, S., & Clark, D. (1992). The pontoon transitional design: A missing link in research on interdisciplinary teaming. *Research in Middle Level Education, 15*(2), 57–81.

Clark, S., & Clark, D. (1994). *Restructuring the middle level school: Implications for school leaders.* Albany: State University of New York.

Dewey, J. (1966). *Democracy and education.* New York: Macmillan.

Dickinson, T., & Erb, T. (Eds.). (1997). *We gain more than we give: Teaming in middle schools.* Columbus, OH: National Middle School Association.

Doda, H. (1977). Teacher to teacher. *Middle School Journal, 8,* 8–9.

Donaldson, G., & Sanderson, D. (1996). *Working together in schools: A guide for educators.* Thousand Oaks, CA: Corwin Press.

Epstein, J. (1981). *Secondary school environments and student outcomes: A review and annotated bibliography.* Report No. 315. Baltimore, MD: Center for Social Organization of Schools, The Johns Hopkins University.

Epstein, J., & Mac Iver, D. (1990). *Education in the middle grades: Overview of national practices and trends.* Columbus, OH: National Middle School Association.

Erb, T., & Doda, N. (1989). *Team organization: Promise, practices and possibilities.* Washington, DC: National Education Association.

Erb, T., & Stevenson, C. (1999). From faith to facts: Turning Points in action—What difference does teaming make? *Middle School Journal, 30*(3), 47–50.

Felner, R., Jackson, A., Kasak, D., Mulhall, P., Brand, S., & Flowers, N. (1997). The impact of school reform for the middle years: Longitudinal study of a network engaged in Turning Points-based comprehensive school transformation. *Phi Delta Kappan, 78*(7), 528–532, 541–550.

Fenwick, J. (1992). *Managing middle grade reform—An "American 2000" agenda.* San Diego, CA: Fenwick and Associates, Inc.

Geertz, C. (1973). Thick description: Toward an interpretive theory of culture. In C. Geertz (Ed.). *The interpretation of cultures* (pp. 3–32). New York: Basic Books.

George, P., & Alexander, W. (1993). *The exemplary middle school* (2nd ed.). New York: Holt, Reinhart, and Winston.

George, P., & Oldaker, L. (1985). *Evidence for the middle school.* Columbus, OH: National Middle School Association.

George, P., & Stevenson, C. (1989). The "very best teams" in the "very best" middle schools as described by middle school principals. *TEAM, 3,* 6–17.

George, P., Stevenson, C., Thomason, J., & Beane, J. (1992). *The middle school: And beyond.* Alexandria, VA: Association for Supervision and Curriculum Development.

Gilligan, C. (1982). *In a different voice: Psychological theory and women's development.* Cambridge, MA: Harvard University Press.

Glaser, B., & Strauss, A. (1967). *The discovery of grounded theory: Strategies for qualitative research.* New York: Aldine.

Glatthorn, A., & Spencer, N. (1986). *Middle school/junior high principal's handbook: A practical guide for developing better schools.* Englewood Cliffs, NJ: Prentice-Hall.

Hargreaves, A., Earl, L., & Ryan, J. (1996). *Schooling for change: Reinventing education for early adolescents.* Washington, DC: Falmer Press.

Hobbs, N., Dokecki, P., Hoover-Dempsey, K., Moroney, R., Shayne, M., & Weeks, K. (1984). *Strengthening families.* San Francisco: Jossey-Bass.

Jackson, A., & Davis, G. (2000). *Turning points 2000: Educating adolescents in the 21st century.* New York: Teachers College Press.

Johnston, J., & Markle, G. (1986). *What research says to the middle level practitioner.* Columbus, OH: National Middle School Association.

Jones, J. (1997). Mature teams at work: Benchmarks and obstacles. In Dickinson, T., & Erb, T. (Eds.), *We gain more than we give: Teaming in middle schools.* Columbus, OH: National Middle School Association.

Kruse, S., & Louis, K. (1997). Teacher teaming in middle schools: Dilemmas for a schoolwide community. *Educational Administration Quarterly, 33*(3), 261–289.

Kvale, S. (1996). *Interviews: An introduction to qualitative research interviewing.* Thousand Oaks, CA: Sage Publications, Inc.

Lalik, R., & Niles, J. (1990). Collaborative planning by two groups of student teachers. *The Elementary School Journal, 90,* 319–336.

Lincoln, Y., & Guba, E. (1985). *Naturalistic inquiry.* Beverly Hills, CA: Sage.

Lipka, C. (1977). *Perceptions of the role of team leaders in Florida middle schools.* Unpublished doctoral dissertation, University of Florida.

Louis, K. (1994). Beyond "managed care": Rethinking how schools improve. *School Effectiveness and School Improvement, 5,* 1–22.

Louis, K., Kruse, S., & Associates. (1995). *Professionalism and community: Perspectives for urban schools.* Thousand Oaks, CA: Corwin Press.

Lounsbury, J., & Clark, D. (1990). *Inside grade eight: From apathy to excitement.* Reston, VA: National Association of Secondary School Principals.

Mac Iver, D. (1990). Meeting the needs of young adolescents: Advisory groups, interdisciplinary teaching teams, and school transition programs. *Phi Delta Kappan, 71*(6), 458–464.

Maeroff, G. (1993). *Team building for school change: Equipping teachers for new roles.* New York: Teachers College Press.

Manning, M. (1993). *Developmentally appropriate middle level schools.* Wheaton, MD: Association for Childhood Education International.

Meier, D. (1995). *The power of their ideas: Lessons for America from a small school in Harlem.* San Francisco: Jossey-Bass.

Merenbloom, E. (1991). *The team process: Handbook for teachers.* Columbus, OH: National Middle School Association.

Merriam, S. (1988). *Case study research in education: A qualitative approach.* San Francisco, CA: Jossey-Bass.

Miller, R. (1987). *Team planning for educational leaders.* Philadelphia, PA: Research for Better Schools.

Mills, R., Powell, R., & Pollak, J. (1992). The influence of middle level interdisciplinary teaming on teacher isolation: A case study. *Research in Middle Level Education, 15*(2), 9–26.

Mitchell, B. (1990). Loss, belonging, and becoming: Social policy themes for children and schools. In B. Mitchell and L. Cunningham (Eds.), *Educational leadership and changing contexts of families, communities, and schools: Eighty-ninth yearbook of the National Society for the Study of Education* (pp. 19–51). Chicago: University of Chicago Press.

Mitman, A., & Lambert, V. (1992). *Instructional challenge: A casebook for middle grade educators.* San Francisco: Far West Laboratory for Educational Research and Development.

Muth, K., & Alverman, D. (1992). *Teaching and learning in the middle grades.* Needham Heights, MA: Allyn and Bacon.

Noddings, N. (1992). *The challenge to care in schools: Alternative approaches to education.* New York: Teachers College Press.

Palmer, P. (1983). *To know as we are known: Education as a spiritual journey.* New York: Harper Collins.

Pounder, D. (1998). *Restructuring schools for collaboration: Promises and pitfalls.* Albany: State University of New York.

Powell, R. (1993). Seventh graders' perspectives of their interdisciplinary team. *Middle School Journal, 1,* 49–57.

Raebeck, B. (1992). *Transforming middle schools: A guide to whole school change.* Lancaster, PA: Technomic.

Rottier, J. (1996). *Implementing and improving teaming: A handbook for middle level leaders.* Columbus, OH: National Middle School Association.

Rottier, J. (2000). Teaming in the middle school: Improve it or lose it. *The Clearing House, 73*(4), 214–216.

Rutter, M., Maughan, B., Mortimore, P., Houston, J., & Smith, A. (1979). *Fifteen thousand hours: Secondary schools and their effects on children.* Cambridge, MA: Harvard University Press.

Senge, P. (1990). *The fifth discipline: The art and practice of the learning organization.* Garden City, NY: Doubleday.

Sergiovanni, T. (1994a). *Building community in schools.* San Francisco: Jossey-Bass.

Sergiovanni, T. (1994, b). Organizations or communities? Changing the metaphor changes the theory. *Educational Administration Quarterly, 30*(2), 214–226.

Sizer, T. (1992). *Horace's school: redesigning the American high school.* Boston, MA: Houghton Mifflin.

Starratt, R. (1994). *Building an ethical school.* Washington, DC: The Falmer Press.

Stevenson, C., & Erb, T. (1998). How implementing Turning Points improves student outcomes. *Middle School Journal, 30,* 49–52.

Van Maanen, J. (1988). *Tales of the field: On writing ethnography.* Chicago: University of Chicago Press.

Vars, G. (1987). *Interdisciplinary teaching: Why and how.* Columbus, OH: National Middle School Association.

Victor, B., & Cullen, J. (1988). The organizational basis of ethical work climates. *Administrative Science Quarterly, 33*(1), 101–125.

Yin, R. (1994). *Case study research: Design and methods* (2nd ed.). Thousand Oaks, CA: Sage.

APPENDIX A
PORTRAITS OF THE THREE TEAMING SCHOOLS

Taylor Middle School: Taylor Middle School is an old, block-long, three-story brick building located in a very economically deprived section of North Philadelphia. A tall, black wrought iron fence surrounds the immediate school site, while small, crammed row homes surround the neighboring area. The one-way streets are dilapidated, crowded with cars, and covered with litter. The windows of Taylor Middle are barred, the steel doors are chain locked, and the outside walls are defaced with graffiti. From the parking lot, which had once been a playground, the skyline of center city Philadelphia can be seen in the distance. Once inside of the school, sunlight reflects off a clean, marble stairway and Honor Roll announcements decorate the halls. Taylor Middle's mission statement—to motivate its students to a high level of achievement, attendance and participation—is prominently displayed in the front foyer above the security guard's station. Taylor educates 1200 5th through 8th graders who are evenly divided among five houses, otherwise known as "small learning communities." Each house is comprised of a combination of grade levels and is usually further divided into two or three teacher member teams. Taylor Middle has incorporated vertical teaming into its schedule for more than eight years now. Most of the teachers work in pairs, block schedule, and have an average class size of 33 students. They do not have ample common planning time, space or training in interpersonal communication or effective organizational skills. Non-teaching, semi-administrative level house leaders accept most of the responsibility for teaming functions, including class schedules, student grouping, and curriculum decisions.

Thomas Middle School: Thomas Middle School, serving 1000 6th, 7th, and 8th graders, is a nationally recognized "School of Excellence." Built in 1972, Thomas sits atop a large hill overlooking the Greater Philadelphia Area. Seventy-four acres of rolling hills, meticulously manicured landscapes, and numerous athletic fields and courts surround the long, two-story school building. The well-designed layout allows for ample parking, lighting, and plenty of trees where students from the woodshop class have hung nicely constructed and decorated birdhouses. The school's interior is clean, bright, and adorned with students' work. Computerized signs and announcements reveal the latest happenings at Thomas Middle. The interdisciplinary teaming organization, comprised mostly of four and five member teacher teams, is horizontally structured along grade levels. In existence at Thomas since the school's inception, the current student to teacher ratio is 130:5 or 155:6 per team. The teams do not have named team leaders, but they do share the same group of students, the same schedule, and the same area of the building. Each teacher also accepts responsibility for planning, teaching, and evaluating the student members of the team. While teachers do have one common planning time per day, they have not had any formal training in interpersonal communication skills, conducting effective meetings, or working with middle level students.

Timmons Middle School: Timmons Middle is a small, rural school nestled quietly in the hills of Northeastern Pennsylvania. Calhoun Township and school district, home to a residential community of middle to upper middle income families, encompasses a 30 square mile region. The small, two floor middle school building is adjacent to, and shares common areas with, the high school. The hallways and classrooms, while close in space, are nicely painted, decorated, and carpeted. The country setting and warm interior add a familiar flare to the site. The students, faculty, and staff at Timmons appear to be somewhat laid-back, easy-going, and friendly. Everyone pretty much knows everyone else by name and is willing to stop and chat. At the same time, they are hardworking, dedicated, and committed to achieving educational excellence. Calhoun school district strives to preserve the characteristics that have made their schools special—small classes, low teacher to student ratios, individualized attention. Timmons Middle is no different. With only 160 students in the 7th and 8th grades, Timmon's interdisciplinary teaming, which has only been in existence for three years, is organized horizontally by grade level. Four teachers—on per core subject—and 80 students comprise each of the 7th and 8th grade teams. The teachers do have one common planning time per day, rotate team leaders on a quarterly basis, and share one team planning room between the two teams. Timmon's schedule does allow for flexibility in classes, student grouping, and instructional methods.

APPENDIX B
INTERVIEWEES IDENTIFICATION KEY

(7 to 10 character code)

1st character = SCHOOL 1 = Taylor 2 = Thomas 3 = Timmons

2nd character = POSITION T = Teacher A = Administrator

3rd & 4th characters =
PARTICIPANT'S NUMBER Ranges from 01 to 15 Total Participants

5th character = GENDER M = Male F = Female

6th character = RACE W = White B = Black H = Hispanic
A = Asian O = Other

7th character = GRADE LEVEL 5 = Fifth 6 = Sixth 7 = Seventh
8 = Eighth

8th & 9th characters =
EXPERIENCE Ranges from 01 to 35 Years Teaching Experience

10th character =
CERTIFICATION E = Elementary S = Secondary

(e.g., 1T01-FW6-13E = Taylor School, Teacher, First Interviewee—Female, White, Sixth Grade—13 Years Teaching Experience, Elementary Certified)

CHAPTER 3

THE EFFECTIVE MIDDLE SCHOOL TEACHER

Inwardly Integrated, Outwardly Connected

Kathleen Roney

ABSTRACT

Good teaching is crucial to effective schooling, yet, a serious lack of research exists with regard to middle level teachers and their effectiveness. The purpose of this study was to explore the question of effective teaching by asking middle level principals, teachers, and students what they believe are characteristics of effective middle level teachers. The questions, how do pre-service teacher preparation programs and daily classroom experiences help or hinder teachers in becoming effective middle level educators, were also investigated. This study followed a qualitative multi-site case study design and offers the reader an emic perspective. Data analysis resulted in four themes under which the 20 characteristics that emerged were placed. The concluding discussion indicates that in effective middle level teaching, there is a critical coherence between the personal self-awareness a middle level teacher possesses and that teacher's capacity to relate to the outside world.

INTRODUCTION

As we know, the overriding mission of schools is to help students learn and to direct them toward productive lives as good citizens. Teachers do this by their instruction and example. The question arises, are students learning? Put another way; Are teachers good at, or effective in carrying out their part in the mission of our schools? In teaching, "Effectiveness has been defined as those characteristics, traits, correlates, products, procedures, and educational strategies that produce a positive change in the total educational environment" (Larke, 1992, p. 133; see also, Brophy & Good, 1986; Hersh, 1981).

In considering the teachers of the young adolescent, that is, the student between the ages of 10 and 15, the question of effectiveness arises. The introductory statement to *A 21st Century Research Agenda* (National Middle School Association, 1997) asserts that there is a need for "substantive discussion among interested parties regarding vigorous and continued research that is based on a thorough and thoughtful research agenda for middle level education" (p. 3). First on the agenda are research questions related to educators committed to young adolescents. Specifically, NMSA poses the question: "What are common characteristics of effective middle level educators?" (p. 11). The purpose of this study was to take up the question of effectiveness and explore the understanding of middle school teachers, students, and principals with regard to characteristics teachers need to possess in order to be effective in working with young adolescents. The questions, how do pre-service preparation programs and daily classroom experiences help or hinder teachers in becoming effective middle level educators, were also investigated. To answer these questions, this study follows a qualitative multi-site case study research design.

REVIEW OF LITERATURE

The definition of an effective teacher has eluded researchers for hundreds of years. By the second half of the 20th Century, Getzels and Jackson (1963) determined that research leading "to the discovery of the specific and distinctive features of teacher personality of the effective teacher" was needed (p. 574). Hunter (1979) claimed that "the process of making and implementing decisions, before, during, and after instruction" increased the probability of student learning, and thus determined the effectiveness of the teacher (p. 65).

In delineating between personal and professional characteristics of effective teachers at any level, Lessen and Frankiewicz (1992) began with an investigative summary of 153 studies prepared by Barr (1948). They noted that Barr identified seven major trait areas in relation to teaching performance: "(1) general classroom management; (2) general instruction skill; (3) scholarship and professional preparation; (4) general personal fitness for teaching; (5) effort toward improvement; (6) interest in work, pupils, patrons, subjects taught, etc.; and (7) ability to cooperate with others" (Lessen & Frankiewicz, p. 125). The first three traits mentioned above relate to professional characteristics while the final four have more to do with the personal characteristics of successful teachers.

Combining personal and professional characteristics, researchers Joyce and Showers (1995) concluded that "all of the studies that have successfully differentiated more and less effective teachers have reported that effectiveness is the product of a complex set of behaviors, rather than the use of a few practices" (p. 88). Their conclusion led them to state that more effective teachers:

- teach the classroom as a whole (they group the students for activities stemming from the foci that are developed).
- present information or skills clearly and animatedly.
- keep the teaching sessions task-oriented.
- are nonevaluative and keep instruction relaxed.
- have high expectations for achievement (give more homework, pace lessons faster, created alertness).
- relate comfortably to the students, with the consequence that they have fewer behavior problems. (Joyce & Showers, p. 91)

As stated by the Carnegie Task on the Education of Young Adolescents (1989) in their seminal report entitled *Turning Points*, "the period of life from ages 10 to 15 represents for many young people their last best chance to choose a path toward productive and fulfilling lives" (p. 20). For those currently working in middle level education, *Turning Points* confirmed the need that teachers have for autonomy at the school and in the classroom. Within the classroom, *Turning Points* entrusted teachers to develop the curriculum and evaluate the students (p. 55). Within the school, it encouraged teachers to participate in budgetary decisions and governance committees, as well as to play a role in the recruitment of new teachers (pp. 55, 60). In order to be effective, the kind of teacher needed, then, is specially trained for the middle school environment.

As active middle school leaders, Doda, George, and McEwin (1987) reflected on the twenty-five-year history of middle schools. "What works today has less to do with modern technology and sophisticated curriculum plans than it does with the person of the teacher and how students experience that teacher on a daily basis" (p. 5). From their experience and research, they offered the following five "truths" about the middle school classroom teacher.

1. Effective middle level teachers do not sit down while they teach. A standing, roving teacher has more opportunity to monitor student behavior. As well, the teacher models an active involvement in the teaching and learning.
2. Effective middle level teachers work to create lessons, which bring students as close to the real thing as possible. Young adolescents are concrete thinkers and need concrete symbols to help them enter into the lesson.
3. Effective middle level teachers have a sense of humor. Middle level teachers keep the affect light when faced with the choice to laugh or scream.
4. Effective middle level teachers think big but teach small. With middle school students this is an option for quality versus quantity.
5. Effective middle school teachers work to weasel their way into the hearts of the young adolescents they teach. Middle school teachers do not underestimate the value of affection in creating bonds with their students. (Doda, George, & McEwin, 1987, p. 5)

Blending three decades of research, theory, and practice, Stevenson (1992) concurred, yet shortened the list and offered four generalizations that teachers can trust in working with young adolescents.

1. Every child wants to believe in himself or herself as a successful person.
2. Every youngster wants to be liked and respected.
3. Every youngster wants physical exercise and freedom to move.
4. Youngsters want life to be just.

Lawton (1993) summarized his commentary on middle school teachers by saying that "to be effective, teachers must follow the philosophy of middle level education" (p. 2). Lawton held that "The most effective middle level teacher has a good knowledge of student development and uses student characteristics and interests to guide planning and implementation of instructional strategies" (p. 3).

Among middle school practices, George and Alexander (1993) reported that "the advisor-advisee program was possibly the most attractive part of the entire middle school concept, but it seems to be the most difficult to implement successfully and carry out effectively over a period of years" (pp. 24–25). Bushnell and George (1993) pondered the reasons why. In their study of teacher effectiveness, these researchers asked 85 teachers and 506 students in the state of Florida what makes a middle school teacher an effective adviser. Their answers are collapsed into five "crucial characteristics" that confirmed what researchers say concerning the important purpose advisor-advisee programs and their teachers serve in middle schools (Clark & Clark, 1994; George & Alexander; George, Stevenson, Thomason, & Beane, 1992; Wavering, 1995).

Effective advisers:

1. Care about the students in their advisory group.
2. Are able to relate to the individuality of various advisees.
3. Are available for their advisees.
4. Have a positive attitude toward advisement.
5. Have their own unique styles of advisement (p. 10).

Turning Points (Carnegie Task Force, 1989, pp. 58–59) outlined that middle school teachers require an understanding of adolescent development, cultural diversity, interdisciplinary programming, and guidance. The report continued that middle school teacher training needs to include a period for observations, paid internships, and mentors, as well as provide for a concentration in one or two subject areas (pp. 59–60). In addition, "A solid background in the subject area(s) and an awareness of the cognitive, affective, and psychomotor characteristics and needs of early adolescents are necessary" (Lawton, 1993, p.6). Following the work of Gay (1978), Lawton added that the middle school teacher also needs to be aware of the "ethnic identification process" of the young adolescent (p. 6).

The belief that "middle level teachers have not been adequately recognized" led Arth, Lounsbury, McEwin, Swaim, and Eighty-three Successful Middle Level Educators (1995, p. 5) to conduct a study of the men and women who teach in middle schools. After listing what they thought were characteristics of effective middle level teachers, the researchers refined and validated their list with the help of 24 principals from across the country. Each principal recommended two middle school teachers to complete a survey of the characteristics. Five of the 48 teachers were subsequently enlisted to participate in individual case studies. According to the participants, the effective middle level teacher posses up to 16 characteristics. The characteristics range from cultural sensitivity to self-confidence, dedication, and creativity in utilizing a "wide variety of resources to improve the learning experiences of young adolescents" (Arth et al., pp. 6–7).

Effective middle level educators need to keep all this in mind when dealing with their young adolescent students on a daily basis. Lawton (1993) offered some final advice. Familiarize yourself with all the courses the students are taking, and help the students form positive attitudes toward the school and classroom. Likewise, serve as a bridge/communicator between the school and home–five positive and constructive written feedback.

In surveying the literature for this study, additional characteristics were found that speak to the personal and professional qualities middle level educators need to possess in order to be effective with young adolescents.

Some of the literature is empirically based, and some is theoretically driven. In Table 1, Davies (1995) depicts an accumulation of those studies that identified characteristics relative to middle level teachers. Davies' summary of research-based characteristics of effective middle level teachers presents the results of quantitative studies of middle level principals, teachers, and/or students.

Table 1. Summary of the Characteristics of Effective Middle Level Teachers

Personal Qualities *Effective teachers*	*Professional Characteristics* *Effective teachers*
• Have positive self-concepts (1, 2, 5)	• Understand young adolescent developmental characteristics (1, 2, 3, 4)
• Display optimism (1, 4, 5)	• Adapt curriculum and instruction to developmental needs (1, 2, 3, 4)
• Show enthusiasm (1, 4, 5)	• Address individual learning needs (1, 2, 3, 4, 5)
• Exhibit a good sense of humor (5)	• Use varied activities and materials (1, 2, 3, 4, 5)
• Demonstrate flexibility (1, 2, 5)	• Ask varied questions and promote thinking (1, 3, 4, 5)
• Respect and accept others (1, 2, 4, 5)	• Promote successful experiences (1, 2, 3, 4, 5)
• Are good listeners and communicators (1, 2, 4, 5)	• Teach communication skills (2, 4)
• Cooperate with other (2, 3, 4)	• Evaluate fairly (2, 4, 5)
	• Encourage self-responsibility (2, 3, 4, 5)
	• Maintain classroom control (2, 3, 4, 5)
	• Monitor learning (1, 4, 5)
	• Structure instruction (1, 4, 5)
	• Easy to understand (4, 5)
	• Know subject matter (1, 2, 4, 5)
	• Self-evaluate for professional growth (2, 3, 4)

Legend:

Research studies supporting identified characteristics (numbers in parentheses, above):

1. Johnston and Markle (1986)
2. National Middle School Association (1981)
3. Walter and Fanslow (1980)
4. National Association of Secondary School Principals (1985)
5. Buckner and Bickel (1991)

(Davies, 1995, p. 151)

THEORETICAL FRAMEWORK

The debate over middle level educational reform has often been polarized between the proponents of the intellectual virtues (the cognitive domain) and the advocates of the emotional virtues (the affective domain). Palmer (1993) highlighted the fruitlessness of this debate, stating: "The practice of intellectual rigor in the classroom requires an ethos of trust and acceptance. Intellectual rigor depends on things like honest dissent and the willingness to change our minds, things that will not happen if the 'soft' values of community are lacking" (p. xvii).

The framework for analysis used in this study is based upon Broudy's (1969, 1971) theory of the paradigms of teaching: didactics, heuristics, and philetics. According to Broudy (1969), "one of the approaches to defining good teaching is in terms of some process that is thought to be a necessary and sufficient condition of it" (pp. 586–587). Nevertheless, in this same work, Broudy contends, "no single model seems to cover all phases of a teacher's role in instruction, classroom management, and personal relations" (p. 587). In a subsequent work, Broudy (1971) holds that the multitude of prescriptions for the improvement of teaching fall into three categories: didactics, heuristics, and philetics. In short, "Didactics asks the teacher to function as an efficient machine; philetics asks him to be a warm, sensitive, concerned person; heuristics demands intellectual security and flexibility" (Broudy, 1972, p. 61).

According to Ericksen (1984), "Good instruction calls for consistency among the three basic aspects of teaching: defining course objectives, managing the classroom hour, and devising methods of testing and evaluation" (p. 16). Didactics deal with the "description, analysis, research, content and planning of the lesson—the goal being the improvement of the teaching reality" (Issing, 1994, p. 172). The discipline of didactic teaching supports the concept of multimedia didactics. Emphasizing the "structure, application and effect of the media and the media system on information and study procedures," Issing (p. 172) anticipated that computers would become the conduit through which didactic teaching takes place. Broudy concurred when he wrote: "the solution is to give over the mechanics of didactics to machines, not because didactics are unimportant, but because they are adaptable to machine operations, whereas heuristics and philetics are not" (1971, p. 11).

Heuristics refers to the "method of teaching that is designed to promote discoveries by the pupil" (Broudy, 1971, p. 2). Heuristic teaching combines Socratic questioning and inquiry with the problem-solving technique advocated by John Dewey (1916). According to Ericksen (1984), "It is vital for students to know something about a field before engaging in the heuristic scramble for solutions to its problems" (p. 93). Using the taxonomy assembled by Bloom, Engelhart, Furst, Hill, and Krathwohl (1956), the educational objectives of analysis, synthesis, and evaluation involve the teacher in heuristic teaching. In these higher-level thinking categories, teachers lead students into learning by discovery.

The concept of philetics is derived from the Greek word *philos* (loving). As a prescription for the improvement of teaching, philetics "urges that the secret of successful teaching is love—the love of the teacher by the learner and presumably vice versa" (Broudy, 1971, p. 4). Palmer (1998) reminded us that "...what scholars now say—and what good teachers have always known—is that real learning does not happen until students are brought into relationship with the teacher, with each other, and with the subject" (p. xvi). Philetics understands the intricate connection between the person of the teacher and the subject of the student.

METHODOLOGY

Following Yin (1994) and Herriott and Firestone (1983), I employed a multi-site qualitative case study design. The study was designed to understand and to describe the characteristics associated with effective middle school teachers, as well as the pre-service and on-the-job experiences of middle level teachers and their feelings of effectiveness. My design takes a nonexperimental, descriptive approach to case study research (Merriam, 1988). It is characterized by a particularistic focus in that I concentrate on middle school teachers, principals, and students.

Data Collection

Permission to conduct the study was granted by the building principals of four middle schools located in a large metropolitan region in the northeastern United States. Grade configuration of the four schools follows the typical middle school six-eight structure. The schools differ according to geographic location, cultural diversity, socioeconomic status, size, and student population. Two of the schools are located in economically deprived, socially underserved, inner-city, urban areas. One of the schools is located in a working class environment of middle income, suburban families. The other school is located in a rural/suburban county of upper-middle and upper class, professional families.

In accord with qualitative case study methodology (Merriam, 1988; Patton, 1990), this study utilized a purposive sampling strategy. The building principal, four teachers, and three students from each school were interviewed. In total 32 interviews were conducted—4 principals, 16 teachers, and 12 students. The data obtained through these interviews allowed me to reach the level of saturation necessary in case study research. The participants varied in gender, age, and ethnicity, and attempted to resemble the demographics of the schools from which they came.

Initially, a survey was sent to all teachers in the four schools participating in this study. The cover letter for the survey invited teachers to volunteer for a follow-up interview. Continuing with the purposive sampling strategy, teachers were chosen at random to be interviewed. Criteria were simply that the teacher had completed at least one full school year of teaching at the middle level, but not necessarily at the particular school. The principals were asked to help recruit students for the interviews. Criteria for students were that they were currently enrolled in the middle school. In addition to the surveys and semi-structured interviews, research procedures for this case study included document analysis, field notes, and a journal.

Data Analysis

Following Miles and Huberman (1994; see also Marshall & Rossman, 1995), analysis procedures involved initial coding of data to determine conditions among the participants and regularities in the setting. Recalling that this is a multi-site case study dealing with multi-data sources, initial strategies for managing the data included constant comparative data analysis (Bogdan & Biklen, 1982; Glaser & Strauss, 1967). That is to say, as categories emerged, data were compared within and between the categories and their properties.

The use of constant comparative analysis enabled me to generate plausible categories, properties, and characteristics of effective middle level teachers. Following Hamel (1993), I present the reader with an emic perspective. I use the exact words of the participants gleaned from the interviews and archival documents. To respect the privacy of the participants, as well as to document the findings, number codes and pseudonyms were assigned to each participant and school site (see Appendix).

Methods of Verification

Following the scholarship of Merriam (1988), I employed a number of strategies to provide strength of confidence. Triangulation of the surveys and interviews with the archival documentation, triangulation of survey responses with interviews, as well as triangulation of the interviews with one another, rendered a holistic understanding of the situation. Use of verbatim statements helped to establish trustworthiness. Low-inference descriptors are used to record precise, almost literal, and detailed descriptions to further minimize error. Finally, member checks of the data and analysis were utilized so to increase the trustworthiness of the interpretations.

ANALYSIS

The recently published agenda for college and university presidents, *To Touch the Future: Transforming the Way Teachers Are Taught* (American Council on Education, 1999), established the following with regard to effective teachers: "The essential competencies of an effective teacher are command of subject, preparation in effective pedagogical practice, and high overall academic performance" (p. 5). Data analysis for this case study resulted in four themes: Understanding the Transitions of the Young Adolescent; Developing Personal Qualities; Developing Critical Relationships; Organizing the Middle School Environment. Twenty characteristics emerged within these themes and include such qualities as flexibility, adaptability, a sense of humor, enthusiasm, classroom and lesson management, and good communication and interpersonal skills. The following presents the reader with an analysis of the themes, as well as a presentation of what the participants offered in terms of teacher preparation programs and on-the-job experiences relative to the characteristics that emerged from this study.

Theme One: Understanding the Transitions of the Young Adolescent

In order to be effective with young adolescents, participants offered that middle school teachers need an understanding of the transitions through which young adolescents pass. As one participant put it, "The middle school teacher has to understand that one day you pull out the crayons and the next day you might be doing Shakespeare" (2T10-FW7-12S). To understand the transitions through which young adolescents pass, one must not only recognize but also be willing to embrace the challenges of this developmental phase. A fundamental love for students during this stage of their adolescent growth is vital. This appears to be in line with what Broudy (1971) refers to as the philetics of teaching.

> **P**: They have to have a sincere love of children and not just the chosen few that are the so-called perfect kids if there is such a thing. They love all of them with the flaws and everything else that they come with, they love them. They don't like them, they don't put up with them, they love them. That's a significant piece. Then, of course,

mastery of the teaching techniques and subject area. But, you know, that's third. But that's strong. It's very important, but that's third. The other factors are really much more significant in my opinion. (1P08-MW6/8-24S)

T: You need to understand the cognition that's going on and the emotions that are involved; and almost be, uh, sort of a parent. You really have to have a really big heart to understand that. You know it's okay that they're not always focused on what's happening in the classroom. (3T18-FW7/8-09E)

S: They care for the students. They answer all their questions. And if they can't answer them, give them a book or something to read and find the answer. If they got a problem, they'll be there to solve it. (4S31-FB6)

In a similar way, respondents agreed that middle level students arrive with a variety of needs that must be addressed. Transitions occurring during this time period require that teachers recognize and help young adolescents through the changes that occur. These changes are a combination of social, emotional, and physical transformations; and, middle school teachers must try to recognize them. While recognizing the challenge, specifically of the heuristics of teaching young adolescents, the participants continue to emphasize the primacy of philetics.

T: I think absolutely at the top of the list is an understanding of what the middle school child, the adolescent child is physiologically going through, emotionally going through ... it is a traumatic event in the life of a child moving from elementary school to middle school. And I mean traumatic to the point of some kids getting stomachaches and migraines. (2T09-FW6-23E)

S: Well, it's kind of fun, but it's also pressuring because it's, like, a new school. Like, you just come out of elementary school and you've got people from two different schools coming here and you're not sure if you're going to make any friends or not. But in the end it's all right, it's very cool. (1S07-FW7)

P: I've actually had kids sit in my office with tears streaming down their faces and laughing about something. I mean, it's a very, very difficult time for them so you have to have people who are able to manage those, you know, that range of behaviors and emotions. Um, I want someone who has a good understanding of the developmental stages and characteristics of middle level kids. That may be the most important reason why middle schools came into existence. (2P16-MW6/8-13E)

Once a teacher has recognized the changes that are occurring, respondents suggested that the teacher needs to offer an understanding and an acceptance of the student. This requires that middle school teachers possess a degree of adaptability and flexibility, as well as a variety of teaching strategies.

> **T**: To be effective you need flexibility, it's very important. I think, even though what you're teaching you may think is precious and the best lesson you have to offer, you have to be prepared that it may not be as precious to them. So you try to focus on the child and the development of the child and not just your content area and making sure you get that done. It's OK if you don't get your full lesson plan done for the day. If you accomplish something, if you've motivated, if you've gotten them to talk, you've done something. So I think flexibility is very important. (2T12-FB7-06E)

> **P**: I think the idea of looking and trying to meet the need for the adolescent and trying to develop your plans around their need, the idea if you have a lesson plan and it's going to take 35–40 minutes, for the middle school that is not going to work. You have to be able to know how to switch gears. You know, every ten or twelve minutes. (3P24-MW6/8-27E)

> **S**: They have to be prepared for anything. You can't just, like, walk in and think that it's going to be just like all flat out on the book and everything. Every grade and every class is different. We just all have our own personalities. (1S06-FW8)

Finally, the participants are realistic in recognizing that mistakes are made along the path to good teaching. Middle school teachers must be involved in reflective practice and learn from their successes as well as their failures.

> **P**: I think people who are, um, flexible not just in dealing with day-to-day situations, but are willing to try new things—um, patterns of scheduling, try new projects. And people who are self-assured enough that they're willing to fail and understand that if I do this it may not work, you know, so let's put it on the shelf and move on. (2P16-MW6/8-13E)

> **T**: I'm a realist. I understand that some kids don't really want to be there. At the end of the year I always ask the kids "let me know, good or bad, I don't care what you say to me because that's just going to make me better next year." Some of them are great. One stuck with

me last year, it was a pretty nasty letter to me, but it stuck with me and I tried to change those things. (1T04-MW7-12S)

Theme Two: Developing Personal Qualities

In their interviews participants mentioned certain personal characteristics that middle level teachers need to possess in order be effective in working with young adolescents. They began with the criterion that teachers must adhere to the advice of Socrates, that is, "know thyself." The principals that were interviewed did not tender any comments with regard to this aspect of middle school teachers. However, the students recognized the value of being known as a whole person.

> **T**: I also think you can't be a real defensive person because you have to be constantly looking at yourself saying: "Okay, everyone just didn't do what I wanted to do, or didn't reach my objective. So I need to look at myself." And you need to be able to be really critical of your own methods and your own teaching; and you have to be able to let someone come in and look at what I'm doing and help me here or give me feedback. You have to be open to feedback. (3T20-FW8-04E)

> **S**: She knows what my limit is and she's been communicating back and forth in my journal that she, like, can give me ideas that she knows that she thinks I'll like. And ideas and stuff that'll work for me because she knows me better. (1S05-FW8)

Furthermore, this study revealed that in order to feel effective in teaching, middle school teachers need to have a sense of humor, an enjoyment of life, and an openness to live and learn more and more about themselves, their subject matter and their middle level students. Arth et al. (1995) found that "Conviction, enthusiasm, and a sense of humor were noted as essential qualities for successfully teaching young adolescents" (p. 24).

> **T**: I think, first of all, the stuff that goes on with kids at this level, I think if you don't have a well-defined sense of humor you're not going to make it. I think you have to be able to laugh at it and help kids to laugh about it because to them, these highs and lows are forever. If they feel bad today they think they are going to feel bad forever and you have to, like, show them in a loving and humorous way that this too shall pass. (1T02-FW6/8-16P)

> **S**: He makes the classroom fun. You laugh a lot in there, and math's been my hardest subject and this year I've kind of come to under-

stand it. I'm not really sure how it happened but, like, the other year has kind of just been like putting problems up from the text book and doing the work. This year it's a lot more involvement and I like it a lot. (2S13-FW8)

P: Absolutely, a sense of humor. Um, not that you don't need that at any level, but particularly here. You know, you absolutely can't take situations and some of the things that these kids do seriously or personally. If you do that, you get into trouble very, very quickly. So, you have to maintain a sense of humor and you have to maintain, um, good balance as to what's important and what is not. (2P16-MW6/8-13E)

Teachers and students alike mentioned certain personal qualities such as patience, honesty, creativity, and empathy as critical in middle level teaching. It became clear that these characteristics deal with the philetics of teaching. Although Broudy (1971) admitted to the difficulty in defining the sort of love recommended in philetics, he explained that "At various times the teacher is urged to be a pal, a big brother, a father figure" (p. 4). Ericksen (1984) held that "Students seek out their teachers as persons whose judgment is respected and whose confidence is trusted as counselor, mentor, and friend" (p. 97). Rogers and Renard (1999) added that once this is established, once empathic, honest, and patient teachers address the fundamental emotional needs of students, students' motivation to learn is enhanced.

T: A lot of patience. Even more so than the primary grades because you really need to put up with an awful lot in the sense that, especially in the inner city here, these kids carry an awful lot of extra baggage with them and you have to understand what's going on in other things. Sometimes what you are trying to teach them, you know, the conflict of Latin America, they certainly don't care when they have these other experiences going on in the house. (4T27-FW6-04E)

T: Being honest with the students—it helps. And then they understand that you are human. Tell them that you had to go home and the baby was sick. I share some personal experiences with them so they understand that this is not my whole life. (2T12-FB7-06E)

S: Just, like, pretend that you are, or just remember when you were in middle school—what you felt like, and what you were going through. And try to, when you talk about the subject that you teach, keep that in mind. And try to explain things in a way that they can understand more. (1S06-FW8)

Theme Three: Developing Critical Relationships

Developing critical relationships offers the reader an additional context within which to think about characteristics considered effective in working with middle school students. Participants affirmed the need for good working relationships with a circle of allies. The critical relationships revealed throughout this study flow from colleagues to friends, and from classroom neighbors to middle school team members. The teachers participating in this study described many benefits to observing their colleagues, chief among them was gaining additional instructional ideas. The teachers indicated that they would like to spend more time observing one another.

> **T**: The most helpful experiences that I've had have been the opportunities to observe other teachers in the building and work collaboratively with them ... we are not in a school where it's, like, "no, I won't give you that, that's my great lesson." Everybody here that I've encountered is willing to share. (1T01-FW8-06E)

> **T**: They [middle school teachers] need to know what it means to team-teach. They need to know what it means to work collaboratively, how to share work, how to share struggles, as well as strengths and learn from that. (4T28-FW6-10E)

Students reflected a positive experience of their teachers as they highlight the benefit of having a variety of personalities among their teachers. The principals participating in this study spoke about the need for teachers to be open to their colleagues and to learn from them so that together they could build up the learning community.

> **S**: [teacher A], he tells these corny jokes and kind of spices up the conversation and stuff. And [teacher B] is the Art teacher, he's just, he acts like he's our age and so it's easy to relate to him. I think they all have their own different personalities and when you put them together they kind of make a kind of really good mix of teachers. (1S06-FW8)

> **P**: I carefully manage the composition on my teams so that I never have a team of totally veteran teachers. I never have a team of teachers who all use the same strategies. What I have seen is that there has been great moderation in some of the most stalwart people because they find themselves as isolates and teachers generally don't like to, they're almost like middle school kids in the fact that they don't like to be out in the bright sunlight. They don't like to stand out as being completely different. (2P16-MW6/8-13E)

In addition to working with students, administrators, and fellow teachers, the importance of parent and family partnerships surfaced. While middle school teachers want to work well with parents and families, they do not know how to go about it. Teachers participating in this study spoke of the difficulty in getting parents involved.

> **T**: You have to make contact with parents nowadays more than ever... That's something an effective teacher has to do, to be in contact with the parents. Let the parents know where the kid is, when he's in trouble. (2T11-MW7-23S)

> **T**: I think over the years, um, parental involvement has diminished so therefore, I think some of the problems with middle school students have increased ... that lack of parent involvement has changed what we're able to do with the kids to some extent. (2T09-FW6-23E)

> **T**: There is a lack of parental involvement. I don't think that means having parents come to PTA meetings. I think it means having parents check homework every night. Having parents care when you call them on the phone and say "your kid acted berserk in school today." You get, "OK, I'll talk to him." You know nothing is going to come of that. (4T28-FW6-10E)

Theme Four: Organizing the Middle School Environment

Characteristics referencing the management of the middle school classroom surfaced among the participants. The Arth et al. (1995) survey of middle level teachers reaffirmed the basic premise of good classroom management. According to these researchers, teachers...

> ...emphasized such things as structure and organization within a classroom, but not at the expense of making learning unpleasant or stifling creativity. They see the benefit of active learning as a means of engaging students in the class in a productive and constructive manner. Building a sense of trust, security, and support with and among students not only gives them a sense of ownership in the class, but also encourages them to take risks. (Arth et al., p. 32)

Respondents to this case study indicated that in order to feel effective in working with young adolescents, middle school teachers need to be prepared not only for the classroom, but for the content of the lesson. Management was the word associated with both.

> **T**: To be the most effective middle school teacher I think organization is at the top of the list. You have to be organized. You have to like

what you're doing. You've got to like middle school age kids. Um, and you have to have a strong background, a general background—it doesn't have to be specific. (2T09-FW6-23E)

P: The results of poor classroom management results in children not achieving, which results in children failing. I feel the most effective classroom teacher is one that plans daily. I mean, everyday tasks of meeting your children, challenging your children to the levels, as well as providing a friend to the children, but a strong disciplinarian to the children. With all these elements I believe a teacher and a child will thrive—it will be great. (4P32-MSE/S-08E/S/A)

Likewise, middle level teachers need to be consistent and flexible, but not rigid. Being prepared and being consistent are only part of the recipe for middle school teachers who seek to develop characteristics effective in working with young adolescents. One of the principals spoke to the issue of certification while the students reflected a sense of security in knowing what is expected of them.

P: I had the experience last year of having a teacher who was secondary certified and the experience wasn't a pleasant one ... I'm not an authority on secondary education, but I have a feeling that the sensitivity and awareness of the students was not always there from the teacher. They expect the children to come in and prepared for the lessons. We are still talking about adolescents who sometimes need to be nudged and coached. (4P32-MBE/S-08E/S/A)

S: Like, they expect us to have it [homework] in. Like, elementary school, they can say, "That's OK, you can do it tomorrow." But they expect us to have it in because they know that we can do it by then. (1S07-FW7)

In like manner, middle school teachers need to be in control of their classrooms and clear about the limits of their discipline policies in order to create a respectful learning environment. The respondents summed it up nicely.

T: Number one, I'm coming from a middle school perspective, you have to have control of the class. No mater how good your ideas are, no matter how enthusiastic you are. Um, if you don't set the right tone in the classroom then nothing's going to happen. (2T11-MW7-23S)

P: The overall cry from all teachers is discipline, discipline, discipline, and discipline! It has to be a community-type of discipline thing where it cannot just be placed upon the administration to look upon discipline. Everyone has to do their role, and this is what we are trying to instill upon our staff members. (4P32-MSE/S-08E/S/A)

S: Some teachers are quiet and they don't really have a lot of control over the class and if that's what their problem is, then just kind of feel free to say well, um, to take control and tell them to stop. (2S14-FW7)

Reflections on Teacher Preparation Programs

In responding to questions about their teacher preparation programs, some teachers attested to positive experiences that helped them understand what was needed to help middle school students learn. Of greatest significance were the methods courses they took. Their responses emphasized the strengths in their preparation with regard to the heuristics of teaching.

T: Definitely helpful because I had reading classes. I had teaching reading methods classes. So that was an excellent teacher and someone who was published widely and he did a lot of things with higher level thinking. I mean, they always brought up Bloom and Madeline Hunter, and all those people, but it was probably the teaching reading and the content area classes that taught things like critical thinking and higher level thinking skills. (2T10-FW7-12S)

T: The, um, methods course that I took, I think it was on ESL, but it still applies to all languages and different methods. For example, expectations. I remember the paper that I did was on how our expectations influence the performance of the students many times. (1T03-FW6/8-14S)

In his study of middle level teachers, Scales (1992) reported that "nearly 3 in 10 of these middle-grades teachers felt their programs had not done a good job in preparing them to understand early adolescent development" (p. 65). Furthermore, while the majority might have reported feelings of adequacy, "their responses suggest this understanding was not translated into classroom behavior and action on curriculum and instruction" (Scales, p. 65). Although they did not use the word "hinder" in relation to their teacher preparation programs, both teachers and principals in this study reflected on the shortcomings of their programs.

T: My background did not prepare me for middle school. Not even the psychology. Everything was focused on the little preschoolers. All

> you want to do is make bulletin boards. I'm damn good at it. Nobody dealt with the psychology of the middle school child. (4T25-FB6/8-20E)

> **P**: There have been some things that I would call glaring weaknesses in the teacher preparation process. One of them is, um, certainly has to do with understanding child development. Um, we see very little evidence that kids have a real understanding coming out of college of not only the physiological development but understanding how kids learn. (2P16-MW6/8-13E)

None of the teachers or principals recalled that their teacher preparation programs specifically helped them prepare for the middle school student. One teacher offered: "I don't know if a program can prepare you for dealing with adolescents. I mean a lot of it has to do with who you are and your experiences" (1T01-FW8-06E). However, the teachers did offer suggestions for improving the programs currently offered to pre-service teachers with respect to the categories in this theme, i.e., self-reflection, sense of humor, enjoyment of students, etc. Their advice on how to combine the philetics, heuristics and didactics of teaching included having a realistic view of the young adolescent, having pre-service experience with middle school students, having courses in higher order thinking skill development, and having a work ethic that takes one beyond the call of duty.

> **T**: They [student teachers] need to see what a kid this age is like because in their heads they're thinking, "Oh, eleven years old, they're so cute at eleven." They can be terrors at eleven. (2T09-FW6-23E)

> **T**: I think the whole idea of the hands-on, higher order of thinking that teachers need to be taught how to do that ... these kids need to be shown, they need to do, in a different generation than when we went to school where we were told to memorize the capitals and that was OK. What's more important is to show kids how to get that information and what to do with it once they have it and why it's important. Teachers need to be shown how to get kids to think for themselves. (4T28-FW6-10E)

Most of the comments the teachers and principals submitted with regard to collaboration skills reflected suggestions and improvements in teacher preparation programs. Their suggestions emphasized training in parent conferencing, extended student teaching, and courses taught by professors who had/have practical classroom experience in middle level education. As one teacher recalled, "The methods courses taught by people who were just recently out of the classroom were the best" (3T20-FW8-04E). Their suggestions concurred with the vision for middle grades teacher preparation prepared by McEwin, Dickinson, Erb, and Scales (1995). These middle school experts outlined that "wise and experienced middle school teachers" need to "...understand the potential of, and work successfully on, an interdisciplinary team, [and to] possess a thorough understanding of the role of family in a student's development" (McEwin et al., pp. 17–19). Likewise, they emphasized that one of the components of the middle grades teacher preparation program must include a variety of site-based experiences in the middle grades (McEwin et al., p. 23). Again, these experts concurred with the suggestions offered by the participants in this case study.

> **T**: I think that it would be wonderful, somehow, if they [teacher prep] could offer a class in dealing with parents, and parents of teenagers, because I think a lot of parents are very troubled themselves, and then that becomes part of your job in helping them deal with their child. (2T10-FW7-12S)

> **P**: I would like to see kids in the classroom beginning in their freshman year, so every year they are building up to student teaching. (3P24-MW6/8-27E)

In a presentation of a developmental approach to teacher learning, Wasley (1999) explained that among the things emerging teachers need, is "help with planning for a week, a month, and a year; moving kids from one activity to the next; ... and focusing lessons on skill acquisition and content knowledge" (p. 12). Most of the teachers had no recollection of their own preparation, but offered lots of suggestions for programs preparing teachers for middle school classrooms. Some participants keyed in on the control issues, others zeroed in on content knowledge, and still others focused on issues of adolescent development that should be included in such programs in order to prepare the middle school teacher for the young adolescent. The following are just two examples of what the teachers and principals participating in this study suggest will improve teacher preparation programs with regard to classroom management.

> **T**: I think any course or any curriculum work that would deal with how to handle this type of kid, what's most effective in control instances, that's 90% of where our energies go. I think as far as teaching middle school, at least at first, the content material. We all come out of that. We are all pretty much on top of what has to be taught, but getting control of the kids and how they are going to react to you, how they react to each other. Any courses that would help in that way. (2T11-MW7-23S)

P: I think that they must be aware of the adolescent growth and psychological aspects of the adolescent youth ... I think that when a teacher comes into the middle years they must realize that they aren't going to have little children sitting in rows and doing what they ask them to do. (4P32-MBE/S-08E/S/A)

Learning from Experience

Given the strengths and the weaknesses of teacher preparation programs, nothing compares to on-the-job experiences as the best teacher. Lucas (1999) explained that the recent California model for retaining new teachers helps because it is a "reflective assessment process based on the premise that teachers learn good practices over several years of study, through consultation with experienced colleagues, and by utilizing reflective practice beyond academic preparation" (p. 45). This model gives the teachers time to test what they have developed and, with the help of their support providers, they can experience success and failure through the process. Reflecting on her experiences as a middle school teacher, one participant in this case study stated that they "helped a lot because one year you do things and you find out if they work or they don't work and you try them again. You know you perfect them as time goes on. Little techniques or just activities that the kids really like, you begin to perfect those" (1T03-FW6/8-14S). Other reflections included:

T: My college education, anything I thought, did not prepare me for my teaching career. The only thing that prepared me was being put in a classroom and each year learning from my own mistakes and experiences. (4T27-FW6-04E)

T: Yeah, they did get into that [higher order skills]. Again, that's something that I think you learn by doing. But it's good to get the academic background and to see where it comes from. And a lot of times I would go back to those books every few years ... I go back and see what they wanted us to learn then. And I found that to be helpful. (2T11-MW7-23S)

T: I had kids starring at me and, you know, the Bloom's taxonomy, the lower level question, just wasn't getting it done. And I think it's like anything else, it comes with a lot of practice. (1T04-MW7-12S)

Once again, some of the teachers reflected that they were more than able to pick up things on their own. "As far as my subject matter, I read myself. I like history a lot, so I read books on my own. I can pick up stuff on my own that way" (4T27-FW6-04E). As the following teachers noted, their sense of honesty, patience, fun, creativity, empathy, etc. is often learned, or perhaps sharpened, on the job.

> **T**: I've always been doing it. It's interesting when they come out with the higher order of thinking, but I remember asking some of the same questions that got people to think: "Well how is this connected to this?" ... I think it's almost just an instinctive thing with teachers because you're naturally curious. You want, you know, you want to see all the connections yourself and you try to get them to see them ... It was not something that was taught. (1T03-FW6/8-14S)

> **T**: I don't think there is a class in college that gets you ready for the affective dimension at all. I think that just comes with being here. The more you deal with these kids at this level, the better off you're going to be when you come in. (1T04-MW7-12S)

Of interest to this study is the emphasis the teachers placed on the responsibility of the administrators in their schools. "The more I'm in education, the more I see that if you don't have an effective administrator, you are in trouble. They set the tone for every building" (2T11-MW7-23S). Valentine, Maher, Quinne, and Irvin (1999) remind us that the 1996 Interstate School Leaders Licensure Consortium outlined four common standards of school leadership. The fourth standard reads: "A school administrator is an educational leader who promotes the success of all students by collaborating with families and community members, responding to diverse community interests and needs, and mobilizing community resources" (p. 55). Indeed, this is an image for which teachers participating in this study gave numerous illustrations. Teachers agreed that administrators help them become more effective when administrators are actively involved in the everyday life of the school and classroom. School administrators inspire hard-working teachers when the teachers can see them walking the halls, in and out of classrooms. Likewise, the teachers highlight the need for administrators to back them up in parent and student conferences.

> **T**: No one should be working with kids that shouldn't be working with kids. I think that's the role of the administrators and evaluators and the supervisors—to weed out the ones who shouldn't be working with kids. They need to be in the classrooms all the time. They need to be walking up and down. They need to be sitting in meetings. They need to be in classrooms. (2T10-FW7-12S)

T: It has to start at the administration. If you know your principal or your boss is behind you 100%, that's going to make you give even more than 100%. (3T18-FW7/8-09E)

T: You have to have the backup in the administrator because some kid is going to cross you and you're going to need help. Some parent is going to come in off the wall and you're going to need to be backed up. And if you're not backed up, and if you don't have the support of the principal, and the kids don't understand what's expected of them and know that it's going to be fairly carried out, you have chaos. You really do. (2T11-MW7-23S)

In remarking on the results of their shadow study, Jones and Tadlock (1999) reported that "The atmosphere in the schools seemed to be better in those schools where the principal seemed to have a good relationship with the staff and the staff had a good relationship with one another" (p.61). The principals in this study, themselves, pondered the unique role and responsibility they have in encouraging their teachers to become more effective.

P: People need to be praised. They need to be told what they are doing is a good thing. They are investing in the lives of other people, that's sacred. That is a sacred thing for me so you don't just walk through, you make the comments to the kids. You know, "you're lucky to have this person." (1P08-MW6/8-24S)

P: I also believe that initially, maybe the first four months, a buddy teacher, somebody to co-op a teacher. I know we are kind of short, we are kind of limited as far as our resources, but if a cooperative teacher was able to go into the classroom at least three out of five days a week to support that teacher, I think that the success rate would be much greater. (4P32-MBE/S-08E/S/A)

P: I think one of the best things we can do is careful selection of new teachers' mentors and make sure that they get indoctrinated, if you will, the correct way in terms of working with the middle school kids. (2P16-MW6/8-13E)

Finally, in addition to receiving administrative praise and support, and talking and exchanging ideas with their colleagues, the teachers echoed the need to belong to professional organizations and to engage in lifelong learning. This can take the form of sitting in on a colleague's class, participating in national conferences and local workshops, or graduate studies leading to an advanced degree. Responses recognizing the need for continued professional development did not distinguish between the didactics, heuristics, or philetics of teaching.

> **T**: I've been to some good workshops. Usually they're taught by some people who are still in the classroom because most colleague professors, that's what they do so they're disconnected from the classroom. So, whenever there is an instructor who is still in the classroom, or at least in the public school arena, I think they offer more valuable resources. (2T12-FB7-06E)

> **T**: The teacher has to constantly learn. They have to be a lifelong learner. They have to be one of those people who are self motivated to constantly seek out information and new ways of doing things so that they don't get stale because it is easy to get stagnant in a job like this. (3T20-FW8-04E)

Summary

As mentioned earlier in the review of literature, only a limited amount of research is available on the topic of effective middle level teaching. Table 1 (p. 8) displays a summary of the characteristics contained in five quantitative studies completed between 1980 and 1991. From among those studies, the quantitative study conducted by NMSA (1981) resulted in 17 characteristics it associated with effective middle level teachers. Buckner and Bickel (1991) designed a survey of 27 descriptors that they brought to middle level students for verification. Arth et al. (1995) sought validation from middle level teachers and principals for the 16 characteristics they considered distinctive of excellent middle level teachers. The more recent Arth et al. study added four characteristics to the list. Through this study, Roney (2000) added six characteristics to top off the list at 34. Note in Table 2 that three out of the four studies share the first 15 characteristics. In short, effective middle level teachers blend knowledge of young adolescents with knowledge of self in working with their colleagues to create developmentally responsive middle level schools so that students acquire the "skills, knowledge, and personal competence ... to be successful now and in the future" (NMSA, 1995, p. 5).

CONCLUDING DISCUSSION

The empirical data collected and analyzed for this study indicate that there is a critical coherence between the personal self-awareness a middle

Table 2. Characteristics of Effective Middle Level Teachers

NMSA (1981)	*Buckner and Bickel (1991)*	*Arth et al. (1995)*	*Roney (2000)*
1. Positive self-concepts	1. Positive self-concepts	1. Self-confident	1. Self-aware & self-motivated
2. Know subject matter	2. Know subject matter	2. Interdisciplinary knowledge of subjects; depth of content knowledge in one or more areas	2. Being prepared with a knowledge base
	3. Maintain classroom control	3. Establishes & maintains disciplined learning environment	3. Being respectful through classroom & lesson management
4. Display optimism	4. Display optimism		4. Be positive
5. Show enthusiasm	5. Show enthusiasm		5. Show enthusiasm
6. Demonstrate flexibility	6. Demonstrate flexibility		6. Adaptable & flexible
7. Act spontaneously	7. Act spontaneously		7. Have fun
8. Demonstrate caring	8. Demonstrate caring		8. Love kids
9. Respect & accept others	9. Respect & accept others	9. Sensitive to differences; respects & celebrates others	
10. Good listeners & communicators	10. Good listeners & communicators		10. Good communication skills
11. Use varied activities & materials	11. Use varied activities & materials		11. Understand need for variety of teaching strategies
12. Promote successful experiences	12. Promote successful experiences	12. Dedicated to welfare & education of young adolescents	
13. Monitor learning	13. Monitor learning	13. Ensures all young adolescents will succeed in learning	

Table 2. Characteristics of Effective Middle Level Teachers (Cont.)

NMSA (1981)	*Buckner and Bickel (1991)*	*Arth et al. (1995)*	*Roney (2000)*
14. Structure instruction	14. Structure instruction	14. Utilizes wide variety of developmentally appropriate instructional strategies	
15. Understand young adolescent developmental characteristics		15. Makes decision based on understanding adolescent development	15. Understand young adolescent developmental challenges & changes
	16. Sense of humor		16. Learns to laugh with others
		17. Works collaboratively	17. Develops critical relationships with colleagues & teams
	18. Evaluate fairly	18. Varies evaluation techniques	
19. Adapt curriculum and instruction to developmental needs		19. Committed to integrated curriculum	
20. Address individual learning	20. Address individual learning		
		21. Works closely with families	21. Collaborates with parents & families
22. Ask varied questions & promote thinking	22. Ask varied questions & promote thinking		
	23. Easy to understand		
	24. Encourage self-responsibility		

Table 2. Characteristics of Effective Middle Level Teachers (Cont.)

NMSA (1981)	*Buckner and Bickel (1991)*	*Arth et al. (1995)*	*Roney (2000)*
		25. Understands & welcomes role of advisor	
		26. Recognizes developmental goals of middle level education	
		27. Develops positive relationships in variety of environments	
		28. Acquires, creates, & utilizes variety of resources	
			29. Patient
			30. Honest
			31. Creative
			32. Empathetic
			33. Perspective
			34. Willing to learn from mistakes

level teacher possesses and that teacher's capacity to relate to the outside world. "The Effective Middle School Teacher: Inwardly Integrated, Outwardly Connected," moves us to a different level in conceptualizing the effective middle level teacher. It advances the theory of identity and integrity in teaching introduced by Palmer (1997). Palmer explained:

> *Good teaching cannot be reduced to technique; good teaching comes from the identity and integrity of the teacher.* In every class I teach, my ability to connect with my students, and to connect them with the subject, depends less on the methods I use than on the degree to which I know and trust my selfhood—and am willing to make it available and vulnerable in the service of learning. (p. 16)

A common belief among the teachers participating in this study is that middle school teachers need to know themselves inside out. This was evidenced by the comments the participants offered regarding a basic awareness of their strengths and weaknesses, as well as their biases and preferences. For example, some participants mentioned the need to be consistent with discipline while other participants recorded a need for skills in classroom management. The teachers acknowledged that the degree to which one possesses skills such as these is critical to one's success at the middle level. Teacher preparation and professional development can assist in their development, but self-awareness is the key to knowing what to develop. The effective middle school teacher needs to be inwardly integrated.

Equally important to the effective middle level teacher is that teacher's ability to relate to others. Data from this case study reveal the importance of teachers connecting not only with their middle school students, but with the families of their students as well. These critical connections also involve teachers in good working relationships with their middle school colleagues, especially in those middle schools where interdisciplinary teaming is employed. *This We Believe* (NMSA, 1995) holds that "Young adolescents form their sense of self in large part from the interactions they have with significant peers and adults" (p. 7). In discussing the role of self in teacher development, Borich (1999) emphasizes that self-confident teachers foster positive pupil self-concepts: "Effective teachers ... appear to share a positive perception of self and others that has a positive effect on pupil self-concept" (p. 102). The effective middle level teacher needs to be outwardly connected.

Palmer (1997) holds that "Good teachers join self, subject, and students in the fabric of life because they teach from an integral and undivided self; they manifest in their own lives, and evoke in their students, a 'capacity for connectedness'" (p.16). Often we hear the claim that "We need systematic evidence that schools are doing their jobs, sensible ways to evaluate teachers' effectiveness and student achievement" (DiPardo, 1999, p. 155). This leads one to understand effectiveness only in terms of student achievement. Is this a sufficient indicator? While effectiveness in relation to achievement may be the question that speaks the loudest, is it the one that sufficiently defines effective?

Palmer (1997) queried: "How can schools educate students if they fail to support the teacher's inner life?" (p. 21). None of the evidence collected for this study indicated that teachers directly placed student achievement in standardized tests on the list of characteristics of effective middle level teachers. Indirectly, they mentioned that one of the signs that they are effective was the successful achievement of their students in the assessments they make as classroom teachers. More precisely, the participants in this study concurred with the Carnegie Task Force (1989) when it wrote: "Teachers will be called upon to promote a spirit of inquiry and to stimulate students to think about and communicate ideas" (p. 43). It is the conclusion of this study that in order to be effective in working with young adolescents, middle level teachers need to be inwardly integrated, that is to say, possessing self knowledge as well as knowledge of their subject. Likewise, the teachers must be outwardly connected to the world of their students, parents, colleagues, and school communities. When teachers achieve this integration and connection, student achievement will follow. Not as an entity in and of itself, more like a by-product of good, effective teaching. One of the many discussed in this study.

Advocating a research methodology that is capable of allowing teachers to tell their stories of teaching and that is able to seek viable interpretations, Freeman (1996) explained: "...teaching is complex and highly contextual, and at the same time deeply coherent and dependent on relationships and the worlds of others..." (p. 102). Freeman continued that "Teacher research should refer to the process by which teachers seek interpretations and give voice to what they know by virtue of their experience, combined with close and disciplined examination of their practice" (p. 107). The principals, teachers, and students interviewed for this study agree wholeheartedly. Through this study, they have offered input into an answer to the original question posed by NMSA (1997) in its research agenda for the 21st century: "What are common characteristics of effective middle level educators?" Ultimately, their responses "will lead to a better understanding of the effects of middle level education on the lives of young adolescents and the communities in which they live" (NMSA, 1997, p. 7).

REFERENCES

American Council on Education. (1999). *To touch the future: Transforming the way teachers are taught.* Washington, DC: Author.

Arth, A., Lounsbury, J., McEwin, C., Swaim, J., & Eighty-three Successful Middle Level Educators. (1995). *Middle level teachers: Portraits of excellence.* Columbus, OH: National Middle School Association and National Association of Secondary School Principals.

Barr, A. (1948). The measurement and prediction of teaching efficiency: A summary of investigations. *Journal of Experimental Education, 16*(2), 203–283.

Bloom, B., Engelhart, M., Furst, E., Hill, W., & Krathwohl, D. (Eds.). (1956). *Taxonomy of educational objectives: The classification of education goals, handbook I: Cognitive domain.* New York: David McKay.

Bogdan, R., & Biklen, S. (1982). *Qualitative research for education: An introduction to theory and methods.* Boston, MA: Allyn and Bacon.

Borich, G. (1999). Dimensions of self that influence effective teaching. In R. Lipka & T. Brinthaupt (Eds.), *The role of self in teacher development* (pp. 92–117). Albany: State University of New York Press.

Brophy, J., & Good, T. (1986). Teacher behavior and student achievement. In M. Wittrock (Ed.), *Handbook of research on teaching* (3rd ed., pp. 328–375). New York: Macmillan.

Broudy, H. (1969). Can we define good teaching? *The Record, 70*(7), 583–592.

Broudy, H. (1971). *Didactics, heuristics, and philetics.* Paper delivered at the University of Illinois, Urbana Campus.

Broudy, H. (1972). *The real world of the public schools.* New York: Harcourt Brace Jovanovich.

Buckner, J., & Bickel, F. (1991). If you want to know about effective teaching, why not ask your middle school kids? *Middle School Journal, 22*(3), 26–29.

Bushnell, D., & George, P. (1993). Five crucial characteristics: Middle school teachers as effective advisers. *Schools in the Middle, 3*(1), 10–16.

Carnegie Task Force on the Education of Young Adolescents. (1989). *Turning points: Preparing American youth for the 21st century.* Washington, DC: Carnegie Council on Adolescent Development.

Clark, D., & Clark, S. (1994). Meeting the needs of young adolescents. *Schools in the Middle, 4*(1), 4–7.

Creswell, J. (1994). *Research design: Qualitative and quantitative approaches.* Thousand Oaks, CA: Sage.

Davies, M. (1995). The ideal middle level teacher. In M. Wavering (Ed.), *Educating young adolescents: Life in the middle* (pp. 149–169). New York: Garland.

Dewey, J. (1916). *Democracy and education: An introduction to the philosophy of education.* New York: Macmillan.

DiPardo, A. (1999). *Teaching in common: Challenges to joint work in classrooms and schools.* New York: Teachers College Press.

Doda, N., George, P., & McEwin, K. (1987). Ten current truths about effective schools. *Middle School Journal, 18*(3), 3–5.

Ericksen, S. (1984). *The essence of good teaching: Helping students learn and remember what they learn.* San Francisco: Jossey-Bass.

Freeman, D. (1996). Redefining the relationship between research and what teachers know. In K. Bailey & D. Numan (Eds.), *Voices from the language classroom: Qualitative research in second language education.* New York: Cambridge University Press.

Gay, G. (1978). Ethnic identity in early adolescence: Some implications for instructional reform. *Educational Leadership, 35*(8), 649–655.

George, P., & Alexander, W. (1993). *The exemplary middle school* (2nd ed.). New York: Holt, Reinhart, and Winston.

George, P., Stevenson, C., Thomason, J., & Beane, J. (1992). *The middle school—and beyond.* Alexandria, VA: Association for Supervision and Curriculum Development.

Getzels, J., & Jackson, P. (1963). The teacher's personality and characteristics. In N. Gage (Ed.), *Handbook of research on teaching* (pp. 232–255). Chicago: Rand McNally.

Glaser, B., & Strauss, A. (1967). *The discovery of grounded theory.* Chicago: Aldine.

Hamel, J. (1993). *Case study methods.* Newbury Park, CA: Sage.

Herriott, R., & Firestone, W. (1983). Multisite qualitative policy research: Optimizing description and generalizability. *Educational Researcher, 12*(2), 14–19.

Hersh, R. (1981). *What makes some schools and teachers more effective.* Unpublished manuscript. University of Oregon.

Hunter, M. (1979). Teaching is decision-making. *Educational Leadership, 37*(1), 62–67.

Issing, L. (1994). From instructional technology to multimedia didactics. *Educational Media International, 31*(3), 171–182.

Jones, M., & Tadlock, M. (1999). Shadowing middle schoolers to understand them better. *Middle School Journal, 30*(4), 57–62.

Joyce, B., & Showers, B. (1995). *Student achievement through staff development: Fundamentals of school renewal* (2nd ed.). White Plains, NY: Longman.

Larke, P. (1992). Effective multicultural teachers: Meeting the challenges of diverse classrooms. *Equity & Excellence, 25*(2–4), 133–138.

Lawton, E. (1993). *The effective middle level teacher.* Reston, VA: National Association of Secondary School Principals.

Lessen, E., & Frankiewicz, L. (1992). Personal attributes and characteristics of effective special education teachers: Considerations for teacher education. *Teacher Education and Special Education, 15*(2), 124–132.

Lucas, C. (1999). Developing competent practitioners. *Educational Leadership, 56*(8), 45–48.

Marshall, C., & Rossman, G. (1995). *Designing qualitative research* (2nd ed.). Thousand Oaks, CA: Sage.

McEwin, C., Dickinson, T., Erb, T., & Scales, P. (1995). *A vision of excellence: Organizing principles for middle grades teacher preparation.* Columbus, OH: Center for Early Adolescence and National Middle School Association.

McMillan, J., & Schumacher, S. (1997). *Research in education: A conceptual introduction* (4th ed.). New York: Longman.

Merriam, S. (1988). *Case study research in education: A qualitative approach.* San Francisco: Jossey-Bass.

Miles, M., & Huberman, A. (1994). *Qualitative data analysis: An expanded sourcebook* (2nd ed.). Thousand Oaks, CA: Sage.

National Middle School Association. (1981). Preparing teachers for the middle grades. *Middle School Journal, 12*(4), 17–19.

National Middle School Association. (1995). *This we believe.* Columbus, OH: Author.

National Middle School Association. (1997). *A 21st century research agenda: Issues, topics & questions guiding inquiry into middle level theory & practice.* Columbus, OH: Author.

Palmer, P. (1993). *To know as we are known: Education as a spiritual journey.* New York: Harper Collins.

Palmer, P. (1997). The heart of a teacher: Identity and integrity in teaching. *Change, 29*(6), 15–21.

Palmer, P. (1998). *The courage to teach: Exploring the inner landscape of a teacher's life.* San Francisco: Jossey-Bass.

Patton, M. (1990). *Qualitative evaluation and research methods* (2nd ed.). Newbury Park, CA: Sage.

Rogers, S., & Renard, L. (1999). Relationship-driven teaching. *Educational Leadership, 57*(1), 34–37.

Scales, P. (1992). *Windows of opportunity: Improving middle grades teacher preparation.* Carrboro, NC: Center for Early Adolescence.

Stevenson, C. (1992). *Teaching ten to fourteen year olds.* New York: Longman.

Valentine, J., Maher, M., Quinne, D., & Irvin, J. (1999). The changing roles of effective middle level principals. *Middle School Journal, 30*(5), 53–56.

Wasley, P. (1999). Teaching worth celebrating. *Educational Leadership, 56*(8), 8–13.

Wavering, M. (Ed.). (1995). *Educating young adolescents: Life in the middle.* New York: Garland.

Yin, R. (1994). *Case study research: Design and methods* (2nd ed.) (Applied Social Research Methods Series, Vol. 5). Thousand Oaks, CA: Sage.

APPENDIX
INTERVIEWEE IDENTIFICATION KEY

(7 to 10 character code)

1st Character = SCHOOLS 1 = Elliott 2 = Girard 3 = Howard 4 = Stevens

2nd Character = PARTICIPANTS S = Student T = Teacher P = Principal

3rd & 4th characters = PARTICIPANT'S NUMBER
Ranges from 01 to 32 Total Participants

5th character = GENDER F = Female M = Male

6th character = ETHNICITY A = Asian B = Black O = Other H = Hispanic W = White

7th character = GRADE LEVEL 6 = Sixth 7 = Seventh 8 = Eighth

8th & 9th characters = EXPERIENCE (Teachers and Principals)
Ranges from 02 to 35 Years Teaching Experience
10th character = CERTIFICATION (Teachers and Principals)
E = Elementary M = Middle S = Secondary P = Special Education

(e.g., 2T01-FB6-13E = Girard Middle School, Teacher, First Interviewee—Female, Black, Sixth Grade—13 Years Teaching Experience, Elementary Certified)

CHAPTER 4

MIDDLE SCHOOL CURRICULUM

Richard Powell and Laura Van Zandt Allen

ABSTRACT

Few things are as complicated and debated as middle level curriculum. Whether the debate pertains to junior high school, interdisciplinary, or integrative ways of knowing, the debate around which is the best approach for young adolescents continues. This paper focuses on historical antecedents to contemporary ways of doing curriculum in middle school. Attention is given to the first and second *Turning Points* documents as means to developing contemporary middle school curriculum. Comparisons are then made between traditional, interdisciplinary, and integrative curriculum. Implications are drawn for future research that draws upon the voices of middle level students to better understand the place that middle level curriculum has in the daily lives of students and teachers.

The problem with middle school curriculum is that we ask students to give answers to questions they do not ask.
—Brazee (1997, p. 187).

INTRODUCTION

One of the most debatable dimensions of middle level schooling is curriculum. For example, some would argue that the middle school curriculum should consist of questions that students ask about the world around them (Brodhagen, 1995). On the other hand, there are educational conservatives who would argue that middle school students need to receive knowledge that is enshrined by the boundaries of subject matter content. There are no ready answers to these highly divergent ways of teaching middle school students, and to these longstanding dichotomies in the middle school movement.

From the meaning of various forms of middle level curriculum to how these forms are best implemented is under continuous and often heated debate. More specifically, there are so many meanings and models for the words *interdisciplinary* and *integrative* that there is little wonder that confusion abounds when, at regional or national middle level conferences, presenters describe "integrative curriculum reform" when in fact they are talking about interdisciplinary reform. Semantical problems are irrefutably replete in the middle level movement. In addition, all middle level educators like to think they are participating in democratic schooling for their students, yet so many who think they are participating in this are still doing schooling in the same age-old form that Dickens (1989) described in *Hard Times*, teaching just the facts in a certain direct way. Students in these situations often have little decision making power other than deciding how the school dance might unfold, or deciding what kind of franchise food might be best in the school cafeteria. Student decision making about curriculum and instruction, in the face of teaching mostly fact-based information in a subject-centered way, is limited if not lacking entirely (Powell, 2001). The confusion over curriculum approaches in middle level schooling is mentioned by Toepher (1997), who writes, *Educators do, indeed, tend to be ambiguous about the definition of curriculum, often confusing curriculum content with approaches to its delivery* (p. 163).

At first the middle grades of 6, 7, and 8 were intended to be scaled-down versions of grades 9–12 (Toepher, 1997). The middle grades, fashionably called junior high school only a few years ago (and for some schools still fashionable), consisted of content-centered departments of teachers, of schools organized around content (e.g., science classrooms all in close proximity, English classrooms in close proximity, and so on), of students situated in academic tracks, and of schools in general emulating the high school model. As more and more attention was given to the affective needs of young adolescents (Carnegie Council, 1989; Eichhorn, 1966), there arose a perceived need to create schools for these adolescents that would ease the transition from elementary to high school, and that would help young adolescents feel more comfortable at school, to be embraced by the school rather than being inserted into it. Thus, the middle school movement grew and has momentarily flourished, although not without debate. Many individuals, including administrators, teachers, and parents, wanted the junior high school model to prevail. This is true today, and the debate about middle school interdisciplinary and integrative curriculum continues to prevail with school districts wavering between the middle school interdisciplinary model and the traditional junior high school model. Much of the debate against the middle level curriculum, particularly that curriculum which grew out of the original *Turning Points* document, should be seen in light of the current movements in standardized and high stakes testing.

The purpose of this chapter is to consider the widespread adoption of the middle school curriculum, to consider the strengths and limitations of this curriculum, and to explore alternative models of middle level schooling other than content-centered and interdisciplinary that have been adopted in selected schools across the country. To accomplish our purpose we first examine historical antecedents to contemporary middle school practices. We then turn to the *Turning Points* phenomenon and we consider its widespread influence on middle school theory and practice. Following this we consider alternative curriculum structures, namely subject-centered, interdisciplinary, and integrative. As we consider alternative curriculum structures we also examine the place that subject matter has in how middle level curriculum plays out in the daily lives of teachers and students. Finally, we consider next steps for research relative to middle level curriculum and instruction.

HISTORICAL ANTECEDENTS TO CONTEMPORARY MIDDLE SCHOOLING

The dawn of the 20th century ushered in an array of substantive turning points for public education. Two revolutionary shifts, now central to the middle school concept, initially developed independently: the redesign of secondary education and the idea of a unified curriculum. The former restructured grade levels from a 1–8, 9–12 pattern into a 6–6 organization and primarily focused on ending high drop out rates, increasing rigor and specialization in the secondary curriculum, and preparing students for work. The latter addressed the need to educate the flurry of students now entering formal schooling and thus advocated a general education, centering curriculum around personal-social issues rather than subject-matter boundaries. Eventually, these new directions would meet and find a rhetorical if not always practical home in the modern-day middle school. Understanding the origins of this genesis promises to help us deal not only with the present conundrums surrounding middle level curricular issues but those facing us in the uncertain years to come.

The Reorganization of Secondary Education

Under the 1–8 structure, the curriculum of the upper grades had largely been viewed as redundant and unchallenging, causing many to refer to these years as a waste of time. Koos (1920) observed that when compared with European schools, "there is a waste of time in our system. The unfavorable position given American schools in these comparisons has had no little to do with the current dissatisfaction with the conventional relationship between our elementary and secondary schools" (p. 1). Moreover, students in the middle years were dropping out of school at alarming rates, preferring meager wages to the boredom of the classroom. Retention studies conducted around 1910 found that almost 100% of those entering first grade completed fifth grade; however, by the sophomore year of high school, 60 to 67% of students left school, with only 8 to 10% graduating high school (Gruhn & Douglass, 1947). Thus, offering a more rigorous, content-specific curriculum seemed a logical step, both to retain students and to get in the most content possible if students did drop out (Beane, 1993). Support for these changes had been endorsed for some time by groups such as the Committee of Ten (1893), who favored a unified six-year high-school course of study beginning with the seventh grade. As a result, the ideology of the secondary school curriculum remained much the same, while the definition of what was now considered "secondary education" expanded to include grades 7 and 8.

With the equal division of elementary and secondary education into the 6–6 plan, a new discussion arose—that of the aims and purposes of what was soon known as the junior high school (grades 7–9). The Committee on the Economy of Time in Education (1913) and later the Commission on the Reorganization of Secondary Education (1918) both recommended that the reorganized secondary school be divided into junior and senior periods of three years each. The decision primarily served the pragmatic need to provide housing for the middle grades rather than any principled desire to best serve young adolescents. It did, however, open the door for the examination of these students as a distinct group who heretofore had remained lost between the agendas of the elementary and secondary schools.

A Unified Curriculum

As discussion regarding the organization of elementary and secondary education mounted, so did conversations regarding the organization of the curriculum. Until this time, the long-standing practice of separating subjects into distinct disciplines had been widely accepted. As the context of education in the United States began to change, however, so did reformer's thoughts regarding the purpose of a public education and the varied processes for achieving this goal.

Individuals and groups in the early 1900s identified many of the same concerns educators face today when advocating for a more unified curriculum. These included the *vast increase in available knowledge and multiplication of learners,* (DeGarmo, 1895, p. 4). Thus, centering curricula around real-world experiences rather than artificial subject matter boundaries garnered support from those such as John Dewey, the Herbart Society, and William Kilpatrick. It was also at this juncture that educators first began to realize the differing needs of K-12 students. Reformers such as Hall (1904) argued that significant differences existed between the elementary and high school student and that curricular and instructional decisions be based on development rather than tradition. As a result, the terms adolescent and pre-adolescent began appearing in educational literature as did the idea that the junior high curriculum should emphasize exploration and individual interest rather than the highly specialized curriculum of the high school. The realization that the majority of students now entering schools were not on the college track added strength to the debate for a practical (vocational) rather than classical curriculum.

By the 1930s, the concept of interdisciplinary curricula had gained widespread currency. Hopkins (1937) estimated that as many as 80% of the nation's schools employed some type of interdisciplinary curriculum, respective of the wide range of terminology used to describe these efforts (i.e., correlation, fusion, core, interdisciplinary, broad fields). Most notable is the famous Eight Year Study (1932–1940), which matched 1475 graduates of thirty experimental high schools with peers who had attended traditional high schools to determine if a curriculum designed around the needs and interests of students was as effective as a conventional curriculum in preparing adolescents for the challenge of higher education (Aiken, 1942). In short, students attending the experimental schools were superior to those from conventional environments, leading investigators to conclude that *the more experimental the school, the greater degree of success in college* (Chamberlin, 1942, p. 209). Faunce and Bossing (1958) point out that "one highly significant outcome of this investigation was its validation of the belief that there is no one pattern of subject preparation for college which is superior to any other pattern" (p. 41).

Despite these findings, the specter of general education continued to overshadow many widespread unification efforts. A curriculum developed for the masses maintained the stigma of "general" versus "specialized" regardless of substantive research to the contrary; thus, an artificial dichotomy took root that is still firmly entrenched today—curriculum may be either unified and general or specialized and college preparatory but not both.

For these reasons, the junior high school curriculum embraced two seemingly divergent aims—the need for more specialized, rigorous coursework and the need to meet developmental needs while preparing students for work and productive citizenry. Cuban (1992) contends that this "uncertainty about mission" (p. 230) has been at the heart of the movement's century-long struggle for success. From the beginning, Koos (1920) notes that "in only two respects do the administrative features [of the junior high school] move toward identity, and these are in the mode of assignment of work to teachers (departmentalization or semi-departmentalization) and in the manner of advancement of pupils (promotion by subject)" (p. 10). Beane (1993) concurs, "Clearly, unless the view of alternatives begins with the fundamental purpose of middle schools themselves, it is most difficult to imagine a substantially different curriculum form in practice" (p. 29). The lack of an identifiable identity failed to distinguish the junior high school from the senior high school; by default then, the curriculum as well as a number of other aspects of the new school often mirrored those found in the upper grades.

In the next section we focus on the movements that instantiated the middle school movement as a design for curriculum and instruction for young adolescents. In this section we turn to the first and second Turning Point documents as the reasoning for this instantiation.

Middle School and the Turning Points Phenomenon

By the 1940s, many advocates supporting the junior high school had declared the reform a failure. This came as little surprise given the incompatibility of the original aims of the school. Criticism revolved around the lack of attention to the developmental needs of students via departmentalization, subject-centered curricula, subject-trained teachers, teacher-centered instruction, tracking, and limited electives (Aubrey, 1945). What the school had accomplished included the retention of students in higher grades (in concert with the establishment of child labor laws), the inclusion of a more rigorous, subject-based curriculum in grades 7 and 8, and the fusion of subject matter (i.e., history, geography, government, and sociology into "social studies"). While a handful of lighthouse schools had incorporated the student-centered curricula prescribed at the onset (i.e., unified curriculum, guidance programs, varied electives), the vast majority did not, electing to retain the function and organization of a "junior" high school. Perhaps most disturbing was the stagnant nature of the institution. Studies from the 1920s to the 1960s revealed little substantive change toward these initial goals. For example, Lounsbury and Douglass (1974) studied the extent of change in junior high schools from 1954–1964 and found almost no increase in practices such as curriculum correlation, problems-based inquiry, and block scheduling. Instead, practices such as counselor-based guidance programs, ability grouping, and direct instruction became increasingly common. Thus, it was this detour away from the original vision of the school along with the general malcontent with the current structure that propelled educators in the 1960s and '70s to set in motion what is now known as the "middle school movement."

As the frenzy surrounding the Sputnik years began to fade, conversations once again rallied around student-centered agendas (e.g., Rogers, 1969). At the middle level, William Alexander (1995), often referred to as the "father of the modern day middle school," argued for restructuring junior high schools into middle schools in his historic speech at Cornell University in 1963. Much more than a name change, middle schools were to be just that—schools designed to meet and bridge the varied needs of students between childhood and adolescence, what Alexander and others referred to as the "in-between-ager" (1968). Curriculum plans proposed during this time emphasized the flexibility of each school to meet the needs of students given the wide range of differences existing in the population; however, they also retained classical subject area boundaries (Eichhorn, 1966). For example, in the *The Emergent Middle School,* Alexander et al (1968) suggested that curricula be classified into three categories of learning opportunities: personal development (i.e., guidance, values, health), skills for continued learning (i.e., reading, problem solving, exploratory), and organized knowledge (mathematics, language arts, social studies, science). In this proposal, some curriculum correlation occurred between the areas of language arts and social studies; however, academic subject boundaries largely remained intact. Another popular plan recommended the retention of traditional academic courses while adding a "core" course in which students studied issues of interest to them in a multidisciplinary format (i.e., Moss, 1969). However, not until the publication of *A Curriculum for the Middle School Years* (Lounsbury & Vars; 1978) was serious attention given to unifying the curriculum. Herein, Lounsbury and Vars advocated a curriculum centered on a problems-based core that included subject-matter content as well as other areas of study. While separate courses in academics and skills remained, the focus was on the core program rather than the converse. Lounsbury and Vars note:

> A major portion of the common learnings should be provided through a core program, most simply described as a problem-centered block-time program. At its best, core provides students with a direct and continuing opportunity to examine in depth both personal and social problems that have meaning to them. It also provides a situation in which a teacher can know a limited number of students well enough to offer the advisement or counseling most of

> them need so badly during the transition years, and in the process they can learn essential human relations and communication skills. (p. 46)

Although few schools implemented this vision of a fully unified curriculum (Gross, 1972; Tils, Vars, & Lounsbury, 1967), the revived concept gained acceptance as a cornerstone of middle school reform. By the early 1980s, the burgeoning National Middle School Association had endorsed a "challenging, integrative, and exploratory" curriculum that allowed for flexibility in grouping, scheduling, and staffing (NMSA, 1982). Other reputable groups followed suit with similar recommendations (i.e., Children's Defense Fund, 1988; California State Department of Education, 1987; National Association of Secondary School Principals, 1986). However, two reports of the 1980s set the stage for sweeping middle level reform: the National Commission on Excellence in Education's *A Nation at Risk*, and the Carnegie Council on Adolescent Development's *Turning Points: Preparing American Youth for the 21st Century.*

The dissemination of *A Nation at Risk* (NCEE, 1983) once again refocused education on the basics, while ushering in the era of accountability. The report referred to the secondary curriculum as "homogenized, diluted, diffused" and without "a central purpose." It also railed against general education as academically weak and inferior to the college-preparatory curriculum. As a result, the Commission recommended that all candidates for high school diplomas be required to take the "new basics," which included three or more years of English, mathematics, science, and social studies plus one-half year of computer science. At the same time, supplementary recommendations regarding the pre-high school years all but supported arguments for change at the middle level. From *A Nation at Risk* (NCEE, 1983),

> The curriculum in the crucial eight grades leading to the high school years should be specifically designed to provide a sound base for study in those and later years in such areas as English language development and writing, computational and problem solving skills, science, social studies, foreign language, and the arts. These years should foster an enthusiasm for learning and the development of the individual's gifts and talents. (p. 40)

What followed *A Nation at Risk* was a prolification of reports and rebuttals on the subject which, in turn, set in motion a decade of reform. This climate of reform was key to enacting many of the substantive changes touted by advocates of the middle school movement since the 1960s.

It was within this environment that the Carnegie Corporation's Council on Adolescent Development released Turning Points: Preparing American Youth for the 21st Century (1989). While a number of reports, texts, and articles had been written on the mismatch between schooling and young adolescent needs, the report secured credibility for the movement on a national level for the first time. Grounded in developmental research, the watershed document made eight recommendations for the restructuring of middle grade schools:

1. Create small communities for learning;
2. Teach a core academic program;
3. Ensure success for all students;
4. Empower teachers and administrators to make decisions about the experiences of middle grade students;
5. Staff middle grade schools with teachers who are expert at teaching young adolescents;
6. Improve academic performance through fostering health and fitness;
7. Reengage families in the education of young adolescents; and
8. Connect schools with communities. (p. 9)

As a result, the 1990s witnessed a marked increase in the implementation of developmentally appropriate practices for young adolescents. McEwin, Dickinson, and Jenkins (1996) documented these changes in practice at the middle level over a 25-year period (studies conducted in 1968, 1988, 1993). Findings included increases in areas such as the establishment of grades 6–8 schools, the organization of teachers in interdisciplinary teams, flexible scheduling, team planning time, teacher-based guidance programs, and middle level teacher education programs, with the sharpest increases occurring between the 1988 and 1993 studies. By the mid-1990s, middle schools outnumbered junior high schools in both name and function. Thus, the Turning Points phenomenon, as it came to be known, was in a number of ways the first concrete realization of the student-centered school advocated for almost a century.

Once schools embraced the philosophy, implementation of one or more of the recommendations followed. Without doubt, the most fashionable change involved organizing faculty into interdisciplinary teams. This was seen by many as a precursor to enacting a number of other reforms such as curriculum correlation, block scheduling, and advisory programs. By others, recommendations were viewed as a menu from which one could pick and choose as needed. For example, by the mid 1990s, the majority of middle grade schools had implemented an interdisciplinary team organization; however, interdisciplinary instruction had not become institutionalized into middle school practice and was an occasional rather than a regular activity. Moreover, 88–90% of middle grade schools continued to utilize direct instruction regularly, with cooperative learning and inquiry teaching incorporated only 35–55% of the time (McEwin et al., 1996).

Beane (1993) argues, "Clearly, the major concern in middle level 'reform' has been on the organization of time and other institutional features rather than on the curriculum" (p. 29). Despite a century of work, a definitive curriculum for the middle grades remained elusive. Dickinson (2001) aptly noted,

> This lack of an appropriate curriculum for the middle school and for young adolescents was extremely debilitating in its effect on the democratic elements of the middle school because it disenfranchised young adolescents with a highly circumscribed, high specialized curriculum dominated by the perspectives of experts ... in fact, this absence of an appropriate curriculum contributed to one of the fundamental dichotomies in the movement—the either/or situation of good places for youth vs. challenging and involving work. (pp. 10–11)

Much of the confusion surrounding this dichotomy surfaced from the emphasis on climatic rather than academic objectives in *Turning Points* (1989). The recommendation to teach "a core academic program" took backseat to other recommendations that focused instead on improving the overall environment for young adolescents. Dickinson (2001) contended that despite Beane's (1993, 1997) and others efforts toward defining what the curriculum of the middle school ought to be during the 1990s, most middle schools remain "shells," existing without a curriculum of their own.

In response, the Carnegie Corporation released a second, equally provocative report. Turning Points 2000 (Carnegie, 2000) stated that "the main purpose of middle grades education is to promote young adolescents' intellectual development" (p. 10). Tellingly, the report recommends teaching "a curriculum grounded in rigorous, public academic standards, relevant to the concerns of adolescents, and based on how students learn best" (Carnegie, 2000, pp. 31–32). An emphasis is placed on addressing a backward curriculum design that intertwines curriculum, assessment, and instruction. Moreover, Turning Points 2000 suggested focusing curricular standards around important concepts (i.e., themes) that are universal and cut across disciplines. While research strongly supports what Dickinson (2001) called "a totally integrated ecology of schooling" at the middle level (i.e., Felner, Jackson, Kasak, Mulhall, Brand, & Flowers; 1997), it remains to be seen whether or not schools can simultaneously address standards and curriculum integration. Pate (2001) argued that these two seemingly divergent aims can indeed coexist and achieve the aims set forth by both. However, Beane (2001) cautioned that, "the push for such ideas put the middle school movement on a collision course with the standards and testing juggernaut" (p. xix). Thus, at the dawn of the 21st century, the struggle to create truly democratic learning environments that integrate the needs of all young adolescents remains much as it has—a much advocated but rarely envisioned dream.

ALTERNATIVE CURRICULUM STRUCTURES

In the previous sections we described the reform of the 1980s and 1990s, and we considered the place that Turning Points has in middle level education. One dimension of middle school curriculum that has emerged from these (and earlier) reforms is alternative curriculum structures. By this we mean how subject matter is organized and taught to young adolescents. Although middle school curriculum often takes many varying forms, there are three general epistemologies that guide these forms. These epistemologies include subject-centered, interdisciplinary, and integrative.

The subject-centered curriculum is the most traditional. Schools that endorse this kind of curriculum often retain the name, junior high school, and resemble what is usually taught in high schools. That is, the curriculum consists of specific subject areas such as Language Arts, science, mathematics, and so on. Schools that have these subject areas are ordinarily divided into subject matter departments, such as the science department or the mathematics department. Teachers, for example, in the math department are then situated with their classrooms in close proximity so that specific areas of the school are known for their subject that is housed there.

The advent to middle school as a concept has attempted to move away from the strictly subject-centered approach to teaching young adolescents. Applebee (1996) gives the name *knowledge-out-of-context* to information taught in a subject-centered context. This is because the subject-centered approach tends to privilege content over the needs of students, thus moving away from a student-centered approach to classroom instruction. Viewed this way the subject-centered approach treats students as blank slates to be filled with content, and direct instruction often prevails in these situations. The direct instruction approach has been criticized as not being able to meet the informational needs of young adolescents. As Brazee (1997) contends, "The problem with the middle level curriculum is that we ask students to give answers to questions they do not ask" (p. 187). What Brazee argues is that subject-centered curriculum is one that is received by students, not created by them and not organized in such a way as to help young adolescents find answers to questions they have about the world around them. Because this world of young adolescents is so immediate the subject-matter in a knowledge-out-of-context situation often fails to help them come to terms with their concerns, issues, and dilemmas that they face each day.

A second epistemology that middle schools have adopted is that called interdisciplinary. This epistemology has become the hallmark of middle schools across the nation. As Lounsbury (1992) writes, "Probably no single word has been more frequently cited in relationship to the middle school than has the word interdisciplinary" (p. 1). In general terms interdisciplinary refers to the bringing together of varying knowledge structures in an effort to help students see connections between these structures. As Vars (1993) writes, "'Interdisciplinary teaching' is instruction that emphasizes the connections, the interrelations, among various areas of knowledge. In its broadest sense it is designed to help students to 'see life whole,' to integrate and make sense out of the myriad of experiences they have, both in school and in the world at large" (p. 1).

Unlike subject-centered schools, interdisciplinary schools are most often divided into core teams of teachers. The departmentalization of subject-centered schools becomes transformed into an interdisciplinary phenomenon, and core teachers (e.g., language arts, science, social studies, mathematics) often have their rooms in close proximity. The interdisciplinary phenomenon, when fully realized, can be a powerful instructional tool for transforming individual teachers professional lives and for helping both students and teachers understand connections between divergent subjects such as English and mathematics, or science and social studies (e.g., Kerekes, 1992). However, not all teams are fully functioning, and interdisciplinary unit building for such teams is more problematic. In these instances teams may meet together but lack the desire or ability to provide students with interdisciplinary units. When teams are unable or unwilling to create interdisciplinary units their instruction then takes on the form of subject-centered teaching, and the idea of middle school becomes minimized.

A third epistemology that some middle schools have adopted is that called integrative. This epistemology views knowledge as nonlinear. That is, knowledge taught to students in an integrative curriculum setting is taught around broader themes and issues that are more germane to students' lives. The knowledge selected to be taught informs a particular theme and is not bound by the linear logic that is so inherent in subject-centered schooling. Learning in an integrative setting can also be called contextualized and situated because the learning is contextualized by a theme or issue, and is situated in the world in which students live out their daily lives (e.g., see Beane, 1997; Brodhagen, 1995). Applebee would call the kind of information taught in an integrative setting knowledge-in-action.

Integrative teaching is labor intensive. This is likely one reason why this kind of curriculum has not become more widespread. Another reason is that traditionalists prefer to have their subject-centered approach which is more predictable and has been a longstanding model in schools across the world. Integrative teaching nevertheless has become a central feature of schools such as Brown Barge Middle School in Pensacola, Florida and Carver Academy in Waco, Texas. These schools attract students and parents who prefer to learn in alternative nonlinear ways.

Teaching integratively also means rethinking the instructional metaphors we use when we teach specific content. For example, as Brodhagen (1995) demonstrates, with an integrative curriculum we no longer give knowledge to students in a straightforward manner; rather, we negotiate the content with them. This is because in an integrative environment we allow students to have a democratic voice in what is taught and how information is acquired. As another metaphorical transition, the integrative environment tries to connect content together far more than what is expected in an interdisciplinary environment. The connection metaphor takes on new meaning in an integrative context. When studying a theme such as Bridges or Flight, the content that informs the theme has to be interconnected. Math, science, literature, building trades, and other topics all become unified, as if there really are no boundaries between these subjects as in traditional settings. As various subjects become connected, they also become coherent, a word Beane (1995) uses when describing the ideal integrative curriculum. Beane notes,

> A coherent curriculum is one that holds together, that makes sense as a whole; and its parts, whatever they are, are unified and connected by that sense of the whole. The idea of coherence begins with a view of the curriculum as a broadly conceived concept—as the curriculum—that is about "something." It is not simply a collection of disparate parts or pieces that accumulate in student experiences and on transcripts. (1995, p. 3)

Another set of metaphors that is misaligned with integrative curriculum includes the *ahead* and *behind* metaphors. These two metaphors are central to subject-centered linear approaches to teaching content. Yet in an integrative curriculum there can be no ahead or behind in learning, rather there is *broader, deeper,* and *uncovering* metaphors. By this we mean that learning nonlinear content cannot have linear metaphors; ahead and behind are linear metaphors for learning. Consequently, we need a new set of metaphors when teaching in a nonlinear environment. When we learn content circumscribed by a theme we cannot move ahead or behind others, but we can move to a deeper and broader level of understanding. Moreover, we can uncover new knowledge about them as we move toward this understanding.

Toward the Democratic Ideology

We now must turn to the question, What is the relationship between the democratic ideology for students and the alternative curriculum structures outlined in the aforementioned discussion and purported in the *Turning Points* documents. Surely, the traditional model of schooling, that which is subject-centered and departmentally-organized is not suited to the democratic ideology. Decisions in these environments about what and how to learn are made by the administration or by teachers, not with the input from students. Turning to interdisciplinary middle level contexts do not necessarily provide a place where the democratic ideology is any more realized (Powell, 2001). Interdisciplinary schools, with their core teams and more intimate settings, might certainly be more humanistic, they are not always more democratic. Beane and Apple (1995) write that democratic schools can be distinguished "from other kinds of 'progressive' schools, such as those that are simply humanistic or child-centered. Democratic schools are both of these things in many ways, but their vision extends beyond purposes such as improving the school climate or enhancing students' self-esteem" (p. 11). Democratic schools, those touted in both *Turning Points* documents, indeed strive to engage students fully and completely by building a community of shared learning, and a community where experiences are developed and owned in part by the students. It is this ownership by students that is the sine quo non of democratic schooling. In democratic schools all students have the opportunity to contribute something. In our studies over the past decade we have found that integrative schools, those that are theme-based and nonlinear in organization of content, are those that incorporate student decision making—those that make students' perspectives, views, and needs the foremost in decision making about what and how learning takes place. Two schools in particular where we have focused our studies, and where we have located democratic learning environments, include Brown Barge Middle School in Pensacola, Florida, and Carver Academy in Waco Texas (Powell, 1999).

Making the school culture and corresponding classroom contexts democratic places where students learn about and internalize key issues such as shared ownership, equity, and personal independence is clearly hard work. What we learned from Brown Barge Middle School and Carver Academy is that democratic schooling, if it is to be realized and functional, should at least engage students in shared ownership of the curriculum by engaging them continuously in decisions that determine what is taught, how it will be taught, and how learnings will be assessed. This will clearly make the school climate more collaborative, consequently more democratic.

RESEARCH POSSIBILITIES

There is much we know about some junior high school and middle school models. We know that junior high schools are predictable in what they expect from teachers and students. We know that when interdisciplinary models more closely emulate junior high schools that the same expectations from teachers and students are equally predictable. What we also know is that these models, those that are inherently subject-centered and authoritarian, connote a semblance of oppression and certainly a lack of shared decision making. Ideologically the middle schools that tout an integrative curriculum (e.g., Brown Barge Middle School) are arguably democratic in that they bring students into decision making about what to learn, and certainly about how content is to be learned.

There is much we have yet to learn about middle schools in general, and integrative middle schools in particular. In particular, we have heard from teachers about their schooling, and we have examined the benefits for teachers that surface from being part of teaching teams. What we need now is to hear from students. This is not always an easy agenda to surmount, yet it is an agenda we must move forward with if we are indeed to more fully understand the place of interdisciplinary schools and integrative schools in students mental lives. We need to explore, in both integrative and interdisciplinary settings, how students' voices are brought into schools' collective voices. And we must strive to understand what this means for students not just during their present tenure in school, but in the future. We need to understand what democratic schooling experiences means for students as they move through later systems that are less democratic in their orientation. Gaining this understanding will assuredly help middle level educators better understand how the middle school movement in general and the Turning Points movements in particular foster the intellectual and personal stature of young adolescents in today's schools.

Relative to interdisciplinary settings, settings that predominate middle school contexts across the nation, we have a need to understand what the interdisciplinary core structure means for students' understanding of content. Does the interdisciplinary setting help students understand the relationships between various disparate content areas? If so, what does this mean for their performance on daily classroom events, and then on standardized exams such as TAAS in Texas and C-SAP in Colorado? The research potential in middle schools is vast and expansive; at the very least this potential should include middle level students' lives as these lives are lived out in the real time of schools. Then we will know more realistically how the *Turning Points* phenomena in fact influence school learning.

REFERENCES

Aiken, W.M. (1942). *The story of the eight year study.* New York: Harper.

Alexander, W.M. (1995). The junior high school: A changing view. In G. Hass & K. Wiles (Eds.). *Readings in curriculum* (pp. 418–425), Boston: Allyn and Bacon.

Alexander, W.M., Williams, E.L., Compton, M., Hines, V.A., & Prescott, D. (1968). *The emergent middle school.* New York: Holt, Rinehart, and Winston, Inc.

Applebee, A.N. (1996). *Curriculum as conversation: Transforming traditions of teaching and learning.* Chicago: University of Chicago Press.

Beane, J.A. (2001). Reform and reinvention. In T. Dickinson (Ed.). *Reinventing the middle school* (pp. xiii-xxii). New York: RoutledgeFalmer.

Beane, J.A. (1997). *Curriculum integration: Designing the core of democratic education.* New York: Teachers College Press.

Beane, J.A. (1993). *A middle school curriculum: From rhetoric to reality.* (2nd ed.). Columbus, OH: National Middle School Association.

Brazee, E. (1997). Curriculum for whom? In J. Irvin (Ed.), *What current research says to the middle level practitioner* (pp. 187–201). Columbus, OH: National Middle School Association.

Brodhagen, B. (1995). The situation made us special. In M. Apple & J. Beane (Eds.), *Democratic schools* (pp. 83–100). Alexandria, VA: Association for Supervision and Curriculum Development.

California State Department of Education. (1987). *Caught in the middle: Education reform for young adolescents in California public schools.* Sacramento, CA: Author.

Carnegie Council on Adolescent Development. (1989). *Turning points: Preparing American youth for the 21st century.* Washington, DC: Carnegie Corporation.

Children's Defense Fund. (1988). *Survey of state policies and programs for the middle grades.* Washington, DC: Author.

Chamberlin, D. (1942). *Did they succeed in college?* New York: Harper and Brothers.

Committee of Ten. (1893). *Report on the Committee of Ten on secondary school studies* (Education Report, 1892–1893, pp. 1415–1495). Washington, DC: U.S. Government Printing Office.

Committee on the Economy of Time in Education. (1913). *Report of the committee of the national council of education on economy of time in education* (Bulletin 1913, No. 38, United States Bureau of Education, pp. 10–19). Washington, DC: U.S. Government Printing Office.

Commission on the Reorganization of Secondary Education. (1918). *Cardinal principles of secondary education* (Bulletin 1918, No. 35, Department of the Interior, Bureau of Education). Washington, DC: U.S. Government Printing Office.

Cuban, L. (1992). What happens to reforms that last? The case of the junior high school. *American Educational Research Journal, 29*(2), 227–251.

DeGarmo, C. (1895). Most pressing problems concerning the elementary curriculum. In C.A. McMurry (Ed.), *The first yearbook of the Herbart Society* (pp. 3–26). Bloomington, IL: Pantograph.

Dickens, C. (1989). *Hard times.* New York: Oxford University Press. (First published in 1854).

Dickinson, T.S. (2001). Reinventing the middle school: A proposal to counter arrested development. In T. Dickinson (Ed.). *Reinventing the middle school.* (pp. 1–20). New York: RoutledgeFalmer.

Douglass, A. (1945). The persistent problems of the junior high school. *California Journal of Secondary Education, 20*(2), 112–120.

Eichhorn, D.H. (1966). *The middle school.* New York: The Center for Applied Research in Education.

Faunce, R.C., & Bossing, N.L. (1958). *Developing the core curriculum* (2nd ed.). Englewood Cliffs, NJ: Prentice-Hall.

Felner, R.D., Jackson A.W., Kasak, D., Mulhall, P., Brand, S., & Flower, N. (1997). The impact of school reform for the middle years. *Phi Delta Kappan, 78*(7), 528–550.

Gross, B.M. (1972). *An analysis of the present and perceived purposes, function, and characteristics of the middle school.* Unpublished doctoral dissertation. Philadelphia, PA: Temple University.

Gruhn, W., & Douglass, H. (1947). *The modern junior high school.* New York: Ronald Press Company.

Hall, G.S. (1904). *Adolescence: Its psychology and its relations to physiology, anthropology, sociology, sex, crime, religion, and education.* New York: D. Appleton and Company.

Hopkins, L.T. (1937). *Integration: Its meaning and application.* New York: D. Appleton-Century.

Jackson, A.W., & Davis G.A. (2000*). Turning points 2000: Educating adolescents in the 21st century* (a report of the Carnegie Corporation of New York). New York: Teachers College Press.

Kerekes, J. (1992). The interdisciplinary unit—It's here to stay. In J. Lounsbury (Ed.), *Connecting the curriculum through interdisciplinary instruction* (p. 97–102). Westerville, OH: National Middle School Association.

Koos, L.V. (1920). *The junior high school.* New York: Harcourt, Brace, and Company.

Lounsbury, J.H. (1992). Interdisciplinary instruction: A mandate for the nineties. In J. Lounsbury (Ed.), *Connecting the curriculum through interdisciplinary instruction* (p. 1–2). Westerville, OH: National Middle School Association.

Lounsbury, J., & Douglass, G. (1974). Recent trends in junior high school practices, in M. Brough and R. Hamm, (Eds.). *The American intermediate school* (pp. 171–175), Danville, Illinios: Interstate Printers and Publishers.

Lounsbury, J., & Var, G. (1978). *A curriculum for the middle school years.* New York: Harper & Row.

McEwin, C.K., Dickinson, T.S., & Jenkins, D.M. (1996). *America's middle schools: Practices and progress.* Columbus, OH: National Middle School Association.

Moss, T.C. (1969). *Middle school.* New York: Houghton.

National Association of Secondary School Principals. (1986*). An agenda for excellence at the middle level.* Reston, VA: Author.

National Commission on Excellence in Education. (1983*). A nation at risk: The imperative for educational reform.* Washington, DC: U.S. Government Printing Office,

National Middle School Association. (1982). *This we believe.* Columbus, OH: Author.

Pate, P.E. (2001). Standards, students, and exploration: Creating a curriculum intersection of excellence. In T. Dickinson (Ed.). *Reinventing the middle school* (pp. 79–95). New York: RoutledgeFalmer.

Powell, R. (2001). On headpieces of straw: How middle level students view their schooling. In T. Dickinson (Ed.), *Reinventing the middle school* (pp. 117–152). New York: Routledge.

Powell, R. (1999). Reflections on integrative curriculum: A conversation with Camille Barr and Molly Maloy. *Middle School Journal, 31*(2), 25–34.

Rogers, C. (1969). *Freedom to learn.* New York: Merrill Publishing Company.

Toepfer, C. (1997). Middle level curriculum's serendipitous history. In J. Irvin (Ed.), *What current research says to the middle level practitioner* (pp. 163–178). Columbus, OH: National Middle School Association.

Van Til, W., Vars, G., & Lounsbury, J. (1967). *Modern education for the junior high school years* (2nd ed.). Indianapolis, IN: Bobbs-Merrill.

Vars, G. (1993). *Interdisciplinary teaching: Why and how.* Columbus, OH: National Middle School Association.

CHAPTER 5

FLEXIBLE SCHEDULING AND YOUNG ADOLESCENT DEVELOPMENT

A Perfect Match

Dave F. Brown

ABSTRACT

Alternative scheduling formats provide structural flexibility to middle schools that promote the design of developmentally appropriate learning environments for young adolescents. Research indicates that flexible scheduling encourages the development of meaningful relationships between teachers and students, increases student understanding through more in-depth study of curricula, and provides time to more effectively address the demands of diverse learners. Alternative schedules create opportunities for curriculum integration and promote more flexibility and creativity in instructional processes. Flexible schedules also increase teacher collaboration and planning and support heterogeneous grouping practices. These are significant changes that match the recommendations of the National Middle School Association.

INTRODUCTION

The knowledge available to educators on how learning occurs has grown considerably over the past ten years. As a result of this knowledge, recent research on effective teaching focuses on addressing social, emotional, and cultural needs as well as the cognitive needs of learners (Cobb & Mayer, 2000; D'Arcangelo, 1998; Gay, 2000; Jensen, 1998; Tomlinson, 1999; Wlodkowski & Ginsberg, 1995). Effective teaching is currently determined by the ability of educators to create learning environments that address learners' needs rather than placing all the responsibility for learning on students. Creating a learner focused classroom benefits young adolescents perhaps more than any other age students. A review of young adolescents' developmental characteristics reveals a set of distinct changes occurring between the ages of 10 to 15:

- considerable changes and variations in stages of physical growth (Simmons & Blyth, 1987; Tanner, 1972; Van Hoose & Strahan, 1988);
- variations in levels of cognitive growth among students as some progress from concrete to formal operational stage (Lounsbury & Clark, 1990; Piaget, 1977);
- heightened social consciousness accompanied by intense egocentrism (Milgram, 1992; Rice, 1999); and,
- frequent examination and questioning of identity. (Erikson, 1968; Marcia, 1980)

Middle level teachers must address young adolescents' physical, social, and emotional concerns prior to gaining the attention and cooperation needed for learning to occur. Many strategies have been provided to individual classroom teachers that address these needs of young adolescents; but the entire school day should be designed to encourage optimal social, emotional, and cognitive development (Caine & Caine, 1994; Knowles & Brown, 2000).

The National Middle School Association (NMSA, 1995) suggested 12 strategies for addressing young adolescents' needs. Among the 12 suggestions are the following four that significantly affect student learning:

- An adult advocate for every student.
- Curriculum that is challenging, integrative, and exploratory.
- Varied teaching and learning approaches.
- Flexible organizational structures. (p. 11)

Two of these four aspects of school structure, curricular decision making and flexible organizational structures, are macro components of middle school and generally regarded by teachers as outside their domain of responsibility and control (Watts & Castle, 1993).

A significant way to address these specific National Middle School Association suggestions is to provide additional time for teachers to interact with students each period, that is, to implement flexible organizational structures as they affect a school's scheduling of class times. The traditionally designed school arrangement of students attending six-to-eight separate classes per day for a time period of approximately 40 to 55 minutes each severely restricts the opportunities for the development of meaningful relationships between students and their teachers. Shortened class periods prohibit opportunities for initiating "challenging, integrative, and exploratory" curricula and do little to assist teachers in using "varied teaching and learning approaches" (NMSA, 1995, p. 11).

Middle schools inherited this traditional approach of splitting the school day into six-to-eight shortened periods (40 to 55 minutes) from high schools that have used this structure since the advent of compulsory schooling (Gruhn & Douglas, 1971). One primary reason for this "factory model" design was to train students to work in factories (Caine & Caine, 1994, p. 14). Another was the belief that students needed to be exposed to a variety of content over the course of 12 years of schooling. A school culture developed and became institutionalized as a result, in which educators and the public embraced the belief that significant learning was best achieved through exposing students to several core subjects for brief periods of time during the day.

THE DEVELOPMENT OF ALTERNATIVE SCHEDULING

A break in the traditional factory model of school structure occurred in the late 1960s when a more flexible plan was introduced by Trump called *flexible modular scheduling* (Goldman, 1983). From the mid 1960s until the 1980s, the traditional scheduling model held on firmly in middle and junior and senior high schools. Only 15% of secondary schools attempted flexible scheduling during the 1960s and 70s (O'Neil, 1995).

Emphasis on the development of students' thinking processes influenced school philosophy in the late 1980s and was an encouragement for schools to adopt alternative scheduling formats (Ennis, 1985). The reintroduction of flexible scheduling models in the 1990s from Carroll (1994), Edwards (1995), and Canady and Rettig (1995) greatly influenced a change in school culture. Subsequently, the National Commission on Time and Learning published *Prisoners of Time* (1994) in which the authors identified five factors that inhibited academic improvement. Among the factors listed were the following:

- The fixed clock and calendar is a fundamental design flaw that must be changed;
- Today's school schedule must be modified to respond to the great changes that have reshaped American life outside school;
- Educators do not have the time they need to do their job properly. (cited in Bevevino, Snodgrass, Adams, & Dengel, 1999, p. 5)

Additional impetus for adopting structural change emanated from cognitive researchers who provided educators with more accurate descriptions of how meaningful learning occurs (Cobb & Mayer, 2000; D'Arcangelo, 1998; Jensen, 1998). Zepeda (1999) reported that as many as half of the high schools across the nation had adopted flexible scheduling formats in efforts to improve learning and teaching.

MIDDLE LEVEL FOCUS

Few junior high and middle schools have altered the structure of the traditional factory model school day of six to eight, 40 to 55 minute periods despite what educators now know about the science of learning and young adolescent development (Valentine & Whitaker, 1997). Valentine, Clark, Irvin, Keefe, and Melton reported in 1993 that 94% of middle schools continued to use a six-to-eight period day. Rettig and Canady (2000) asked the following:

> We wonder if middle school students are being expected to deal with too many subjects, often presented in fragmented ways, during a school day or year? In terms of what we know about the characteristics and problems of the middle school student ... do we need to revisit what we are asking a 13-year-old student to do, which in many middle schools, is to be responsible for eight or nine different classes, notebooks, texts, tests, and other class requirements, often every school day? As teachers, would we oppose such expectations of ourselves? (p. 11)

With these words, Rettig and Canady describe another distinct disadvantage of using a traditional model of structuring the school day for young adolescents—it fails to address their developing social, emotional, physical, and particularly, cognitive needs. Jackson and Davis (2000) provide support for altering the structure of middle schools with specific goals in mind for young adolescents:

> It is to enable every student to think creatively, to identify and solve meaningful problems, to communicate and work well with others, and to develop the base of factual knowledge and skills that is the essential foundation for these "higher order" capacities. (p. 11)

Reaching these specific goals requires those who operate middle schools to design them such that young adolescents have many opportunities and additional time to develop trusting relationships with teachers. Jackson and Davis (2000) add, "The relationships established within the middle school affect both the quality of student learning and the quality of teaching" (p. 122). Social and emotional bonds between students and teachers can be more fully developed through establishing more time for students and teachers to become engaged in learning processes. Many strategies exist for improving these bonds; however, restructuring the daily schedule may be the most effective means.

WHAT IS FLEXIBLE SCHEDULING?

Alterations in the structure the school day schedule from several equally divided periods to a format that provides fewer, but longer flexible periods is called *flexible scheduling* (Bevevino et al., 1999). Within these longer time periods, a number of learning components may be altered:

- Curricula may be delivered in an integrated manner.
- More individualized instruction may occur.
- students can be provided with more time for reflection and collaboration in their learning.

Emphasis should be placed on flexibility in designing alternative scheduling practices. Teachers on a team using a flexible scheduling format can make changes daily or weekly in altering students' movement between classes based on their progress in areas of integrated study. Students may spend 35 minutes in a class or two and one half-hours based on the desired outcomes and progress toward those during the time period.

Several labels are often used interchangeably to refer to alternative scheduling formats:

- Modular scheduling (Rettig & Canady, 2000).
- Intensive scheduling (Bevevino et al., 1999).
- Copernican plan (Canady & Rettig, 1995).
- block scheduling, which may include any of the following variations:
    a. 4 × 4 semester plan,
    b. 2 × 4 semester plan,
    c. alternating day plan also known as A/B block or 1/2 day (Hackman & Valentine, 1998).

Each of these labels refers to an alternative to the traditional six-to-eight equal time periods; however, alternative schedules are not necessarily designed as flexible time periods. Block scheduling plans are often rigid time frames of 60-to-90 minute periods, thereby preventing the necessary flexibility needed to adjust to students' learning needs and teachers' instructional needs. The primary structures in many high schools are permanent block arrangements that prevent teachers and students from utilizing flexible time sequences. Hackman and Valentine (1998) suggested that the, "Copernican and 4 × 4 block schedules may provide numerous advantages for high schools, but they possess a serious flaw that makes them very problematic for implementation at the middle level..." (p. 8).

The *4 × 4 semester* block format, for example, provides students four separate single-subject classes a day; each one meeting for 80-to-90 minutes. Students begin four new courses each semester. A few middle schools have adopted the 4 × 4 semester plan to match their high school programs (Brown, 2001). The *alternating-day* schedule is also designed with four classes a day that meet for approximately 80 minutes each. The difference between the alternating day and the 4 × 4 schedule is that students in an alternating day program meet with all their classes for a full year on alternating days of the week. The *Copernican Plan* is another alternative scheduling format that incorporates extended periods generally more than 60 minutes each. This plan is designed to provide considerable flexibility in the number of days that courses meet. Teachers may deliver courses in as few as 30-to-60 day formats or in trimesters or quarters (Canady & Rettig, 1995).

The ideal structure for middle schools that intend to meet the developmental needs of young adolescents while addressing progressive learning theory and curriculum integration is flexible interdisciplinary scheduling. The *flexible interdisciplinary* schedule is designed to provide enough flexibility to meet the goals of the true middle school. Extended flexible time frames are used to encourage team teachers to develop and promote curriculum integration. Large blocks of time from one-to-three hours are available each day to promote the study of specific themes. Teachers may collaborate to extend periods of integrative studies for any length of time based on students' or teachers' needs.

Advantages of Flexible Scheduling

The implementation of flexible scheduling arrangements in middle schools creates a number of advantages in designing optimal learning environments for young adolescents. A primary advantage is the simple gift of additional time to insure "meaningful learning" (Caine & Caine, 1994, p. 7). Sizer (1992) suggested a need for extended class sessions to promote greater student understanding. An examination of the research on teaching for understanding and brain-based learning reveals that students need extended periods of time for hands-on and minds-on learning experiences (Wolfe & Brandt, 1998). The implementation of constructivist activities naturally involves longer time for learning (Brooks & Brooks, 1993). Proponents of problem solving, critical and creative thinking, and research processes realize that learning is a highly reflective process that involves time (Costa, 1991; Kauchak & Eggen, 1998). Meaningful learning also requires that students have time to make connections between prior knowledge and background schemata (Caine & Caine). The factory model approach to delivering six-to-eight academic disciplines to students in a disconnected manner for short time periods does little to promote genuine understanding. Learners forced into traditional scheduling patterns receive information in concise formats that leads to what Caine and Caine (1994) refer to as "surface knowledge" (p. 7).

Another advantage for extending learning periods is to insure that students have time to make connections among separate content areas. Perkins (1992) explained,

> ...Teaching of the subject matter involves much more than teaching bits and pieces of content. Learners need an integrative sense of the subject matter. They need an overarching mental image of its structure, so that they see how its strands interweave to make a whole fabric. (p. 117)

Traditional American school scheduling practices are based on the belief that knowledge is limited; that is, what students need to know prior to adulthood is a limited set of principles based primarily on Euro-centric views (Hirsch, 1988). Educators who accept this notion embrace a belief that students learn through memorizing isolated facts. This philosophy leads to teaching pieces of information that are seldom connected thus reducing the possibilities for holistic understanding. A more realistic view in the current information age is that knowledge is infinite and fluid, changing as more information and research in the various fields is produced and published (Perkins, 1992). Educators who accept the premise of an infinite flow of information focus on teaching students essential strategies for learning; such as problem solving; creative and critical thinking; and, analysis and research skills. These emphases permit students to strengthen thinking and learning processes as they make the connections among essential principles (Knowles & Brown, 2000).

Effective middle school educators design and deliver curricula in an interdisciplinary format that permits students to make the connections among principles and concepts (Beane, 1993). Flexible schedules provide the time structures to promote interdisciplinary investigations among disciplines and in coordination with students' interests. Longer blocks of learning also provide students opportunities to master material rather than merely being exposed to information. The time available for reflection and practice is increased through flexible scheduling models.

Flexible scheduling structures limit the number of students that teachers assist throughout the year. Sizer (1992) contends that teachers should be responsible for educating a maximum of 80 students a year. Traditional schedules require teachers to educate as many as 150 students. The ability to meet the learning needs of this many students is overwhelming. The personal relationships required between teachers and students to insure meaningful learning has a broad research base (Bosworth, 1995; Goodman, Sutton, & Harkevy, 1995). Significant relationships can be more fully developed when teachers work in a flexible scheduling format that limits the number of instructional periods to three or four a day. A necessary accommodation to seeing students for longer time periods is that teachers develop cooperative relationships with students to improve learning and lessen discipline problems.

National Middle School Association (1995) advocates "Varied teaching and learning approaches" and "Assessment and evaluation that promote learning," for young adolescents (p. 11). Imagine the possibilities for strengthening curriculum, instruction, and assessment when class periods are extended past 60 minutes. Students can engage in a multitude of active learning processes when additional time is available; such as,

- Collaborating with other students to improve understanding .
- Reflecting on and developing hypotheses.
- Completing primary research investigations.
- gathering primary and secondary data to answer research queries.
- designing and presenting elaborate final projects.

These are active learning processes that have the potential to address students' social, emotional, cultural, and cognitive learning domains in a much more significant way than these areas can be addressed in short isolated time periods. Gallagher (1999) cited a study in which researchers discovered "...That on average only 28 minutes of a 50-minute period at the high schools ... were devoted to teaching" (cited in Rettig & Canady, 2000, p. 13). The other 22 minutes were consumed by housekeeping activities such as collecting and reviewing homework or taking attendance. Every middle level educator who teaches in a traditional schedule understands the frustrations of lost time to nonacademic endeavors.

One powerful reason to adopt a flexible scheduling arrangement in middle school is the opportunity to address the needs of students with a variety of learning profiles among students. Tomlinson (1999) suggests numerous instructional ideas that provide differentiated learning activities. The variations in skill levels among students are quite pronounced at the middle school level. Meeting the needs of these varied learners cannot be accomplished over the course of a 42-to-55 minute schedule. An extended period provides opportunities for individualized conferences and assistance, plus time for student-to-student collaboration. Additionally, schools that strive to create educational equity for all students through the adoption of heterogeneous grouping practices can better meet the learning needs of all students through the flexible schedule design. Teachers can create realistic and achievable expectations for all learners when they have the additional resource of time available to them through flexible extended periods.

RESEARCH ON THE IMPACT OF ALTERNATIVE SCHEDULING

Degree of Support for Alternative Scheduling

The ideas mentioned above are powerful claims about the potential of flexible scheduling to positively affect student learning and teacher instructional processes. Despite the possible positive effects, in one study, researchers reported that a mere 40% of sixth and seventh grade classrooms and even less (27%) of eighth grade classrooms had implemented flexible scheduling formats by the middle 1990s (McEwin, Dickinson, & Jenkins, 1996). Rettig and Canady (2000) report that flexible scheduling is the least implemented of suggested developmentally appropriate middle school practices.

Yet, in many middle and high schools where flexible scheduling designs have been implemented, teachers and administrators perceive the change as positive. Teachers in three high schools using the 4 × 4 semester plan noted three positive aspects: greater instructional flexibility, longer planning periods, and more time for in-depth study of content (Queen, Algozzine, & Eaddy, 1998). Hottenstein (1998) found that alternative scheduling formats, "...had a positive impact on school climate," and were valued by administrators, teachers, and students in surveys from 24 high schools in several states (cited in Queen, 2000, p. 216). Hottenstein (1998) discovered that teacher approval of block scheduling increased from 52% prior to implementation to 87% after a year of use. Three educators discovered teacher "burn-out" was reduced as a result of their school moving to block scheduling (Hannaford, Fouraker, & Dickerson, 2000, p. 213).

Despite many positive beliefs, teachers are concerned about increasing planning time and altering instructional delivery techniques as class periods almost double in length (Swope, Fritz, & Goins, 1998; Santos & Rettig, 1999). Some veteran teachers are apathetic about altering their instructional processes after years of success with other methods (Corley, 1997). Some teachers are concerned that students may not be receiving enough content in a 4 × 4 block schedule since classes only meet for a semester (Brown, 2001; Hackman & Waters, 1998). These fears and others have caused some teachers to abandon alternative scheduling models after short implementation periods (Adams & Salvaterra, 1998).

Effects on Instruction

Several studies indicate that as a result of using longer blocks, teachers implement more active instructional processes (Brown, 2001; Dow & George, 1998; Fogerty, 1996; Seed, 1998; Shortt & Thayer, 1999). Smith (1998) reported that a majority of middle level teachers in one building perceived that a move to block scheduling gave them greater control over instructional time. Middle level teachers at two schools reported designing more lessons to promote critical and creative thinking through more hands-on manipulative activities. In this same study, teachers reported providing more time for student reflection and student-to-student collaborative learning as a result of having longer periods (Brown, 2001). Middle level students in one flexible schedule program reported covering topics in greater depth and being exposed to more creative lessons (DeRouen, 1998). Reither (1999) surveyed administrators in one alternative scheduled high school who reported that teachers were using more student-directed projects, simulation activities, cooperative learning, and wider use of computer activities. With all of these reported instructional changes, are students actually making academic and cognitive gains as a result of alternative scheduling models?

Effects on Student Learning and Behavior

Many researchers, parents, teachers, and legislators believe that changes in teacher instructional behaviors can subsequently positively affect the academic growth of students. Despite interest in this outcome, two particular studies found no significant differences in achievement test scores or end of course tests for high school students enrolled in alternative scheduling versus traditional scheduling formats (Queen, 2000; York, 1997). In one high school, however, students' AP scores increased. In another high school, block-scheduled students' SAT verbal scores rose slightly, while mathematics scores slightly decreased (Hottenstein, 1998). Other studies reveal that students' test-score data comparisons between blocked and traditionally scheduled schools show mixed results (Queen; Reither, 1999;

Shortt & Thayer, 1999). Other indicators of student achievement show positive results. In some schools, for instance, the percentage of students receiving better grades has increased, a drop in failure rates were noted, and a considerable rise in the number of honor roll students was noted (Dow & George, 1998; Hottenstein, 1998; Rettig & Canady, 2000).

It may be valuable for schools to use more meaningful data than test scores to evaluate alternative scheduling formats. Other significant indicators include changes in student behavior, success for students with special needs, lower retention rates, improved instructional practices, and more positive student/teacher relationships. These types of positive data sets have been reported in response to implementing alternative scheduling.

One study of a high school revealed half the number of discipline referrals from the previous year (Dow & George, 1998). Similar positive results associated with students' behavior were noted at the middle school level in a Virginia middle school (Smith, Pitkin, & Rettig,1998). Smith (1998) found that suspensions at a middle school were reduced by as much as 20% during the first year of alternative scheduling implementation. A considerable drop in retention of seventh and eighth graders also occurred following the change to block scheduling in several Virginia middle schools (Smith, 1998). Brown (2001) discovered that middle level teachers perceived better student/teacher relationships as a result of seeing fewer students for longer blocks of time. These results reveal that alternative scheduling formats have a positive effect on more than academics, which may lead to improved academic performance.

CONCLUSION

Several valuable reasons exist for redesigning middle schools' schedules into longer blocks of flexible periods. Researchers have discovered that flexible scheduling improves schooling for young adolescents by encouraging the development of meaningful relationships with students; increasing student understanding through more in-depth study of curricula; and, providing time for teachers to more effectively address the learning demands of diverse learners and students with special needs. Researchers also recognize that alternative schedules empower teachers with additional responsibilities for curricular design, encourage teachers to utilize more flexibility and creativity in instructional processes, increase teacher collaboration and planning, and support heterogeneous grouping practices (Hackman & Valentine, 1998; Nolan, 1998; Rettig & Canady, 2000; Seed, 1998). These are significant changes that match the recommendations of the National Middle School Association (Erb, 2001) and the Carnegie Corporation

(Jackson & Davis, 2000) for improving the lives of young adolescents through developmentally appropriate practices.

Altering daily schedules is a significant change to a long tradition of the factory model design of schooling that has become a part of American educational culture. Changing the attitudes and beliefs of teachers can be a long, slow, difficult process. Helping parents to understand the value of this change can be even more challenging. All stakeholders must be involved in discussions about the philosophy and value of using alternative scheduling formats. Faculties interested in adopting an alternative schedule must begin gathering data, investigating other programs, and establishing specific time lines at least a year prior to implementation (Williamson, 1998). Comprehensive in-service training is required for teachers to embrace this significant change and insure successful implementation (Bevevino et al., 1999; Smith et al., 1998; Williamson). Although several standard alternative scheduling options are available, each middle school faculty must choose or design a plan that is flexible enough to meet their needs. The issue of time availability has haunted teachers for years, as they search for strategies to meet the needs of all students within an academic year. Alternative scheduling formats may provide the time needed for greater success for students and teachers.

REFERENCES

Adams, D.C., & Salvaterra, M.E. (1998). Structural and teacher changes: Necessities for successful block scheduling. *The High School Journal, 81*(2), 98–106.

Beane, J.A. (1993). *A middle school curriculum: From rhetoric to reality.* Columbus, OH: National Middle School Association.

Bevevino, M.M., Snodgrass, D.M., Adams, K.M., & Dengel, J.A. (1999). *An educator's guide to block scheduling.* Needham Heights, MA: Allyn and Bacon.

Bosworth, K. (1995). Caring for others and being cared for: Students talk about caring in school. *Phi Delta Kappan, 76,* 686–693.

Brooks, J.G., & Brooks, M.G. (1993). *In search of understanding: The case for constructivist classrooms.* Alexandria, VA: Association for Supervision and Curriculum Development.

Brown, D.F. (2001). Middle level teachers' perceptions of the impact of block scheduling on instruction and learning. *Research in Middle Level Education Annual, 24,* 121–141.

Caine, R.N., & Caine, G. (1994). *Making connections: Teaching and the human brain.* Menlo Park, CA: Addison-Wesley.

Canady, R.L., & Rettig, M.D. (1995). *Block scheduling: A catalyst for change in high schools.* Princeton, NJ: Eye On Education.

Carroll, J.M. (1994). The Copernican plan evaluated: The evolution of a revolution. *Phi Delta Kappan, 76,* 105–113.

Cobb, C.D., & Mayer, J.D. (2000). Emotional intelligence: What the research says. *Educational Leadership, 58*(3), 14–18.

Corley, E. (1997, February). *Teacher perceptions regarding block scheduling: Reactions to change.* Paper presented at the annual meeting of the Midwestern Educational Research Association, Chicago, IL.

Costa, A.L. (Ed.). (1991). *Developing minds: A resource book for teaching thinking* (Vol. 1, rev. ed.). Alexandria, VA: Association for Supervision and Curriculum Development.

D'Arcangelo, M. (1998). The brains behind the brain. *Educational Leadership, 56*(3), 20–25.

DeRouen, D.A. (1998). Maybe it's not the children: Eliminating some middle school problems through block scheduling and team support. *The Clearing House, 71*(3), 146–148.

Dow, J., & George, P.S. (1998). Block scheduling in Florida high schools: Where are we now? *National Association of Secondary School Principals Bulletin, 82*(601), 92–110.

Edwards, C.M., Jr. (1995). The 4 x 4 plan. *Educational Leadership, 53*(3), 16–19.

Ennis, R. (1985). Goals for a critical thinking curriculum. In A.L. Costa (Ed.), *Developing minds: A resource book for teaching thinking* (pp. 68–71). Alexandria, VA: Association for Supervision and Curriculum Development.

Erb, T. (2001) (Ed.). *This we believe ... And now we must act.* Westerville, OH: National Middle School Association.

Erikson, E.H. (1968). *Childhood and society.* New York: W. W. Norton.

Fogerty, R. (Ed.). (1996). *Block scheduling: A collection of articles.* Arlington Heights, IL: IRI Skylight Training and Publishing.

Gallagher, J. (1999). Teaching in the block. *Middle Ground, 2*(3), 10–15.

Gay, G. (2000). *Culturally responsive teaching: Theory, research, and practice.* New York: Teachers College Press.

Goldman, J.J. (1983). Flexible modular scheduling: Results of evaluations in its second decade. *Urban Education, 18,* 191–228.

Goodman, J.F., Sutton, V., & Harkevy, I. (1995). The effectiveness of family workshops in a middle school setting: Respect and caring make a difference. *Phi Delta Kappan, 76,* 694–700.

Gruhn, W., & Douglas, H. (1971). *The modern junior high* (3rd ed). New York: Ronald Press.

Hackman, D.G., & Valentine, J.W. (1998). Designing an effective middle level schedule. *Middle School Journal, 29*(5), 3–13.

Hackman, D.G. , & Waters, D.L. (1998). Breaking away from tradition: The Farmington High School restructuring experience. *National Association of Secondary School Principals Bulletin, 82*(601), 83–92.

Hannaford, B., Fouraker, M., & Dickerson, V. (2000). One school tackles the change to block scheduling. *Phi Delta Kappan,82,* 212–213.

Hirsch, E.D. (1988). *Cultural literacy: What every American needs to know.* New York: Random House.

Hottenstein, D.S. (1998). *Intensive scheduling: Restructuring America's secondary schools through time management.* Thousand Oaks, CA: Corwin Press.

Jackson, A.W., & Davis, G.A. (2000). *Turning points 2000 Educating adolescents in the 21st century.* New York, & Westerville, OH: Teachers College Press and National Middle School Association.

Jensen, E. (1998). *Teaching with the brain in mind.* Alexandria, VA: Association for Supervision and Curriculum Development.

Kauchak, D.P., & Eggen, P.D. (1998). *Learning and teaching: Research-based methods* (3rd ed.). Needham Heights, MA: Allyn and Bacon.

Knowles, T., & Brown, D.F. (2000). *What every middle school teacher should know.* Portsmouth, NH & Westerville, OH: Heinemann & National Middle School Association.

Lounsbury, J., & Clark, D. (1990). *Inside grade eight: From apathy to excitement.* Reston, VA: National Association of Secondary School Principals.

Marcia, J. (1980). Ego identity development. In J. Adelson (Ed.), *The handbook of adolescent psychology* (pp. 159–187). New York: Wiley.

McEwin, C.K., Dickinson, T.S., & Jenkins, D.M. (1996). *America's middle schools: Practices and progress—a 25 year perspective.* Columbus, OH: National Middle School Association.

Milgram, J. (1992). A portrait of diversity: The middle level student. In J.L. Irvin (Ed.), *Transforming middle level education* (pp. 16–27). Needham Heights, MA: Allyn & Bacon.

National Commission on Time and Learning. (1994). *Prisoners of Time.* Washington, DC: Author.

National Middle School Association. (1995). *This we believe: Developmentally responsive middle level schools.* Columbus, OH: Author.

Nolan, F. (1998). Ability grouping plus heterogeneous grouping: Win-win schedules. *Middle School Journal, 29*(5), 14–19.

O'Neil, J. (1995). Finding time to learn. *Educational Leadership, 53*(3), 11–15.

Perkins, D. (1992). *Smart schools: From training memories to educating minds.* New York: The Free Press.

Piaget, J. (1977). *The development of thought: Elaboration of cognitive structures.* New York: Viking.

Queen, J.A. (2000). Block scheduling revisited. *Phi Delta Kappan, 82,* 214–222.

Queen, J.A., Algozzine, R., & Eaddy, M.A. (1998). Implementing 4 x 4 block scheduling: Pitfalls, promises, and provisos. *The High School Journal, 81*(2),107 -14.

Reither, G. (1999). When there aren't enough hours in the day.... *Momentum, 30*(2), 63–7.

Rettig, M.D., & Canady, R.L. (2000). *Scheduling strategies for middle schools.* Larchmont, NY: Eye on Education.

Rice, R.P. (1999). *The adolescent: Development, relationships, and culture* (9th ed.) . Needham Heights, MA: Allyn & Bacon.

Santos, K.E., & Rettig, M.D. (1999). Going on the block: Meeting the needs of students with disabilities in high schools with block scheduling. *Teaching Exceptional Children, 31*(3), 54–9.

Seed, A. (1998). Free at last: Making the most of the flexible block schedule. *Middle School Journal, 29*(5), 20–21.

Shortt, T.L., & Thayer, Y. (1999). Block scheduling can enhance school climate. *Educational Leadership, 56*(4), 76–81.

Simmons, R.G., & Blyth, D.A. (1987). *Moving into adolescence.* New York: Aldine de Gruyter.

Sizer, T. (1992). *Horace's school: Redesigning the American high school.* Boston: Houghton Mifflin.

Smith, S.G. (1998). *A multi-case study of flexible block scheduling in three middle level schools: Perceptions of administrators and counselors.* Unpublished doctoral dissertation, University of Virginia, Charlottesville.

Smith, D.G., Pitkin, N.A., & Rettig, M.D. (1998). Flexing the middle school block schedule by adding non-traditional core subjects and teachers to the interdisciplinary team. *Middle School Journal, 29*(5), 22–27.

Swope, J.A., Fritz, R.L., & Goins, K.L. (1998). What are marketing teachers and principals saying about block schedules? *Business Education Forum, 53*(2), 36–7.

Tanner, J.M. (1972). Sequence, tempo, and individual variation in growth and development of boys and girls aged twelve to sixteen. In J. Kagan & R. Coles (Eds.), *Twelve to sixteen,* (pp. 1–23). New York: W. W. Norton.

Tomlinson, C.A. (1999). *The differentiated classroom: Responding to the needs of all learners.* Alexandria, VA: Association for Supervision and Curriculum Development.

Valentine, J.W., Clark, D.C., Irvin, J.L., Keefe, J.W., & Melton, G. (1993). *Leadership in middle level education. Vol. 1: A national survey of middle level leaders and schools.* Reston, VA: National Association of Secondary School Principals.

Valentine, J., & Whitaker, T. (1997). Organizational trends and practices in middle level schools. In J.L. Irvin (Ed.), *What current research says to the middle level practitioner* (pp. 277–283). Columbus, OH: National Middle School Association.

Van Hoose, J., & Strahan, D. (1988). *Young adolescent development and school practices: Promoting harmony.* Columbus, OH: National Middle School Association.

Watts, J., & Castle, S. (1993). The time dilemma in school re-structuring. *Phi Delta Kappan, 75,* 306–310.

Williamson, R.D. (1998). *Scheduling middle level schools: Tools for improved student achievement.* Reston, VA: National Association of Secondary School Principals.

Wlodkowski, R.J., & Ginsberg, M.B. (1995). *Diversity and motivation: Culturally responsive teaching.* San Francisco: Jossey-Bass.

Wolfe, P., & Brandt, R. (1998). What do we know from brain research? *Educational Leadership, 56*(3), 8–13.

York, T. (1997). *A comparative anaylsis of student achievement in block and traditionally scheduled high schools.* Unpublished doctoral dissertation, University of Houston, Houston.

Zepeda, S.J. (1999). Arrange time into blocks. *Journal of Staff Development, 20*(2), 26–30.

PART II

MOVING MIDDLE LEVEL REFORM INTO THE 21ST CENTURY

CHAPTER 6

NEW TEACHER STAFFING AND COMPREHENSIVE MIDDLE SCHOOL REFORM

Philadelphia's Experience

Elizabeth Useem

ABSTRACT

This study examines the problem of teacher recruitment, preparation, and retention in the context of schoolwide reform in seven of Philadelphia's 43 middle schools. The seven schools are implementing the Talent Development Middle School model of Johns Hopkins University's Center for Research on the Education of Students Placed at Risk (CRESPAR), one of the most promising national designs for urban middle school improvement. Data from interviews of all teachers (60) new to the schools in 1999–2000 confirm the long-held perception in the city that teachers assigned to middle schools are disappointed in their placement and ill-prepared for their placement. They were grateful for the training and mentoring they got from the Talent Development program, experiences that significantly increased their commitment to staying in the school. However, concerns about the District's residency requirement, salary, discipline, supplies, and other factors were prompting large numbers of them to seek employment elsewhere.

INTRODUCTION

Middle grade educators can now choose from among several promising "whole school change" models that simultaneously push the academic rigor and personal nurture called for in *Turning Points 2000* (Jackson & Davis, 2000), *This We Believe* (National Middle Schools Association, 1982, 1995), and the manifesto of the National Forum to Accelerate Middle-Grades Reform. These designs include the Turning Points Design Model coordinated by the Center for Collaborative Education in Boston; the Talent Development model created at Johns Hopkins University; Different Ways of Knowing coordinated by The Galef Institute in Los Angeles; the W. K. Kellogg Foundation's Middle Start initiative; the Success for All Middle School Project at Johns Hopkins University; and Making Middle Grades Matter, an initiative of the Southern Regional Education Board (Bradley & Manzo, 2000).

Successful implementation of such schoolwide improvement models, especially those with a strong academic component, assume that schools have a reasonably qualified and stable staff of classroom teachers. Recent documentation of the strong positive connection between teachers' knowledge and skill and students' learning levels underscore the importance of such staffing (Darling-Hammond, 1999; Darling-Hammond, 2000; Haycock, 1998; Haycock, 2000; Wenglinksy, 2000). Many models invest heavily in teacher training and the use of new classroom materials, an investment that is expected to yield benefits for students over a period of years as the teachers become familiar with new and presumably more effective approaches to instruction. Yet efforts to improve urban middle and high schools in the U.S. have been severely hampered by the inadequate preparation levels of many teachers, the common practice of assigning teachers to courses for which they have no specialized knowledge, and the rapid turnover of schools' instructional staff from year to year (Balfanz & MacIver, 2000; Cooney, 1998; Haycock & Ames, 2000; Ingersoll, 1999; McEwin & Dickinson, 1995; Ruby, 1999, 2001; Strauss, 1999; Useem, Christman, Gold, & Simon, 1997).

At the middle school level (grades 6–8), the problem of teacher qualifications is especially serious since many states, including Pennsylvania, permit elementary-level certified teachers to instruct core subjects in the seventh and eighth grade (Cooney, 1998; Olson, 2000; Useem, Barends, & Lindermayer, 1999; Watson, 2001). The need to understand and address the issue of middle school staffing has become more urgent as standards-based curricula are introduced and more stringent promotion and graduation requirements for eighth graders and twelfth graders take hold.

This study examines the problem of teacher recruitment, teacher preparation, and teacher retention in the context of schoolwide reform in seven of Philadelphia's 42 public middle schools. The seven schools are at varying stages of implementing the Talent Development Middle School model of Johns Hopkins University's Center for Research on the Education of Students Placed at Risk (CRESPAR), one of the well-regarded comprehensive school designs aimed at raising performance of low income and minority middle schoolers. This model combines high academic standards and personalization by introducing a standards-based common core curriculum for all students; small teacher teams; an emphasis on engaging teaching strategies; high quality curriculum materials; intensive professional development in subject areas keyed to the curriculum; including in-class coaching from master teachers; and extra-help opportunities for students below grade level. Students have demonstrated significant achievement gains in the schools that have fully implemented the model (Balfanz & MacIver, 2000). The Philadelphia Education Fund, a nonprofit education reform organization, serves as Hopkins' regional partner in the Philadelphia area for this national initiative.

STAFFING IN PHILADELPHIA'S MIDDLE SCHOOLS

Philadelphia's public middle schools have long had difficulty attracting teachers. Pennsylvania does not have a required middle level teaching certificate although an optional certificate became available in 2001. Instead, teachers are generally certified for the elementary level (grades K-6) or are licensed for one or more subject areas at the secondary level (grades 7–12). The state allows elementary-certified teachers to teach the seventh and eighth grade as long as their "teacher certification preparation program and repertoire of subject knowledge and instructional skills are commensurate with the learning outcomes that a given course is intended to achieve" (Pennsylvania Department of Education, 1990). In reality, however, the state does not enforce this vaguely worded regulation. In Philadelphia, teachers are frequently assigned to classes of seventh and eighth graders in subject areas for which they are manifestly underqualified. Applicants to the District who are elementary-certified for grades K-6 or who have secondary certification(s) usually prefer placements in elementary schools (this includes the District's 46 K-8 schools) and high schools respectively, accepting middle school positions only as a last resort.

Suburban districts that can choose from a surfeit of applicants can select secondary-certified teachers or elementary-trained people who have advanced degrees in a subject area or special expertise in teaching middle grades students. Only three of the 19 teacher preparation programs in colleges and universities in the Philadelphia area offer any sort of middle grades preparation program (Useem, Barends, & Lindermayer, 1999).

The proportion of teachers new to the District in the city's 43 middle schools during the 1999–2000 school year averaged 13.5%, ranging from a low of zero vacancies in four schools (that either were small or had fewer low income students) to a high of 40% in one school. When the four schools that have some element of student selection are removed from the analysis, the average is 14.4% new staff members. In eleven of the 43 schools, more than 20% of the teaching staff was new to the District and the school. Philadelphia's middle schools still had 78 teaching vacancies in May of the school year, an understated figure since some principals had given up listing the position. By contrast, high schools across the District had only 18 vacancies at that point.

Overall, teachers in the District's middle schools are much less experienced than high school teachers in the system, and experience levels vary substantially by the poverty rate of the school. In the six middle schools with the highest levels of poverty (with 95% or more of the students eligible for free or reduced-price lunch), teachers average only seven years of experience. In the highest-poverty high schools, that figure is 13 years. In the District's lowest-poverty middle schools (46–70% low income), the median years of teachers' experience is 13 years, compared to 24 years in the lowest-poverty high schools (42–61% low income). Similarly, middle schools rely more heavily on uncertified teachers than other school types (Useem & Neild, 2001). Middle school teachers are more likely than teachers in other school levels to choose to transfer out of their schools to elementary, K-8 schools, or high schools, and they tend to migrate to schools with higher test scores and more advantaged student bodies (Chester, Offenberg, & Xu, 2001).

DATA AND METHODS

While analyses of large-scale surveys and reviews of state certification requirements have painted a general picture of teachers' thin preparation for teaching academic subjects in the middle grades, the literature on the issue lacks fine-grained qualitative studies that take into account the complexities of middle level teachers' credentials and course assignments. It is easier to study the question of "out of field" teaching among high school teachers whose certification is in a specific discipline(s) than it is to study the issue for middle grades' teachers whose states allow them to teach in all core subject areas with just an elementary license. With this in mind, this study looked at their academic preparation of new teachers in middle schools implementing a high-standards comprehensive school change effort.

In February and March of the 1999–2000 school year, I interviewed all of the 60 teachers new to the School District of Philadelphia who began teaching in these seven middle schools during that academic year. The teachers were questioned about their preparation for instructing in the middle grades, their experience being recruited and hired in the District, their course assignments, their appraisal of the Talent Development training and curricular program, and their plans for remaining in the school or the District. The 15 to 30 minute structured interviews took place during the school day. All of the teachers in the target population agreed to participate.

The 60 teachers were assigned to teach in one of the seven schools choosing to implement the Talent Development model (Table 1). These schools are fairly typical of Philadelphia middle schools, entities that vary in size from 238 to 1500 students. Poverty rates of the student bodies in the seven schools range from a low of 71% to a high of 90%. The number of classroom teachers per school ranged from 19 teachers in an unusually small middle school to a high of 64 in one of the District's largest middle schools. There is no reason to believe that these 60 teachers are any different from new teachers assigned to other middle schools in the District, particularly since they did not claim to choose the school because of the Talent Development program. Thus, the findings discussed here can most likely be generalized to all new middle school teachers hired for the 1999–2000 school year in Philadelphia.

Table 1. Talent Development Middle Schools, 1999–00

School	*Grades*	*No. Students*	*No. Teachers*	*% Low Income*	*% First Year Teachers*	*Average Years in Building*	*No. Teachers Interviewed*
1	5–8	1125	60	86	9.5	9.7	5
2	5–8	977	54	86	16.1	8.9	13
3	5–8	1472	64	90	22.1	8.3	15
4	6–8	850	38	86	21.3	9.0	12
5	6–8	1189	58	71	3.0	15.1	3
6	6–8	989	47	81	21.0	9.0	9
7	7–8	238	19	90	na	na	3

THE NEW TEACHERS IN PHILADELPHIA'S MIDDLE SCHOOLS: BACKGROUND CHARACTERISTICS

Three fourths of the new teachers were female, consistent with the district-wide pattern of 74% female. A little more than a third (35%) were African

American, 60% were Caucasian, and 5% were Hispanic, also similar to the breakdown of the District's teachers. (The districtwide breakdown is 34% African American; 62% Caucasian; and 2.6% Hispanic.) Sixty percent were currently residing within Philadelphia's city limits, and 35% had graduated from a Philadelphia public high school. Two fifths were pursuing graduate work; 22% had completed a Master's degree, and 38% had completed only a BA or BS degree and had not yet embarked on graduate study.

A quarter of these new teachers started teaching right after college graduation. The others had some prior occupational experience after receiving their Bachelor's degree: 25% had taught in private or parochial schools or in another public school system; 17% had work experience in another occupation; 27% had been substitute teachers; and 5% had taught in preschool.

Almost two thirds of the new recruits (65%) were certified as elementary teachers. A much smaller number, 8%, were secondary certified in one or more subject areas. A significant group, 27%, had emergency certifications as Apprentice teachers, two thirds of whom were currently enrolled in an elementary education certification program. These 60 teachers had received or were working toward their teaching certificates at 25 different institutions of higher education, a fact that reflected the District's attempts to recruit at a wide range of colleges. (The largest percentage, 18%, were trained at Temple University.) The majority (77%) began teaching in the month of September of the 1999–2000 school year with the rest being hired throughout the school year.

Only a small percentage of the new teachers had prepared for and wanted to teach at the middle school level. Of those who had completed student teaching (Apprentice teachers had no student teaching experience), nearly three-fourths (74%) did their student teaching in grades K-5. Another 12% had student taught in the sixth grade, half of whom had divided their student teaching time between sixth and a lower grade. Only 14% had student taught in the seventh or eighth grade. Twelve percent were student teachers in a high school. A mere six of the 60 teachers (10%) said they preferred teaching the middle grades to any other school level.

THE RECRUITMENT AND HIRING EXPERIENCE

When applying for a teaching position in Philadelphia, applicants who are certified must take a written examination, in addition to the national Praxis tests, undergo an oral examination before a panel of two or three interviewers (usually principals), and then go through a centrally administered school assignment/selection process. As is the case in most large urban districts, the hiring process has long been perceived as unnecessarily drawn out, cumbersome, and frustrating. The District, however, has made some progress in streamlining and speeding up the process, and, like most other large districts, it has instituted several incentives aimed at boosting recruitment. In 1999, the residency requirement that stipulates teachers must move into the city after one year of teaching was loosened to three years, and a hiring bonus of $4500 was put into place. Teachers receive $1500 after six months on the job and another $3000 after three years of employment with the District. A new "enhanced compensation system" will enable teachers who demonstrate certain levels of skill and knowledge to receive higher pay. In March 2001 the District also passed a two-pronged bonus system that will: (1) pay teachers in 19 hard-to-staff schools an additional $2000; and (2) pay teachers in certain scarce subject specialties such as math, science, special education, and foreign languages an additional $1500.

The interviews yielded some initial findings about the impact of the loosening of the residency requirement and the hiring bonus, both of which were put into place during the summer these candidates were being hired. A quarter of the new teachers (26%) said the change in the residency requirement was very important in influencing them to teach in Philadelphia's public schools. Another 14% said it was somewhat important and 60% said it was not important. Many in the latter group, however, claimed that this requirement would become important to them in the future and would be a primary reason for their choosing to seek employment outside of the city. A number said that living in the city was problematic now or would be in the future because their current or prospective spouses had jobs in distant suburbs where employment has boomed in recent years.

With regard to the bonus, 21% of the new teachers said it was very important, 37% reported it was somewhat important, and 42% claimed it was not important. These teachers had applied to the system before the bonus was announced, so for most it came as a pleasant surprise ("it helped pay for my wedding"; "it helped me buy a computer") but was not a key factor in their decision to teach in Philadelphia. The bonus did appear to be a significant incentive for people who had been thinking about applying for a long time such as teachers in lower-paid positions in parochial schools.

Approximately two thirds of the 60 teachers interviewed gave a rating of "good" or "excellent" to the offices of Recruitment (65%) and Examinations (69%), reflecting the efforts that have been made to re-engineer those aspects of the hiring process. Most of the new teachers gave favorable reviews to their initial recruitment experience, including the taking of the system's written and oral tests, but tended to be much more critical of the way in which their application was processed and the way their personnel benefits were handled. Many talked about experiences with lost paperwork, lack of clear and consistent directions and information, difficulty getting through on the telephone, and bureaucratic bungling.

Their greatest dissatisfaction, however, was with the school selection process. Only 28% of the new teachers rated the services of that office as "good" or "excellent." Since these teachers had not wanted a middle school assignment, their unhappiness with the process is not surprising. The centralized "school picking" procedure has long been a source of irritation, even trauma, for new recruits. The collective bargaining agreement between the District and the Philadelphia Federation of Teachers (PFT) allows school-based hiring only in those schools where two-thirds of the faculty have voted to allow it, an option chosen by just 12 schools in December 2000, the first opportunity this option was made available to them. The typical practice in Philadelphia is for prospective teachers to pick a school from among the remaining vacancies on a given day, usually during the summer months. Information is not provided about the schools in advance. Candidates choose in the order of their ranking on one of several lists, a ranking based, in part, on their local examination score.

Principals or their designees can come to the school selection sessions and make a pitch for their individual schools, an option utilized by a relatively small number of administrators. The new teachers have to select on the spot from one of the schools still listed or risk losing a placement in any position. By the time these teachers were called to pick a school, they found themselves with few options since nearly all of the coveted elementary openings were already taken.

The interviews revealed that new teachers typically did not choose schools according to the school's philosophy, the school's reform program (such as Talent Development), the culture of the school among the staff and parents, the quality of the principal's leadership, the achievement levels of the students, or a school's "performance index score" that includes student test scores and absenteeism levels among students and teachers. Unless they had done serious research ahead of time on very short notice—difficult since the list of schools with vacancies is available only a day or two ahead of a school selection date—they had little opportunity to learn this sort of information about the schools. Lacking this information, their desire for a reasonable commute led them to choose a school as close as possible to their home.

While less important than geographic location, the pitch made for a particular school by a principal or another administrator or teacher from the school also influenced prospective teachers' choice of a school. In addition, some of the new teachers were privy to information about the school as a result of personal experience (student teaching, subbing, formerly attending that school, familiarity with the neighborhood) or of hearing about it from friends or family members. Another influential factor was their perception about the safety of the neighborhood. In some cases, the teachers' union staffers advised the recruits about which among several schools to select. Others said they chose "blind," knowing almost nothing about the school.

ASSIGNMENT TO COURSES AND GRADE LEVELS

The Talent Development trainers stress the notion that teachers should have only two preparations, either in two content areas in the same grade with the same students, or teaching one subject in two adjacent grade levels in a "looping" arrangement that enables teachers to stay with the same group of students over two years. The data show that some progress has been made in that direction. Nearly two thirds of the new teachers (64%) were assigned to just one grade although 14% had schedules that spanned three or four grade levels. Seventy percent were placed in one or two subject areas. Nearly a quarter of the new teachers (23%) were teaching three different subjects, and 8% (5 people) found themselves trying to cover four different content preparations. Not surprisingly, new teachers with multiple preparations and grade levels were unhappy with their assignment. The least satisfied were those assigned to teach a non-core course to as many as 24 separate classes in order give other teachers their preparation times.

New teachers' course schedules varied significantly from school to school. In four of the schools, more than 78% of the teachers taught only one grade. One principal assigned three fourths of the new teachers (77%) to one content area with an eye to developing content knowledge and pedagogical strategies in a field. Another school had succeeded in assigning 10 out of its 12 new teachers to two subject areas at just one grade level.

Only a modest percentage of teachers appeared to be well prepared to teach in the content areas and grade levels to which they were assigned (Table 2). Depending on whether the field was math, science, social studies, or reading/English language arts (RELA), I classified only 10% (in social studies) to around 17% (in science and RELA) as well trained to teach in a particular field, a designation based on self-reports of their higher education coursework and experience, i.e., a major or minor in the field or at least four academic courses in that area. I categorized approximately two-fifths to a half of the new teachers (42% and 52% respectively) as "somewhat prepared," meaning that they had an elementary certificate with two or three academic courses in the content area plus a teaching methods course in that discipline.

More than a third, however, were categorized as "poorly prepared," including 42% of the new teachers in RELA. This designation was applied to those who had from zero to two courses in that content area and no teaching methods course in the field, or a methods course but only zero or one course in the content area, or three courses in the subject but no pedagogy coursework. In most of these cases, the teachers themselves volunteered that they were not qualified to teach in that subject area at the grade level to which they were currently assigned.

NEW TEACHERS' ASSESSMENTS OF THE TALENT DEVELOPMENT TRAINING AND CURRICULUM

Despite being new to the school, the teachers interviewed for this study had high rates of participation in the Talent Development professional training opportunities. Nearly two-thirds (63%) said they had received in-classroom coaching in one or more curriculum areas from a Talent Development "curriculum coach." These coaches are either teachers on special assignment from the School District or are staff from Johns Hopkins. In some cases, expert teachers within the schools support the initiative by coaching new teachers as well. They conduct demonstration lessons, provide materials and handy tips, and give feedback.

Table 2. Percent of Teachers Qualified to Teach, By Subject Area: Grades 6–8

Level of Preparation	*Reading & English/ Language Arts*	*Mathematics*	*Science*	*Social Studies*
Well Prepared	16%	14%	17%	10%
Somewhat Prepared	42	52	43	50
Poorly Prepared	42	34	40	40

Note: Teachers' preparation level referred only to subject areas they were actually teaching.

Similarly, 68% had attended after-school and/or Saturday workshops in one or more curriculum areas (available for pay or for graduate course credit) or had enrolled in the Skillful Talent Development Teacher graduate course (in pedagogy and classroom management) at St. Joseph's University. The workshops, geared to the specific curriculum being used by the teachers, previewed upcoming units, lessons, and experiments, attending both to teachers' content knowledge and pedagogical strategies. Only three of the 60 teachers attended one of the August institutes in a content area, reflecting the fact that most of them were hired late in the summer or after school started. Altogether, an impressive 80% of the new teachers participated either in the coaching or in the workshops or the course in one or more subject areas.

Overall, the new teachers gave favorable appraisals of the training. Between 82 and 92% of the teachers rated the in-class coaching as "good" or "excellent" with the highest marks given to the coaching in mathematics. Ratings of the workshops were also high with the "good" or "excellent" designation of 76% to 91%, depending on the subject area.

Ratings of the usefulness and effectiveness of the Talent Development curriculum and materials were largely favorable but more mixed than ratings of the training. Only 56% claimed that the science curriculum was "good" or "excellent," not surprising since the development by Johns Hopkins of a full-blown curriculum was not yet complete. All five people teaching the social studies curriculum in the upper grades (adopted in only three of the schools thus far) gave it a good or excellent rating. Three fourths gave similar marks to the RELA program, and 63% did so in mathematics. Sixty-three percent of those responding to an open-ended question about Talent Development's value in supporting their growth as a new teacher (49 of the 60 teachers) claimed that it was "very valuable."

THEIR PLANS FOR THE FUTURE: TEACHER RETENTION

The 60 new teachers were asked a series of questions about their future employment plans. Only 40% said they would like to continue teaching in their current school next year or for the next three years, 22% said "maybe," and 38% said they would not like to stay at that school. When queried whether or not they would like to return to the School District of Philadelphia next year, a larger number, 63% said "yes," 25% said "maybe," and only 12% said "no." Some were hoping to land a job in an elementary or high school within the District.

Teachers who had received in-class curriculum coaching and/or had attended Talent Development workshops or courses were far more likely to say they would like to stay in their current school, at least for the short term. Of the 24 teachers who said they wanted to return to their current school, 21 (88%) had availed themselves of curriculum coaching in one or more subject areas. Only three (12%) who wanted to stay had not received coaching. Of the 23 teachers who said they wanted to leave the school, 11 (48%) had coaching and 12 (52%) had not. Those who said "maybe" were nearly equally divided. Put another way, of the 38 teachers who had coaching, 21 (55%) said they wanted to stay in their school compared to only three (14%) of the 22 who had not had coaching. Teachers with coaching, then, were about four times more likely to report wanting to return to their school next year or for the next few years. (The correlation between these two variables is 0.29; $p = 0.02$).

The same relationship exists between participation in Talent Development workshops in one or more curriculum areas or in the Skillful Talent Development Teacher course. (Again, the correlation coefficient is 0.29; $p = 0.02$) Of those who wanted to stay at the school, 88% had attended workshops versus only 12% of those who had not. When participation in coaching and workshops is aggregated into a "total participation" variable, the correlation between that variable and a desire to return to the school is 0.34 ($p = 0.01$). That is, the more intensive a teacher's participation in Talent Development activities, the greater is his or her proclivity to return to that middle school.

Teachers were asked whether they would leave the District within the next five years if they got an acceptable offer elsewhere. Two thirds (67%) said they would leave, 22% said they were not sure, and only 12% said they would stay no matter what. The residency requirement loomed large in this discussion. A third of the teachers said the residency requirement would cause them to leave the District, another third said it might cause them to leave, and only 35% claimed that the residency requirement would not lead them to seek employment outside of the city system.

When asked in an open-ended question about the factors that might cause them to leave the District, half of those interviewed cited the residency requirement (about which many were vehemently opposed, including some who had grown up in the city) and nearly one third pointed to the problems of student behavior and discipline or school climate issues. A little more than a quarter (28%) brought up salary. The lack of materials and supplies was cited as a reason by 17%. Smaller percentages mentioned lack of support from the principal on discipline (8%) or other financial issues such as the city wage tax, the lack of tuition reimbursement for continued education, and high auto insurance (7%).

NEW TEACHERS IN THE SEVEN SCHOOLS: SUMMING UP

Data from these interviews with all of the teachers new to seven middle schools and to the School District of Philadelphia confirm the long-held belief in the system that teachers assigned to middle schools enter these schools feeling unprepared and disappointed in their placement. Most are certified to teach at the elementary level, and the majority of the emergency-certified Apprentice teachers are enrolled in elementary education programs. Only six of the 60 wanted a placement in a middle school and only six had done their student teaching in grades seven or eight. Although placed in schools that had opted to undertake a demanding comprehensive school reform effort, the teachers and school administrators had no genuine opportunity to meet and choose one another prior to the placement. Lacking a chance to investigate key features of a school's culture and philosophy, new teachers chose a school primarily according to its geographic location in the city.

Approximately 33 to 40% of these teachers were assigned to teach courses where their academic preparation was manifestly thin, and another 40 to 50% had academic credentials that fell short of adequate preparation for the classes in their schedules. Almost a third of them had teaching loads that spanned three or four core subject areas. Some of the principals, however, were successful in limiting the number of separate courses and grades.

Although most of the teachers were pleased and surprised at the support they found from their colleagues—many raved about the collegial professional community they found at their schools—the majority hoped to find another school assignment within one to three years, usually at the elementary level, either within the District or in nearby suburbs. The District's requirement that teachers live in the city after three years of employment was the primary reason given for wanting to leave the system. (Residency requirements are not common. Chicago, Providence, and Pittsburgh are among the cities with such requirements, but these limits on hiring are increasingly rare.) Discouragement with student behavior and discipline issues was the second most common reason given, with salary a close third. Only seven teachers said they would choose to stay in the system over the long haul even if they got an acceptable offer from another district. Long-term loyalty to an institution or city did not frame their plans for the future; instead, like others in their generation, they appeared to be managing their personal and professional lives with a cool eye to options in a wide regional job market.

Within this context, the Talent Development effort tried to develop teachers' subject matter expertise through in-classroom support from curriculum coaches, after-school and Saturday workshops, and a course in classroom management and pedagogy. An impressive proportion of the new teachers, 80%, participated in some form of the training. Many expressed concerns about aspects of the curricular features of Talent Development but, for the most part, they felt they benefitted from the professional development opportunities and appreciated the fact that there was a common core curriculum and supporting materials. (Many middle schools in the District do not have a schoolwide core curriculum.) Most significantly, teachers who had taken advantage of the coaching and/or the workshops and courses were much more likely to say they wanted to return to the school next year. These data, then, provide evidence of the importance of school-based professional development in retaining teachers in high-poverty middle schools.

The challenge facing developers and implementers of comprehensive urban middle school change models is clearly a daunting one. A high proportion of new faculty arrive at the school unprepared to teach standards-based courses in core subject areas. Trainers work intensively with these teachers, many of whom leave the school in the following years, along with veteran colleagues. An even more common problem, documented by researchers at Johns Hopkins, is that teachers are routinely switched from subject area to subject area from year to year, undercutting the development of their content knowledge and pedagogical skills (Balfanz & MacIver, 2000; Ruby, 1999, 2001). They note that such a pattern requires that a quasi-permanent training structure be in place in schools such as these. The good news, though, is that participation in this schoolwide reform effort appears to dampen turnover rates.

A PROMISING PROGRAM: TEMPLE UNIVERSITY'S "EXCELLENCE IN TEACHING PARTNERSHIP"

Temple University has tried to increase the number of prepared middle grades teachers in the city through its partnership with the School District of Philadelphia's Office of Human Resources, three of the District's middle schools, and the Philadelphia Education Fund. Their Excellence in Teaching Partnership (ETP) initiative prepares undergraduates for middle grades positions and then places them upon graduation in middle schools within the District. Temple established a middle grades endorsement program for students majoring in elementary or secondary education in 1998. This program offers coursework in middle grades teacher preparation, arranges for students to have practicum and student teaching experiences in the three high-poverty middle schools located near the campus, offers professional development opportunities for teachers in those schools, and works with the District to assure the rapid hiring of the graduates to teach in these or other middle schools.

The ETP program has resulted in a notable increase in the numbers of qualified middle grades teachers for the city. In 1997–98, Temple did not place a single student teacher in the District's middle schools. By the 2000–2001 school year, 19 student teachers from Temple were teaching in middle schools and another 71 undergraduates were in practicum placements in middle schools. Seventy percent of those who have completed the program have gone on to teach in the District. The three middle schools have developed a ready supply of new recruits who are familiar with and willing to teach in their schools: as of the Fall of 2000, ten student teachers from the program had become full-time teachers in those schools.

DIRECTIONS FOR CHANGE

Schoolwide reform efforts that seek to make middle schools more academically rigorous and more personalized for students depend on reasonably qualified and stable teaching staffs. At this point, new teachers in Philadelphia middle schools enter their buildings handicapped by inadequate preparation in core academic subjects and inexperience working with young adolescents, conditions that encourage their frequent and rapid departure from those schools. New state and District standards accompanied by new graduation and promotion requirements along with upgraded requirements for students' eventual employment spotlight the need to address this alarming circumstance.

This situation can be addressed by policy changes at four levels: the state, the school district, the school, and higher education institutions. The state of Pennsylvania could enforce its current regulation that permits elementary-certified teachers to instruct courses in the seventh and eighth grades only where their preparation and proficiency level is "commensurate with the learning outcomes" of the course. In addition, the state could redesign its new optional middle level certificate in a way that guarantees subject matter specialization in two academic areas, not a smattering of coursework in multiple areas of the curriculum. And the state could work toward requiring specialized preparation for teaching the seventh and eighth grade, either by inserting competencies appropriate for the middle grades within the secondary subject-area certificate, adding on specialized coursework to the elementary certificate (in either undergraduate or graduate programs), or through a middle level certificate. Pennsylvania could also take the lead in offering financial incentives of various kinds to encourage teachers to work in low income middle schools. Lastly, greater fiscal support for the Philadelphia schools from the state would enable the system to pay competitive salaries that attract and retain teachers. To its credit, the state has passed more stringent academic requirements for certification and for admission to teacher education programs.

The District too could alleviate the shortage of trained teachers at all grade levels by changing its residency requirement, instituting tuition reimbursement for graduate-level work, developing a loan forgiveness program, automating the hiring process, and speeding up the hiring time line (Philadelphia Commission on Children and Youth, 2001). It could also aggressively implement the new hiring option that would enable schools to choose their own staffs from a pool of veterans wishing to transfer or new teachers who are pre-qualified by the District.

At the school level, principals could stem the outflow of new teachers by deepening new teacher induction supports. Where schoolwide reform efforts such as Talent Development are being implemented, principals could require new teachers to participate in at least some form of the training, particularly on-site support that does not interfere with new teachers' other induction and continuing education obligations. Assignment of new teachers to a limited number of course preparations and grade levels both during the first and in subsequent years is another strategy for developing expertise and self-confidence in particular subject areas.

Colleges and universities in the Philadelphia area could undertake aggressive efforts to recruit a higher proportion of students into teaching at the seventh and eighth grade levels and to develop high quality teacher preparation programs specifically designed for that level. The Temple University program offers a model of such training, along with its partnership with the School District of Philadelphia, to streamline the hiring of their graduates.

The present difficulty of developing a qualified and stable staff in Philadelphia's middle schools is not an inevitable condition. It is a product of specific policies set in place in years past. New standards, new accountability systems, upgraded academic requirements for teacher certification statewide, and a vastly expanded metropolitan job market, should propel policymakers to redesign incentives and regulations with the goal of placing and retaining proficient teachers in inner city middle schools.

ACKNOWLEDGMENT

An earlier version of this article was presented as a paper at the Annual Meeting of the American Educational Research Association, Seattle, Washington, April 2001.

REFERENCES

Balfanz, R., & MacIver, D. (2000). Transforming high poverty urban middle schools into strong learning institutions: Lessons from the first five years of the Talent Development Middle School. *Journal of Education for Students Placed at Risk, 5,* 137–158.

Bradley, A., & Manzo, K. K. (2000, October 4). Middle grades: Feeling the squeeze. *Education Week,* (Special Supplement).

Chester, M.D., Offenberg, R. M., & Xu, M. D. (2001, April). *Urban teacher transfer: A three-year cohort study of the School District of Philadelphia faculty.* Philadelphia, PA: Office of Accountability and Assessment, School District of Philadelphia. Paper presented at the Annual Meeting of the American Educational Research Association, Seattle, WA.

Cooney, S. (1998). *Improving teaching in the middle grades: Higher standards for students aren't enough.* Atlanta, GA: Southern Regional Education Board.

Darling-Hammond, L. (1999). *Teacher quality and student achievement: A review of state policy evidence.* Seattle, WA: Center for the Study of Teaching and Policy, University of Washington.

Darling-Hammond, L. (2000). Reforming teacher preparation and licensing: Debating the evidence. *Teachers College Record, 102,* 28–56.

Erb. T. (2001). *This we believe: Developmentally responsive middle level schools.* Westerville, OH: National Middle Schools Association.

Haycock, K. (1998). Good teaching matters: How well-qualified teachers can close the gap. *Thinking K-16, 3,* 1–14. Washington, DC: The Education Trust.

Haycock, K. (2000). No more settling for less. *Thinking K-16, 4,* 3–12. Washington, DC: The Education Trust.

Haycock, K., & Ames, N. (2000, July). *Where are we now? What is the challenge for middle grades education?* Plenary Address, National Educational Research Policy and Priorities Board Conference on Curriculum and Instruction in the Middle Grades: Linking Research and Practice. Washington, DC.

Jackson, A., & Davis, G. (2000) *Turning points 2000.* New York: Teachers College Record.

Ingersoll, R. (1999). The problem of underqualified teachers in American secondary schools. *Educational Researcher, 28,* 26–37.

McEwin, K., & Dickinson, T.S. (1995) *The professional preparation of middle level teachers: Profiles of successful programs.* Westerville, OH: National Middle Schools Association.

National Middle Schools Association. (1982, 1995). *This we believe: Developmentally responsive middle level schools.* Westerville, OH: Author.

Olson, L. (2000). Finding and keeping competent teachers. Who should teach? *Quality Counts 2000,* 12–18. Washington, DC: Education Week.

Pennsylvania Department of Education. (1990). CSPG #86.

Philadelphia Citizens for Children and Youth & The Alliance Organizing Project. (2001). *Who will teach our children?* Philadelphia, PA: Author.

Ruby, A. (1999, April). *An implementable curriculum approach to improving science instruction in urban middles.* Center for Research on Students Placed at Risk (CRESPAR), Johns Hopkins University. Paper presented at the Annual Meeting of the American Educational Research Association, Montreal, Canada.

Ruby, A. (2001, April). *Stability and change among science teachers during the implementation of comprehensive school reform: Lessons from Philadelphia's middle schools.* Center for Research on Students Placed at Risk (CRESPAR), Johns Hopkins University. Paper presented at the Annual Meeting of the American Educational Research Association, Seattle, WA.

Strauss, R.P. (1999). Who gets hired to teach? The case of Pennsylvania. In M. Kanstoroom & C. E. Finn, Jr. (Eds.), *Better teachers, better schools* (pp.175–201). Washington, DC: Fordham Foundation Press.

Useem, E., Barends, R., & Lindermayer, K. (1999). *The preparation of middle grades teachers in an era of high stakes and high standards: Philadelphia's predicament.* Philadelphia, PA: Philadelphia Education Fund.

Useem, E., Christman J.B., Gold, E., & Simon, E. (1997). Reforming alone: Barriers to organizational learning in urban school change initiatives. *Journal of Education for Students Placed at Risk 2,* 55–78.

Useem, E., & Neild, R.C. (2001). *Teacher staffing in the School District of Philadelphia: A report to the community.* Philadelphia, PA: Philadelphia Education Fund.

Watson, S. (2001). *Recruiting and Retaining Teachers: Keys to Improving the Philadelphia Public Schools.* Philadelphia, PA: Center for Policy Research in Education, University of Pennsylvania.

Wenglinsky, H. (2000). *How teaching matters.* Princeton, NJ: Educational Testing Service.

CHAPTER 7

RETHINKING MIDDLE LEVEL TEACHER EDUCATION FOR THE 21ST CENTURY

A Systems Approach

Juan Necochea, Laura P. Stowell, Janet E. McDaniel, Maureen Lorimer, and Charlotte Kritzer

ABSTRACT

A systems approach to teacher education can illuminate the essential components and their relationships to the whole in order to determine what needs to be done to increase the probability of preparing effective teachers for middle level schools. This chapter identifies seven interactive, independent, and overlapping components—social justice and excellence, caring communities, modeling exemplary practices, middle level knowledge base, partnerships, habits of mind and heart, and home/school/community links—of a systems model of teacher education likely to result in better prepared middle level teachers for diverse settings.

INTRODUCTION

Now that we have become accustomed to thinking of ourselves as living in the 21st century, many of us have moved beyond the reflection that was in vogue at the turn of the millennium. It has been almost a relief to be back to "business as usual" in our daily lives, including our professional lives as middle level educators and middle level teacher educators. Unfortunately, this is not an altogether healthy state of affairs, as the energy we generated with the beginning of the century provided some promise that we could reinvent and revitalize our twentieth-century institutions. One institution that could benefit from such attention is the preparation of teachers of young adolescents.

The call for specific preparation for middle level educators is a well-established component of the middle school concept. Reform reports have consistently called for educators committed to and expert at teaching young adolescents (Carnegie Council on Adolescent Development, 1989; Jackson & Davis, 2000; National Middle School Association, 1995). Textbooks for use in pre-service and in-service teacher preparation are plentiful (e.g., George & Alexander, 1993; Stevenson, 1998). Standards for basic and advanced middle grades teacher preparation are recognized by national accrediting societies (National Middle School Association, 1996). Yet research demonstrates that we have failed to provide most young adolescents with the well-prepared teachers they deserve. State licensor regulations overwhelmingly persist in allowing overlapping, optional or nonexistent middle level preparation (McEwin & Dickinson, 1996). As a result, three of four teachers of young adolescents begin their careers with no specialized preparation to be teachers of the students in their care (McEwin, Dickinson & Jenkins, 1996; Scales & McEwin, 1994).

While the middle school movement has charted much progress toward providing schooling appropriate for young adolescents, is it any wonder that this movement is at a state of "arrested development" as the 21st century proceeds (Dickinson, 2001)? Few middle school teachers are conversant in young adolescent development; they have not heard of middle school organization and philosophy; they lack experience with age-appropriate curriculum, instruction, and assessment. Although it is not their fault, it is no wonder that so many poorly-prepared teachers find themselves leaving middle schools for the elementary or high schools that are more comfortable for them. The "revolving door" ushers them in and out of middle schools with frightening regularity (Dickinson, 2001, p. 7).

The premise of this chapter is that applying a comprehensive systems approach to middle level teacher preparation could help move the middle level movement out of the "arrested development" in which it lies. We will first outline our vision of a systems approach for middle level teacher education. We then illustrate seven major components that we believe are necessary as we rethink our work in the new century.

A SYSTEMS APPROACH TO MIDDLE LEVEL TEACHER PREPARATION

Middle level advocates at the turn of the 21st century call for profound structural changes in middle level classrooms and schools as well as a drastic departure from the status quo in teacher licensor, curriculum, student assessment, and instruction (Dickinson, 2001; Jackson & Davis, 2000). Jackson and Davis (2000) apply "systems thinking" to middle school reform in an effort to explain how the "interacting and interdependent group of practices ... form a unified whole" as the critical change elements converge to influence the transformations in a holistic and unified manner (p. 27). Applying a system lens to middle school reform allows a better understanding of the interwoven nature of the implementation process, thus the ability to more accurately discern how changes or adjustments in one element (e.g., staff development) might affect the other (e.g., instruction) in a complex interactive manner. Additionally, since middle schools are embedded organizations (or subsystems) in larger social-political structures, which make middle school reform an extremely intricate process, system thinking provides a mechanism to better grasp the norms and rules that govern educational change in an apparent chaotic world of middle level reform. Therefore, middle level reformers will have a clearer picture of both positive and negative interactive influences of system components in the change process toward excellence and equity for educating early adolescents in middle schools.

Following this systems thinking paradigm, this chapter is intended to present the complex interactive, intertwined, and interdependent components of effective teacher preparation for middle schools. However, a caveat is in order here. An effective teacher preparation pre-service program is a necessary but insufficient condition to affect middle school reform, for there are a host of other factors (e.g., funding, governance, incentives, teacher induction) at work that could have adverse influences on the change process. This line is thinking is consistent with Covey's (1990) notion of the interconnectedness of organizations:

> Everything is related to everything else, as in any ecosystem. In an ecosystem, not only do we deal with everything, but everything is very interrelated and interdependent. An initiative in one area affects every other area. Some management paradigms assume that an organization is a kind of disconnected, mechanical, nonorganic, nonecological environment. But all organizations

are ecosystems within larger biospheres and thus part of nature. Nature doesn't have compartments in it. It is one indivisible whole. (p. 187)

Although reformers must recognize those other influences in the change process, it is beyond the scope of this chapter to discuss all "ecosystems" fully. As in many past educational reform efforts, however, the devil is in the details. In this chapter, we incorporate the components of effective middle level teacher preparation for excellence that seem to "hang together" in the manner described by Keefe and Howard (1997):

> A system is a gestalt, a group of components that 'hang together because they continually affect each other over time and operate toward a common purpose.' Systems include biological organisms (like the human body), natural entities (like the solar system), human organizations (like families, teams and schools), and inventions (like the telephone or the factory). The systemic structure of an organization is not just its flowchart or its processes and procedures, but the pattern of interrelationships among the key components of the system. (p. 4)

Applying a systems lens to the world of middle level teacher education is accomplished by carefully examining the critical interrelated and interdependent components that could result in improved classroom practices, thus the need to distill the interactive influences and relationships of the key elements of effective teacher preparation (Keefe & Howard, 1997; Morris, 1997; Senge, 1990; Wheatley, 1994). Although it is wise to follow Senge's (1990) recommendation for learning organizations to focus on the elements that would provide the most leverage in a system, a common plight of teacher education reformers is to emphasize one or a few aspects of the whole while "neglecting to see how this will impact or be interconnected to other parts of the system ... that serve as institutionalized barriers that impede the change process" (Necochea & Cline 2000, p. 319). A systems approach to teacher education illuminates the essential elements and their relationships to the whole in order to determine what needs to be done to increase the probability of preparing effective teachers for middle level grades. As Jackson and Davis (2000) note, systems tend to seek equilibrium, therefore the tendency of organizations is to favor "keepers of the status quo" and to resist innovations. Institutionalized norms, rules, and belief systems tend to govern how "business is done here" (Keefe & Howard, 1997).

Figure 1 reflects the seven interactive components of a possible systems model of teacher education likely to be effective in preparing teachers for diverse settings. The interactive components—social justice and excellence, caring communities, modeling exemplary practices, middle level knowledge base, partnerships, habits of mind and heart, and home/

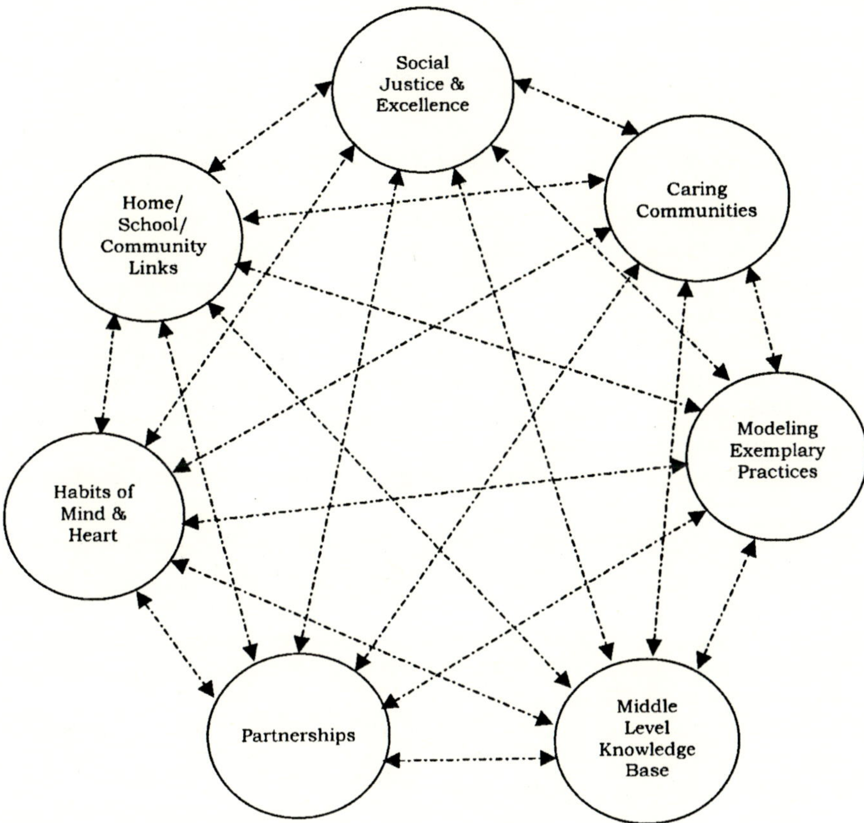

Figure 1. Systemic Teacher Education Model

school/community links—for this model are drawn from our own experiences in teacher education as well as the middle school reform literature.

The interconnected, interactive and interdependent nature of the system is demonstrated by the arrows connecting all components to form the whole. Although the components are presented individually for simplicity of analysis, this separation is rather artificial, for the relationships are not necessarily mutually exclusive. They often overlap, with influences going in all directions simultaneously. In middle level teacher education, Senge's (1990) notion of leverage could be beneficial in terms of starting somewhere in reforming pre-service practices and "getting the most bang for your buck" in influencing the system. Referring to system influence, Wheatley (1994) states:

> We need to learn more about this "interweaving of processes" that leads to structure. In ways we have never noticed, the whole of a system manages itself as a *total* system through natural processes that maintain its integrity. It is critical that we see these processes. It will shift our attention away from the parts, those rusting holdovers from an earlier age of organization, and focus us on the deeper, embedded processes that create whole organizations. (p. 118)

In preparing middle level teachers to be more effective in diverse settings, we envision a model that is context-embedded in specific teacher preparation programs. For this reason, a universal configuration of components might be an exercise in futility and perhaps even counterproductive. A model that is effective in one setting should serve more as a heuristic guide rather than dogma, for those wishing to transform their middle school teacher education programs must undergo their own systems analysis that applies to their own contexts.

Although we often illustrate some of these components with examples taken from our own practice, we recognize that their application to other settings must be sculpted according to the configuration and needs of the local context. Therefore, we offer these components in the spirit of sharing, not assuming that our practice at California State University San Marcos could or should be appropriate for others. We see these seven concepts as the starting point for the conversation that we hope to stimulate among other middle level teacher educators.

Social Justice and Excellence

What better time to confront the inconsistencies and paradoxes of society and ourselves than young adolescence? This is the time of life in which a person is increasingly conscious of himself or herself in relation to the society at large. In *A Talk to Teachers*, James Baldwin (1985) wrote:

> The paradox of education is precisely this—that as one begins to become conscious, one begins to examine the society in which he is being educated. The purpose of education, finally, is to create in a person the ability to look at the world for himself, to make his own decisions ... But no society is really anxious to have that kind of person around. What societies really, ideally, want is a citizenry which will simply obey the rules of society. If a society succeeds in this, that society is about to perish. The obligation of anyone who thinks of himself as responsible is to examine society and try to change it and to fight it—at no matter what risk. This is the only hope society has. This is the only way societies change. (p. 325)

Young adolescents are developmentally capable, given the opportunity and support, to engage in the complex issues associated with pursuing social justice. Early adolescence is a time of great change: physical, psychological, cognitive, social and moral growth. Early adolescents are also becoming more aware of their own thinking (meta-cognition) as well as coming to see knowledge as not absolute but rather as constructed by people and thus relative (Perry, 1970). In short, early adolescents are cognitively capable of reasoning about the reality and ideal of social justice, of thinking about why/how they come to that reasoning, and whether that reasoning is helpful/accurate for a specific situation.

Young adolescents are also more reflective about themselves, their identities and personality development. They are beginning to see themselves in relation to others and the world. Gilligan (1982) argues that females in particular develop their identities in relation to response from others. Another significant aspect of identity development is how one is seen as part of an ethnic group. Students begin to think about themselves in relation to ethnicity. A second aspect of identity and ethnicity is how middle level students come to think about others based on ethnicity. Quintana (1998) points out that middle level students are operating on a level where they develop a social perspective of ethnicity. For middle level students, this means an understanding of subtle aspects of ethnicity beyond food, fashion, and folklore to deeper aspects of differences in values, world-view, and especially socioeconomic connections to ethnicity. Perhaps what is more important, it means an awareness that ethnicity is a key factor in social relations (e.g., ethnic differences in friendship patterns especially having friends of one's own ethnic group) and an awareness of ethnic-based discrimination and prejudice.

What is our role as educators in the fight for social justice? New teachers point out that teaching for social justice and excellence for all works in the abstract (i.e., university classrooms), but they must adhere to standards, ensure their students pass standardized tests and after all, keep their jobs. Teaching a rigorous curriculum and teaching for social justice are not mutually exclusive. Teaching students skills necessary to participate in society is primary. As Delpit (1998) has said, "After all, no revolutionary society would have much use for a physician who was committed to social change but couldn't keep patients alive! I believe that teaching the skills and perspectives needed for real participation in a democratic society is one of the most revolutionary tasks that an educator committed to social justice can undertake" (p. 51). Social justice is about ensuring that the disenfranchised have access to political power and that educational excellence is within their reach. Knowledge and skills in literacy, mathematics, science, geography, political science, and history are essential for not only participating in society but also changing it.

However, teaching for social justice and excellence is more than teaching academic skills. Teaching for social justice and excellence means educating the mind and the heart. Wink (1997) calls it "the pedagogy of the caring heart and the critical eyes" (p. 147). It means attending to the emotional as well as cognitive aspects of education. It means attending to the individual and how the individual relates to the social group. It means attending to relationships inside and outside of the classroom. It means attending to power relationships and the dynamics of race, class and gender. It means teaching for introspection, reflection and change. It means becoming part of the educational system and then working to change it. Working for change with a direction. Change for the sake of some higher purpose: for social justice and excellence.

What does this mean for middle level teacher education? Teachers tend to teach the way they were taught. When candidates enter a teacher preparation program, they have around sixteen years of school experience—predominantly with status quo teaching. For most of them, for most of the time, teaching and education have *not* been political acts. In a very short period of time, we are trying to change all their years of socialization. We may model the critical aspects of middle level education like teaming, integrated curriculum, advising and the like. But everything is done with an explicit political and ideological stance. We must see schools as laboratories where students learn to challenge unjust societal conditions so that they further a transformation to a more just and equitable society. What goal do the methods we model serve? Are these approaches tools and, as such, are they amoral rather than moral or immoral? Farr and Tone (1994) reminded us that "standing with a hammer in one's hand and knowing its name doesn't make one a builder or tell one how to use it" (p. xiii). We would add to this adage that holding the hammer does not tell one *why* to use it. We concur with Van Til's (1994) worry that "too many teachers are more interested in learning the tricks of the trade [rather] than the trade." Our position is that teachers and teacher educators need to know both *how* and *why* to use the tools or trick of the trade that one possesses; otherwise one is a mere technician rather than a professional.

Working toward social justice and excellence is a state of mind as well as a state of action—both of which must be sustained despite the temptation to take the path of least resistance, the replication of the inequities in the status quo. Although middle school teachers will not arrive in their lifetimes at the end of "the arc of social justice" envisioned by Martin Luther King Jr., neither can we move society closer to that goal by giving in (McDaniel, Necochea, Ríos, Stowell, & Kritzer, 2001). As Oakes and Lipton (1999) remind us, "To struggle *for* social justice is to engage *in* social justice" (italics in original) (p. 369). Middle level teacher educators can do their part to achieve equity for young adolescents by preparing future teachers to be effective in and committed to that struggle.

Caring Communities

Jackson and Davis (2000) acknowledge a critical aspect of middle level education: relationships matter (p. 121). They remind us of the benefits of developing smaller learning communities where caring relationships are more likely to develop. Small is better, but it is not enough. Creating teams does not ensure that students feel needed and cared for by that team. Everyone needs to feel cared for and part of some group, especially in middle level classrooms. It is easier for students to learn from people who they feel care about them and whom they care about. A recent study asking underachieving middle school students about their school experiences places their relationship with the teacher at the top of the list of ways to help them succeed (Muir, 2000). Students won't learn from teachers whom they think don't care about them. It is essential that we treat students as if we genuinely like and respect them, even when disciplining them.

In order to teach all children, the teacher must have a connection with every student. Building positive relationships between students and teachers and then building a classroom community reinforces for adolescents and adults the importance of the affective domain of learning. Young adolescents are not just academic beings. In fact, at this time in their lives, adolescents are primarily social beings, a fact has been known for decades. In *A Place Called School*, John Goodlad (1984) found that junior high students value their school friendships and social relationships far more than school subjects and teachers. When asked, "What is the one best thing about this school?" more than a third of the students in Goodlad's study responded "my friends" and 15% named sports activities. About two thirds of what students appreciated about school was the opportunity to meet and mix with their peers. In fact, at 8%, "nothing" outranked "classes I am taking" (7%) and teachers (5%). Goodlad also found that junior high students' satisfaction with school stemmed from their perceived success in peer group relationships rather than from characteristics of the school itself (p. 254). Rather than bemoaning these facts, middle level educators can capitalize on students' natural tendencies to be social for the students' advantage. Indeed, "successful schools for young adolescents choose to become environments that promote social development" (Persico, 1996, p.39).

Students also see more easily how they and their education are connected to the smaller groups that they participate in, as well as how they connect to the larger society. Connectedness is part of the support system students need to succeed in education. "Of all the riches denied to disadvantaged children, perhaps the most important is a network that would allow them to thrive in school and give them a sense of belonging . . . They have not become part of the networks that add to the intellectual enrichment of children" (Maeroff, 1998, p. 426).

To become committed to the establishment of caring communities during their teacher preparation, pre-service teachers should experience the benefits of a sense of community themselves. They are unlikely to feel part of a learning community if their teacher preparation program consists of a cafeteria-style array of courses taught be faculty who act as independent operators within the typically competitive environment of institutions of higher education. Teams of instructors who plan the teacher education curriculum together and who demonstrate caring relationships with one another and with their students can serve as models for future middle level teachers. Community-building activities in middle level teacher education are no less meaningful than in middle level schools. Establishing connections with instructors and peers that will continue into the first years of teaching may make the difference between persistence and giving up when the weight of those first years catch up with novice teachers.

Modeling Exemplary Middle School Practices

Prospective middle level educators easily understand the need to master the practical aspects of their job, but they often do not appreciate why they need to bother with background knowledge or theory. Practice and theory go hand in hand. Teachers learn from experience and how to cope with the daily routine problems. The best teachers are able to respond to change and be reflective practitioners. To do this, teachers need more than the daily routine procedures. Good theory not only empowers the teacher, but also helps teachers to ask the right questions when times change and new problems must be analyzed. This is why creating a responsive middle level teacher preparation program for a pre-service teacher is a long and sometimes arduous process. If teacher preparation programs seek to be exemplary, they must find the right "mix" of theory and practice.

In addition, we argue that teacher preparation programs must practice what they preach. In other words, we should not require teacher candidates to do anything that we are not first willing to do ourselves in the preparation program. Practicing what we preach is a challenge because it is always easier to "say" than to "do" (McDaniel, Ríos, Stowell, & Christopher, 1994). A common complaint among pre-service teachers is that their teacher preparation programs had "too much theory" and not enough practice. One way to make sure there is a balance between theory and practice is by modeling. There are several ways that middle level teacher education programs can bring the theoretical and practical bases of middle schooling into the pre-service experiences of prospective teachers. Here we address one example among other possible ways: interdisciplinary team teaching.

The reform reports that form the bedrock of the middle school movement at the turn of the century (Carnegie Council on Adolescent Development, 1989; Jackson & Davis, 2000; National Middle School Association, 1995) consider interdisciplinary teaming to be an essential component of effective middle schooling. We contend that having teams of teacher educators who make connections among their own academic disciplines (educational psychology, curriculum and instruction, content area pedagogy) makes an indelible impression on prospective middle grades teachers. Further, organizing future teachers into cohorts of students who support each other and who bond with their team of instructors gives these soon-to-be teachers an experience they not only understand in theory but that they feel in practice. We believe that is it not only wise of middle level teacher preparation to take the theory of teaming and put it into practice, but that it is in fact negligent to *not* model interdisciplinary teaming for improving teacher education.

Once pre-service teachers experience interdisciplinary teaching in their preparation program, they begin to make the multiple connections that could result in deeper understanding, much the same way that young adolescents do in their own schooling. As noted in *This We Believe* (National Middle School Association, 1995), "Curriculum is integrative when it helps students make sense out of their life experiences. This requires curriculum that is itself coherent, that helps students connect school experiences to their daily lives outside the schools, and encourages them to reflect on the totality of their experience" (p. 22). No less than young adolescents, pre-service middle level educators also see the "totality" of their program when they experience it through the practice of interdisciplinary teaming that results in greater articulation, reflection, and a more holistic experience.

While the benefits of teaming to middle level students are clear in terms of both cognitive growth and school climate, teachers also reap countless rewards from this structure (Knowles & Brown, 2000). Teams of middle level teacher educators find the rewards of working together well worth the considerable expenditure of planning time and the ongoing negotiation required to keep a team going (Grossman & McDaniel, 1990; Ríos, McDaniel, & Stowell, 1998).

We have found thematic instruction to be an obvious (albeit not easy) path to demonstrating the power of team planning to prospective middle level teachers. Organizing the teacher education curriculum around powerful "themes with teeth" creates an expectation that future middle level teachers will become team members themselves so that they can be more effective collaborators in their middle schools (Stowell, McDaniel, & Ríos, 1995). Team teaching helps to establish the "climate of continuous learning and experimentation bolstered by care and support" that Van Zandt Allen and McEwin (2001, p. 304) regard as crucial to successful middle level teacher education programs. There are many other features of reinvented middle schools (Dickinson, 2001) that reinvented middle level teacher education programs could (and in our view, should) model. Among these are advisory, student choice, attention to equity issues, service learning, democratic classrooms, student-centered instruction, authentic assessment, partnerships, and flexible scheduling. By meshing practice and theory into a seamless whole, teacher education programs increase their potential to provide lasting skills to succeeding generations of middle level teachers.

The Knowledge Base of Middle Level Education

Middle level teacher preparation programs must provide a thorough foundation in the well-established knowledge base of middle schooling and young adolescence. As early as 1947 and as recently as 2001, well-respected researchers and reformers have called for schools that address this knowledge base, and for teachers who are able to work effectively in these schools (Dickinson, 2001; Gruhn & Douglass, 1947). The consensus on this knowledge base is so strong that experienced middle level educators are (as well they should be) able to recite it like a litany: understanding of early adolescence; knowledge of middle level philosophy and organization; ability to develop integrative middle level curriculum; commitment to developmentally and culturally responsive practices in instruction and assessment; and collaborative relationships among educators, families, and community. In addition, prospective middle level teachers should affix this knowledge base to academic preparation in two or more teaching fields, with early and sustained field experiences in the middle grades, and through a partnership between university-based and school-based middle level educators (McEwin & Dickinson, 1997). In our own practice, we endeavor to incorporate all these bases of middle level preparation into our teacher education program. Here we will highlight our practices in teaching our students about the physical, intellectual, and social, emotional and moral aspects of young adolescent development.

Turning Points 2000 (Jackson & Davis, 2000) summarizes years of recommendations to the effect that teacher preparation programs provide "substantial comprehension of young adolescents' developmental characteristics and needs" (p. 96). The diverse physical characteristics, depth and breath of intellect, range and volatility of emotions, important social interactions, and changing moral values of young adolescents are critical issues at the core of any middle level teacher education program. To promote maximum understanding of these essential concepts, teacher preparation must include authentic activities that assist the pre-service practitioner to connect the field's knowledge base with the realities of the classroom.

We begin our school year in late August by matching each pre-service teacher with an experienced teacher who shares the beginning of the middle school year experience. For a week, the pre-service students observe the organization of the middle school with regard to schedule, curriculum, and teaching practices. They pay particular attention to how teachers begin to build community with and among their students, and how teachers address issues of multicultural, multilingual education in their classrooms. Later in the semester, the pre-service students engage in a shadow study (Stevenson, 1998) at their student teaching sites. With the opportunity to compare findings on "a day in the life" of students of diverse achievement, interest, ethnicity, language background, and grade level, the prospective teachers are able to relate their theoretical knowledge of young adolescent development to the practical world of kids in school. As Jackson and Davis (2000) stated, "Teachers should know about how the developmental realities play out against a backdrop of race, ethnicity, religion, gender, socioeconomic status, family, and community" (p. 100). Authentic opportunities to translate issues of development into appropriate instructional plans that emphasize the diversity of learners and their needs must be included in all middle grades teacher preparation programs.

Partnerships

Just as relationships matter between teachers and their young adolescent students, so do relationships matter among teachers, administrators, and other stakeholders in the middle school. Successful middle schools are not the result of "spontaneous combustion;" rather, they are the result of the sustained intellectual, social and emotional effort of teams of committed people. Building the knowledge, skills, and dispositions necessary for teamwork must start in teacher education if we are to achieve the promise of middle schools. However, middle level teacher preparation does not occur in a vacuum. Partnerships between teacher education programs and exemplary middle schools provide powerful entryways into the profession for future teachers as well as powerful opportunities for continuing professional development for experienced teachers.

The last half of the twentieth century saw a movement away from the university-based laboratory schools of the past in favor of partnerships between universities and public schools located in a variety of authentic community settings. Professional development schools combine the energy of pre-service teachers, the wisdom of knowledgeable and dedicated teachers, the support of administrators, and the bridging-both-worlds experience of teacher educators in the pursuit of reinvented middle schools. The simultaneous renewal of teacher education and middle schools is achievable through such unique partnerships (Van Zandt Allen & McEwin, 2001). It is not only the young adolescents in reinvented middle schools who learn—Dickinson and Butler (2001) remind us that "on a good day everyone grows" (p. 321). For pre-service teachers who are choosing to teach in part due to a love of lifelong learning, this is a very attractive prospect indeed.

The agenda of social justice that we pursue is inextricably attached to strong partnerships with experienced middle school educators. Although teaching for social justice may start at the university, it is unrealistic to expect prospective teachers to apply it in their student teaching classrooms without the support that comes from these experienced teachers. Cochran-Smith (1991) argues that a powerful way for student teachers to learn to reform teaching is to "work in the company of experienced teachers who are themselves struggling to be reformers in their own classrooms, schools and communities" (p. 279). Pre-service teachers must learn how to work on different ways of seeing, being and teaching in the school environment with parents, teachers and administrators. Experienced teachers can demonstrate that changing teaching and education is challenging, often discouraging, and it takes time. Experienced teachers can also show how to work to change schools without alienating colleagues. Pre-service teachers often approach a new school with optimism, "answers" and a lot of prejudgement. They need to be mentored into becoming effective agents of social justice and excellence.

Working and talking regularly with experienced teachers who share the goal of teaching for social justice and excellence allows student teachers to participate in their ways of knowing and reforming teaching. These relationships lead student teachers to see that larger school reform efforts are deeply entangled with their own biographies as educators, the decisions they make and permit others to make about the children in their classrooms, and the discussions that occur at their schools (Cochran-Smith, 1991, p. 285).

In order for student teachers to observe and engage in the kind of work Cochran-Smith (1991) describes, they must be present for longer periods of time than most field experiences permit. Pre-service teachers must hear the conversations, the questions and the struggles of experienced teachers who know that reform takes time. Time is essential for student teachers to learn not only the intricacies of teaching, but also the paradoxes of teaching for social justice and excellence in middle schools that are not yet on the path to reinvention.

Home/School/Community Links

The caregivers in young adolescents' lives are also important partners in the educational process. The two *Turning Points* reports (Carnegie Council on Adolescent Development, 1989; Jackson & Davis, 2000) advocated for strong connections to parents and other adults who care about them. Hersch (1998) pointed out that most young adolescents feel disconnected from home, parents and society. Yet, they crave that connection: they want adults to reach out to them. Young adolescents should be the center of concentric circles of caring in which the home, school, community, and other institutions (e.g., places of worship) support, protect and care for them.

Effective education for young adolescents must include more than communities within the school, especially when students come from diverse ethnic and linguistic backgrounds. Goodlad (1984) suggested an ecological perspective of school. This is in concert with Dewey's (1916/1961) notion that the learning in school must be continuous with that out of school: "There should be a free interplay between the two. This is possible only when there are numerous points of contact between the social interests of the one and the other" (p. 358). An ecology of education is one in which there is give and take between the school and the institutions, agencies and people of the community. It is more than the cliché, "It takes a village to raise a child." Rather, the child is an active member of that village, has something to give back and plays a role in shaping that village as well. All students should see the school as an extension of their home and community.

Young adolescents don't look at school as primarily a place to *get ready* for what matters in life. What matters is what is happening to them *right* now. Therefore, there is no time like the present to work within the community outside of the classroom. "The world outside the classroom is a limitless resource of diverse people, purposeful activity and the innumerable artifacts of a culture—cars, buildings, bridges, art. Our children grow out of and into this world. They are its products as well as its architects" (Gillis, 1992, p. 130). Bringing young adolescents and the community together through service learning rewards both. The creativity, compassion, and optimism of young adolescents provide the fuel for their work in communities. With a well-designed curriculum that builds on their community action, middle school students will have more powerful learning experiences than those available to them within the classroom walls. Young adolescence is a time particularly well matched to service learning (Fertman, White & White, 1996). Prospective teacher educators must learn the pedagogy of service learning so that it becomes another teaching-learning strategy that is consonant with their beliefs about student empowerment. The case for service learning in teacher education is strong (Anderson, Swick, & Yff, 2001). In middle schools where active learning is a practice and not just a slogan, middle level pre-service teachers should find opportunities to practice service learning so that it becomes a part of their beings as middle level educators.

Habits of the Mind and Heart

One critical aspect of teacher preparation is the development of what we call "habits of the mind and heart." Fashioned after Deborah Meier's (1995) "habits of mind" and Robert Bellah and colleagues (1996) "habits of the heart," these are the ephemeral and elusive beliefs and practices that we believe middle level teachers of the 21st century must possess. Pre-service middle level teachers must begin to form philosophical underpinnings during their teacher preparation coursework that will guide them throughout their teaching careers. These habits are not quick to manifest themselves, nor are they mastered by virtue of one lesson in a methods course. These habits should serve as spiritual renewal to help develop the knowledge, skills, and dispositions for effective middle level teaching. Incorporating these habits into their daily practice will carry pre-service teachers through their journey as middle level educators. These habits will also help them endure the vicissitudes of the pendulum swings of educational reforms.

Reflective Practice

Individuals who look critically at all aspects of their work and then make modifications or adjustments find that they are working most effectively. Teachers use a variety of tools for reflective practices. Teacher education should encourage the formation of reflective practice by the use of personal journals, review of student work, peer observations, quick writes, group writings, reactions to assigned readings, analysis of case studies, etc. as way to improve the teaching and learning process. Making reference to reflection, Dewey (1938/1963) state:

> What avail is it to win prescribed amounts of information, to win the ability to read and write, if in the process the individual ... loses the ability to extract meaning from his future experiences as they occur? (p. 49)

Indeed, teacher preparation should include daily reflections, in a variety of forms of expression, for the purpose of extracting personal meanings from their "learning-to-teach" experiences.

Positive Attitude

A positive attitude for teaching adolescents is a necessary element for becoming an effective middle level teacher. Because of its elusive nature, teacher attitude is difficult to teach, but by all means needs to be incorporated into teacher education programs to instill a sense that middle school teachers can make a significant difference in the lives of young adolescents. In our teacher preparation program, for example, we examine teacher attitude through whole and small class discussions of teachers who made a difference in our lives. It is interesting to us how easily our students remember the "good and bad" teachers from their pasts, and the central role that teacher attitude played.

Furthermore, as teachers ourselves, we draw from our own years in middle schools by sharing stories of educational change and making a difference. Our own personal narratives as progressive educators give our students examples of how a positive attitude can help them navigate the turbulent waters of middle school reform.

Lifelong Learners

Middle level teacher educators must be lifelong learners. Advanced degrees, membership in professional organizations, professional conferences, and district workshops all provide opportunities to rethink and refine teaching practices. Reading educational journals and other publications will also rejuvenate teachers with new ideas or reinforce effective practices. In our middle level program, our students read current journals and periodicals, attend the state middle school conference, and join professional organizations. Additionally, we exemplify lifelong learning ourselves by presenting at conferences, staying abreast of research, publishing, and learning new ways to collaborate as colleagues.

Agents of Change

Teachers must be at the heart of the reform movement if fundamental change is to occur. Pre-service teachers have lots of positive energy and are ready to take on the world and its many challenges. We encourage our pre-service teachers to look closely at the role they can play once they are fully employed and working at a school site. We share stories of former students and the important changes they made to their schools. Taking on the role of team leader, or sitting on a specific committee, becoming a member of a school site council, attending local board meetings or PTA meetings are all avenues for sharing a voice/opinion. We teach our students that they must become "the change you want to see in middle schools." We expect our students to "come to their first teaching experience with . . . a willingness and the preparation to participate actively in the school's governance system" (Jackson & Davis, 2000, p. 96).

Democratic Educator

Within the classroom, middle school teachers have a tremendous amount of authority and power. We emphasize that teachers much use their authority and power to create democratic classroom environments. By creating a democratic classroom, the teacher builds motivation and increases the opportunities for quality relationships. Within a common sense framework, we provide activities in teacher preparation that foster student empowerment, encourage student voice and choice, and set the tone for a positive learning environment. Middle level teachers need to promote principles and practices that prepare students for democratic citizenry.

Professionalism

In the day to day operations of a school, countless interactions test the professionalism of middle level educators. Although some will be positive and easy, others will be challenging and emotionally charged. Pre-service teachers must embrace a commitment to professionalism as fundamental to their role as educators. In teacher preparation we cannot predict every scenario that may occur in a teacher's career. We challenge students to seek positive outlets for vexing situations. Teaching is a "people-centered career," thus educators must establish professional relationships with students, parents, colleagues, administrators, paraprofessionals, and other school personnel.

"Habits of the mind and heart" should be at the core of any quality teacher education program and are especially essential in middle level teacher preparation. Prospective middle level educators not only need knowledge and skills, but also dispositions that can make their chosen career a fulfilling one. These "habits of the mind and heart" are the intangible threads that help middle level teacher make sense of the complex and sometimes chaotic world of educating young adolescents.

CONCLUSION

Like Oakes and Lipton (1999), we "do not believe that the world is a neutral place or that teaching is a neutral profession" (p. xix). In our minds, it follows that teacher education cannot be a neutral enterprise. The stakes for young adolescents are high. Middle level educators have known for decades that middle schools provide the last, best chance for those who are on the verge of a "downward spiral" (Jackson & Davis, 2000, p. 8). If society fails its youth, then Dr. King's arc of social justice will be supplanted by the downward spiral. There is a tremendous responsibility to share. Families, community organizations, places of worship, business owners, government leaders, and yes, educators have a piece of the action. Good teachers know that at the heart of the teaching-learning experience is a teacher who is well prepared. Good middle school teachers have the knowledge, skills, and dispositions that enable them to awaken each day ready to grow, ready to care, ready to risk, *ready to teach.* They know that the young adolescents who share their classrooms are ready to grow, ready to care, ready to risk, and *ready to learn.*

How can we as teacher educators not awaken each day likewise ready to grow, to care, to risk, to teach and to learn—in short, to prepare those teachers who will be entrusted with the education of young adolescents? To do so requires that we rethink middle level teacher education. We began this chapter by noting the relief that has come with being "over the millennium." But "business as usual" will not do, in our minds. Having so recently reflected on the changes of the last 100 years, we cannot help but think ahead to the next 100 years. The arc or the downward spiral—which is it to be? Middle level teacher education—all parts of the system, all working to be more than the sum of their parts—must be transformed if young adolescents and their teachers are to have the 21st century that they so richly deserve.

REFERENCES

Anderson, J.B., Swick, K.J., & Yff, J. (2001). *Service-learning in teacher education: Enhancing the growth of new teachers, their students, and communities.* Washington, DC: American Association of Colleges for Teacher Education.

Baldwin, J. (1985). *The price of the ticket.* New York: St. Martin's Press.

Bellah, R.N., Madsen, R., Sullivan, W.M, Swidler, A., & Tipton, S.M. (1996). *Habits of the heart :Individualism and commitment in American Life.* Berkeley: University of California Press.

Carnegie Council on Adolescent Development. (1989). *Turning points: Preparing American youth for the 21st century.* New York: Carnegie Corporation.

Cochran-Smith, M. (1991). Learning to teach against the grain. *Harvard Educational Review, 61*(3), 279–310.

Covey, S.R. (1990). *Principle-centered leadership.* New York: Summit Books.

Delpit, L. [Quoted in Ayer, W., Hunt, J. A., and Quinn, T. (1998)]. *Teaching for social justice: A Democracy and Education reader* (p. 51). New York: Teachers College Press.

Dewey, J. (1916/1961). *Democracy and education: An introduction to the philosophy of education.* New York: Macmillan.

Dewey, J. (1938/1963). *Experience and education.* New York: Collier Books.

Dickinson, T.S. (Ed.). (2001). *Reinventing the middle school.* New York: Routledge Falmer.

Dickinson, T.S., & Butler, D. (2001). On a good day everyone grows. In T.S. Dickinson (Ed.). *Reinventing the middle school* (pp. 321–328). New York: Routledge Falmer.

Farr, R., & Tone, B. (1994). *Portfolio and performance: Helping students evaluate their progress as readers and writers.* Fort Worth, TX: Harcourt Brace.

Fertman, C.I., White, G.P., & White, L.J. (1996). *Service learning in the middle school: Building a culture of service.* Columbus, OH: National Middle School Association.

George, P.S., & Alexander, W.M. (1993). *The exemplary middle school* (2nd ed.). Fort Worth, TX: Harcourt Brace.

Gilligan, C.F. (1982). *In a different voice.* Cambridge, MA: Harvard University Press.

Gillis, C. (1992). *The community as classroom.* Portsmouth, NH: Heinemann.

Goodlad, J.I. (1984). *A place called school.* New York: McGraw Hill.

Grossman, P.L., & McDaniel, J.E. (1990, April). *Breaking boundaries: Restructuring preservice teacher education as a collaborative school–university venture.* Paper presented at the meeting of the American Educational Research Association, Boston, MA.

Gruhn, W.T., & Douglass, H.R. (1947). *The modern junior high school.* New York: Ronald Press.

Hersch, P. (1998). *A tribe apart: A journey into the heart of American adolescence.* New York: Fawcett Columbine.

Jackson, A.W., & Davis, G.A. (2000). *Turning points 2000: Educating adolescents in the 21st century.* New York: Teachers College Press.

Keefe, J.W., & Howard, E.R. (1997). *Redesigning schools for the new century: A systems approach.* Reston, VA: National Association of Secondary Principals.

Knowles, T., & Brown, D. (2000). *What every middle school teacher should know.* Portsmouth, NH: Heinemann.

Maeroff, G. (1998). Altered destinies: Making life better for schoolchildren in need. *Phi Delta Kappan, 79* (6), 424–434.

McDaniel, J.E., Necochea, J., Ríos, F.A., Stowell, L.P., & Kritzer, C. (2001). The arc of equity in reinvented middle schools. In T. Dickinson (Ed.), *Reinventing the middle school* (pp. 56–75). New York: Routledge.

McDaniel, J.E., Ríos, F.A., & Stowell, L.P. (1995). California State University San Marcos. In C.K. McEwin & T. Dickinson (Eds.), *The professional preparation of middle level teachers: Profiles of successful programs* (pp. 57–63). Columbus, OH: National Middle School Association.

McDaniel, J.E., Ríos, F.A., Stowell, L.P., & Christopher, P.A. (1994). Do as we do and as we say: Modeling curriculum integration in middle level teacher education. *Middle School Journal, 26*(2), 14–20.

McEwin, C. K., & Dickinson, T. S. (1996). *Forgotten youth, forgotten teachers: Transformation of the professional preparation of teachers of young adoelscents.* New York: Middle Grades School State Policy Initiative, Carnegie Corporation of New York.

McEwin, C.K., & Dickinson, T.S. (1997). Middle level teacher preparation and licensure. In J. I. Irvin (Ed.), *What current research says to the middle level practitioner* (pp. 223–229). Columbus, OH: National Middle School Association.

McEwin, C.K., Dickinson, T.S., & Jenkins, D.M. (1996). *America's middle schools: Practices and progress—A 25 year perspective.* Columbus, OH: National Middle School Association.

Meier, D. (1995). *The power of their ideas: Lessons for America from a small suburban school in Harlem.* Boston: Beacon Press.

Morris, D.R. (1997). Adrift in the sea of innovations: A response to Alexander, Murphy, and Woods. *Educational Researcher, 26*(4), 22–26.

Muir, M. (2000, November). *What do underachieving middle school students believe motivates them to learn?* Paper presented at the annual meeting of the National Middle School Association, St. Louis, MO.

National Middle School Association. (1995). *This we believe: Developmentally responsive middle level schools.* Columbus, OH: Author.

National Middle School Association. (1996). *NMSA/NCATE-approved curriculum guidelines.* Columbus, OH: Author.

Necochea, J., & Cline, Z. (2000). *Race ethnicity and education, 3*(3), 317–332.

Oakes, J., & Lipton, M. (1999). *Teaching to change the world.* Boston: McGraw Hill.

Perry, W.G., Jr. (1970). *Forms of intellectual and ethical development in the college years.* San Diego, CA: Academic Press.

Persico, M. (1996). Our responsibility is teaching responsibility. *Middle School Journal, 28*(2), 39–42.

Quintana, S.M. (1998). Children's developmental understanding of ethnicity and race. *Applied and Preventive Psychology, 7*, 27–45.

Ríos, F.A., McDaniel, J.E., & Stowell, L.P. (1998). Making the path by walking it. In A. Cole, R. Elijah, & G. Knowles (Eds.), *The heart of the matter: Teacher educators and teacher education reform* (pp. 237–254). Ann Arbor, MI: Caddo Gap Press.

Scales, P.C., & McEwin, C.K. (1994). *Growing pains: The making of America's middle school teachers.* Columbus, OH: National Middle School Association.

Senge, P.M. (1990). *The fifth discipline: The art and practice of the learning organization.* New York: Doubleday.

Stevenson, C. (1998). *Teaching ten to fourteen year olds* (2nd ed.), White Plains, NY: Longman.

Stowell, L.P., McDaniel, J.E., & Ríos, F.A. (1995). Fostering change for democratic middle schools through teacher education. *Middle School Journal, 26* (5), 3–10.

Van Til, W. (1994, November). (Untitled remarks.) In T. Dickinson (Chair), W. Van Til, G. Vars, & J. Lounsbury (Eds.), *A historical perspective on the middle grades curriculum conversation.* Symposium conducted at the meeting of the National Middle School Association, Cincinnati, OH.

Van Zandt Allen, L., & McEwin, C.K. (2001). Reinventing middle level teacher preparation via professional development schools. In T.S. Dickinson (Ed.), *Reinventing the middle school* (pp. 302-317). New York: Routledge Falmer.

Wheatley, M.J. (1994). *Leadership and the new science.* San Francisco: Berrett-Koehler.

Wink, J. (1997). *Critical pedagogy: Notes from the real world.* White Plains, NY: Longman.

CHAPTER 8

MIDDLE LEVEL LEADERSHIP FOR THE 21ST CENTURY

Principals' Views on Essential Skills and Knowledge; Implications for Successful Preparation

Vincent A. Anfara, Jr., Kathleen M. Brown, Rebecca Mills, Kimberly Hartman, and Robert J. Mahar

ABSTRACT

Despite the consensus that leadership is essential to current school reform initiatives, deep philosophical and political disagreements remain about what kind of educational leaders are needed, what knowledge and skills they should possess, and how they should be professionally prepared. Rhetoric about their importance is often accompanied by sufficient attention to their professional development. The purposes of this study were to identify the essential performance-based skills needed for middle level leadership in the 21st century, and to assess the impact of these on administrator preparation programs. An analysis of the qualitative data (surveys and interviews) revealed that effective middle level principals have a positive outlook about their work, are more teacher-oriented, are supportive of parent/community involvement, have a high tolerance for ambiguity, and are intentional in their efforts to assemble, develop, and maintain a dedicated staff. Additionally, formal education in administration and participation in professional associations appeared to have no bearing on principal effectiveness.

INTRODUCTION

"Almost all educational reform reports have come to the conclusion that the nation cannot attain excellence in education without effective school leadership" (Crawford, 1998, p. 8). We know that effective school leaders: (1) recognize teaching and learning as the main business of school, (2) communicate the school's mission and vision clearly and consistently to all constituents, (3) promote an atmosphere of trust and collaboration, and (4) emphasize professional development (see Bauck, 1987; George & Grebing, 1992; Weller, 1999). Despite the consensus that leadership counts, deep philosophical and political disagreements remain about what kind of educational leaders are needed, what knowledge and skills they should possess, and how they should be professionally prepared. Many policymakers, for example, criticize the preparation of school administrators in colleges and universities as outmoded and ineffective, unable to address adequately the complexities of school leadership.

As middle level education moves into the 21st century new questions need to be asked and old ones revisited. Middle level principals are essential to current school reform initiatives; yet rhetoric about their importance is often unaccompanied by sufficient attention to the new knowledge and skills they will need or how they might acquire these to forward a contemporary, complex reform agenda. Emphasizing this renewed interest in the role of the principal, Olson (2000) noted:

> After years of work on structural changes, standards and testing and ways of holding students and schools accountable, the education policy world has turned its attention to the people charged with making the system work.... But nowhere is the focus on the human element in public education more prevalent than in the renewed recognition of the importance of strong and effective leadership. (p. 1)

The purposes of this study were: (1) to report what the respondents in this study identified as the essential performance-based skills and knowledge needed for middle level leadership in the 21st century; and (2) to assess and project the impact of these knowledge and skill areas on administrator preparation programs. This study examined these issues by surveying and interviewing middle level principals about personal characteristics, job roles and tasks, and professional beliefs related to middle schools and the middle school philosophy.

REVIEW OF LITERATURE

There is a lack of research focused on the middle level principalship. Between 1981 and 1983 the National Association of Secondary School Principals (NASSP) conducted a national study of the middle level principalship which resulted in two publications, *The Middle Level Principalship, Volume I, A Survey of Middle Level Principals and Programs* and *The Middle Level Principalship, Volume II, The Effective Middle Level Principal.* Analyzing the data from these two studies, Bauck (1987) attempted to determine the differences and similarities between typical and effective middle level principals. He concluded that while effective middle level principals are teacher oriented and encourage parent and community involvement in the school, they do not feel that formal education or participation in professional organizations have contributed to their success (see Table 3 in the concluding discussion for a more complete list of his findings). Since 1983 no large scale studies have been undertaken.

In 1999 Valentine, Maher, Quinne, and Irvin noted that the role of the principal has shifted noticeably in the 20th century. More importantly they wrote, "As the principalship moves into a new millennium, characterizing the principalship with a few key words is more difficult than ever" (p. 56). With this in mind, we review the literature on the middle level principal to establish the key roles that principals have played to this point in time. Basically, this literature sets forth ideas about the functions and personal nature of effective middle level principals as well as connecting principal leadership to school change.

Kilcrease (1995), in her study of middle level principals, concluded that administrators performed three broad functions that enabled them to be successful: (1) providing a program especially adapted to diverse student needs, (2) promoting continuity of education, and (3) introducing needed innovations in curriculum and instruction. In addition, middle level administrators must have the skills to ensure that teaming and shared decision making processes work well in the school (George & Grebing, 1992) and perception about the attitudes and leadership skills among their teaching staff (Whittaker & Valentine, 1993). Not surprisingly, several theorists and researchers assert that middle level principals should be knowledgeable about young adolescents, their development, and their learning styles (Eichorn, 1987; George, 1990; Schmidt, 1998). Of course, the reform literature also strongly advocates that middle level principals possess a special set of skills, knowledge, and attitudes.

The literature about the personal nature of middle level principals is not usually research based; however, it sets forth such expectations as personal confidence (Rubinstein, 1990), trustworthiness (Tarter, 1995), and instructional leadership. The latter category is best explained by Williamson (1991) who defined the role of the middle level principal as an inspirational leader, human resource developer, and change agent. The principal must help develop and convey the school vision, work with students, teachers, support staff, parents and the community to improve the school. Middle level principals must be able to inspire others to strive for excellence.

Neufeld (1997) asserted that middle level principals, especially those in urban schools, can reform schools if they transform themselves from managers to leaders along with learning new knowledge and skills. Montgomery (1995) concurs that principals working with teachers can make great changes. "If only the principal will grow, the school will grow. To change something, someone has to change first" (Barth, 1985, p. 92). Middle level principals must be catalysts for change if middle level schools are to meet the varied and diverse needs of young adolescents.

Hipp (1997) extends the idea of principal and teacher collaboration and makes suggestions for principals to reinforce teacher efficacy. These suggestions include, among others: (1) modeling behavior, (2) promoting teacher empowerment and decision making, (3) managing student behavior, (4) creating a positive climate for success, and (5) inspiring caring and respectful relationships.

Responsibilities of a 21st century middle level principal are complex and far-reaching; however, middle level principals must ensure that young adolescents do not face what *Turning Points* refers to as the possibility of a "diminished future" (Carnegie Task Force on Education of Young Adolescents, 1989, p. 8).

PERFORMANCE STANDARDS FOR ADMINISTRATORS

Many professional organizations have developed performance standards that are meant to govern the work of school administrators. A careful examination of these organizations' standards reveals an amazing consistency in the knowledge, skills, and dispositions characteristic of effective school administrators. The first widely distributed set of preparation guidelines/standards for administrators was released in 1983 by the American Association of School Administrators (AASA). In 1993 the National Policy Board for Educational Administration (NPBEA) published *Principals for Our Changing Schools* which outlined 21 knowledge and skill domains deemed essential for effective school leadership. In 1996 the work of the Interstate School Leadership Licensure Consortium (ISLLC) came to the forefront and is presently being adopted by state agencies around the country. Its standards for school administrators were built around the premise that good leaders are those who can improve teaching and learning.

Of all of the national organizations that focus on school administration issues it appears that only one has focused its attention on middle schools. In 1986 (revised 1991 and 1997) the National Association of Elementary School Principals (NAESP) published *Elementary and Middle Schools Proficiencies for Principals.* NAESP recognized that middle level schools are extremely complex organizations that require a wide range of leadership proficiencies. This professional organization also noted that "trends toward school-based management, shared decision making, and a more intense focus on student performance ... require school leaders to acquire new skills" (p.1).

While NAESP notes that it is unrealistic to expect that all principals will possess all of the proficiencies cited in their report, an outstanding principal is characterized by 96 proficiencies. According to this list of proficiencies the outstanding middle level principal: (1) involves the school community in identifying and accomplishing the school's mission; (2) recognizes the individual needs and contributions of all staff and students; (3) applies effective interpersonal skills; (4) conducts needs assessments; (5) advances the profession through participation in professional organizations, (6) uses active listening skills, (7) works to build consensus; (8) understands group dynamics; (9) maintains a visible presence in the classroom; (10) engages the staff in the study of effective teaching practices; (11) uses both formative and summative evaluation skills; (12) uses collaborative planning to identify objectives that accomplish the school's mission; (13) develops and implements effective schedules; (14) understands the school district budget and its implications for the school; and (15) uses effective strategies to deal with political forces that affect the school (*Proficiencies for Principals,* 1997, p. 3).

In addition to these proficiencies NAESP also identified four prerequisites for success as an elementary and middle level leader. These include: (1) advanced understanding of the teaching and learning processes; (2) thorough understanding of child growth and development; (3) broad base of knowledge, including a solid background in liberal arts; and (4) sincere commitment to educational equity and excellence at all levels for all children (*Proficiencies for Principals,* 1997, p. 3).

METHODOLOGY

This study of middle level principals employed a dominant-less dominant research design (Creswell, 1994) with qualitative methods as the dominant paradigm. This study is part of a larger research project on middle level principalship, designed to explore and further the knowledge base related to the nature of the middle level principalship. Research questions included: (1) What are the essential skills and knowledge identified by middle level principals for school leadership in the 21st century?, and (2) When, where, and how do middle level principals obtain these performance-based skills and knowledge?

Data Collection

Data were collected using surveys and semi-structured interviews. Initially surveys were sent to 125 middle level principals in the states of Pennsylvania and New Jersey. With the support of school superintendents and intermediate unit leaders, 72 surveys were returned for data analysis. The surveys gathered information related to the principals': (1) educational, professional, and personal background; (2) knowledge of middle school philosophy; (3) experience with school reform and change; (4) attitudes toward parent involvement in school; (5) and knowledge of special education issues.

The survey contained both open and closed-ended questions. Responses, which were scaled, were then analyzed using descriptive statistics. Unscaled (open-ended) responses were clustered into themes or categories. The descriptive statistics, used throughout the analysis, help confirm the findings.

From the pool of survey respondents, 17 principals indicated that they were willing to be interviewed. Eight of these seventeen principals work in schools recognized as "blue ribbon" schools by the U.S. Department of Education. It is important to note that the seventeen interviewees are highly representative of the larger sample of survey respondents with regard to gender, age, experience, race/ethnicity, prior school experience, and the like. These in-depth, semi-structured interviews allowed the middle level principals to expand upon their survey responses, discuss more freely what it means to be a middle level principal, and to explain their understanding of effectiveness in relation to middle level leadership. The researchers attempted to follow the dictates of phenomenological interviews, "to let them [middle level principals] tell us what we need to know rather than to ask them what we think, a priori, we would like to know" (Pollio, 1991, p. 4). The interviews were tape-recorded and transcribed for purposes of analysis.

Research Context

Keefe, Clark, Nickerson and Valentine (1983) described the typical effective principal as "a man ... between the ages of 45 and 54 who has spent 10 to 14 years as a principal, 9 to 11 of which have been in his current school. The effective principals appear to be older and more experienced than the norm for middle level principals. They spend more time in professional growth activities ... and are active in professional associations" (p. 11). The typical middle level principal in this study is a white male (85%), 48 years of age who holds a master's degree (79%) obtained in the 1970s and 1980s (79%). He is a seasoned educator with 13 years of teaching experience and prior administrative experience as an assistant principal (74%). He is certified on the secondary level (62%).

Seventy percent of the principals who participated in this study are members of NASSP with only 37% belonging to the National Middle School Association (NMSA). Fifty-four percent are committed to administering a middle school for no longer than five years. When assessing the responses of the participants in this study it is important to note that neither Pennsylvania nor New Jersey recognizes middle school certification for school administrators. According to the laws in each state, a principal who is licensed at either the elementary or secondary levels may administer a middle school. A more complete portrait of the sample used in this study is available in Table 1.

Table 1. Portrait of Participating Middle Level Principals (n = 72)

RACE/ETHNICITY	• White 61 (85%) • Black 4 (6%) • Hispanic 1 (1%) • Not Reported 6 (8%)			
GENDER	• Male 54 (75%)		• Female 18 (25%)	
AGE	Range = 28–65 years Mean = 48 years			
HIGHEST DEGREE	• MA/MS 31 (43%) • MEd 26 (36%) • EdD 13 (18%) • PhD 2 (3%)			
YEAR OF DEGREE	1960s 2 (3%)	1970s 28 (39%)	1980s 29 (40%)	1990s 13 (18%)
CERTIFICATION	• Secondary 62%		• Elementary 38%	
TEACHING EXPERIENCE	Range = 2.5–25 years Mean = 13 years			

Table 1. Portrait of Participating Middle Level Principals (n = 72) (Cont.)

PRIOR ADMINISTRATIVE EXPERIENCE	• Assistant Principal 55 (77%) • Administrative Experience 5 (7%) • Curriculum Specialist 5 (7%) • No Prior Administrative Experience 7 (9%)	
ADMINISTRATIVE EXPERIENCE IN YEARS	Range = 1–31 years Mean = 9 years Mode = 1 year (8 respondents)	
TENURE FOR MIDDLE SCHOOL APPOINTMENT	• 1–3 Years: 12 (17%) • 4–5 Years: 33 (46%) • 6–10 Years: 12 (16%) • 10+ Years: 15 (21%)	
FORMAL MIDDLE SCHOOL TRAINING	No 39 (54%)	Yes 33 (46%)
MEMBERSHIP IN PROFESSIONAL ORGANIZATIONS	• NASSP 50 (70%) • ASCD 43 (60%) • NMSA 27 (37%) • STATE MSA 17 (24%)	

The typical middle school in this study was public, included grades six through eight, and was located in a suburban setting. As noted in Table 2, principals reported widespread use of teaming, interdisciplinary teaching, transition programs, exploratory curriculum, and block/flexible scheduling.

Table 2. Middle School Demographics (n = 72)

SCHOOL LOCATION	Suburban 54 (75%)	Urban 15 (21%)	Rural 3 (4%)	
GRADE CONFIGURATION	6–8 47 (65%)	5–8 11 (16%)	7–8 8 (11%)	7–9 6 (8%)
TYPE OF SCHOOL	Public 72 (100%)	Private 0 (0%)	Other 0 (0%)	
MIDDLE SCHOOL PROGRAMS IMPLEMENTED	• Teaming 66 (92%) • Interdisciplinary Teaching 64 (89%) • Transition Programs 57 (79%) • Exploratory Curriculum 53 (74%) • Block/Flexible Scheduling 43 (60%) • Advisory 26 (36%)			

Data Analysis

The process of data analysis began with repeated readings of the transcripts and the compilation of survey results. Each researcher read and reread the data to identify "the repetitive refrains, the persistent themes" (Lightfoot, 1983, p. 15), to code the data according to these emerging themes, and to make sense of the whole in terms of the context. The five researchers involved in this project met to discuss and debate their individual interpretations of the data. Themes were compared and tested against the data collected. Wasser and Bresler (1996) noted that processes such as those we followed involve "multiple viewpoints ... held in dynamic tension" (p. 6) and referred to this process as the "interpretive zone." After much discussion the seven themes that are presented in this study emerged, meeting the test of honoring the middle level principals' experiences.

Readers will notice the code (see Appendix A) used to identify the source of each verbatim interview account (i.e., 01WM-50/17-6/8S80). Translated this code means: Interviewee #1 is a white male who is 50 years old with 17 years of administrative experience. He works in a sixth through eighth grade middle school that is located in a suburban area with a faculty of 80 teachers.

Integrity of Data and Analysis

To help ensure the internal validity or dependability (Lincoln & Guba, 1985) of our results, we used triangulation of interview and survey data, the presentation of verbatim quotes, the use of multiple researchers (and coders), audit trails (Merriam, 1988), and member checks. The themes presented in this article were "member checked" by six of the seventeen principals interviewed.

ANALYSIS: LEADERSHIP FOR THE 21ST CENTURY AND THE MIDDLE SCHOOL PRINCIPAL

An analysis of the qualitative data revealed that effective middle level principals: (1) have a very positive outlook about their work, experience a high degree of job satisfaction, and view school problems as surmountable; (2) are more teacher-oriented, as evidenced by their concern for providing teachers with planning time and professional development; (3) are supportive of parent/community involvement in their schools; (4) have a high tolerance for ambiguity and uncertainty; and (5) are intentional in their efforts to assemble, develop, and maintain a staff of dedicated educators who want to be in a middle school. Additionally, the analysis revealed that formal education in educational administration appeared to have no bearing on middle level principal effectiveness, and that levels of participation in professional associations appeared to be unrelated to principal effectiveness. The analysis that follows develops each of these themes more fully.

MIDDLE LEVEL LEADERSHIP FOR THE 21ST CENTURY: ESSENTIAL SKILLS AND KNOWLEDGE

A Positive Outlook/High Job Satisfaction

Effective middle level principals express a positive outlook and a high degree of job satisfaction (Clark & Clark, 1994). Respondents to this study were no exception; they expressed their enjoyment in working with young adolescents as well as a positive attitude toward meeting what many characterized as the "challenge" of serving as the principal of a middle school. For example, one experienced suburban principal said, "It's exciting to see [students] enter adolescence and change from children to adults.... Change is something big in the life of middle school youngsters. They're going through this change, and we have to know that and appreciate that" (14WM-56/06-6/9S90). Similar sentiments were expressed by all respondents.

Even when they discussed adolescents as a "tough age group," responses were softened with statements about the principals' excitement about the challenge and/or empathy for students' developmental difficulties. For example, principals said:

> You need a different kind of parameter for the middle school so that you make sure it turns out right for them. Great opportunity to present them with successes. I just think there is just a lot of energy and a lot of willingness and readiness to learn. (09BF-50/05-6/8S80)

> For me personally, I think that the kids are most challenging at this age... they're very impulsive; they're very self-centered, and they can be cruel to each other and to adults at times, and I think it's a neat age to work with and try to get them to understand what they're doing, how they're doing it, and look at themselves and see if they can do it a better way. (03WM-45/13-7/8R25)

> In our urban school, we do a lot of proactive work through our curriculum.... Plus we have a lot of intervention work through the team. Mental health issues, drug and alcohol issues.... So you have to take the lay of the land and figure out "are we meeting the needs of the kids?" and sort of mold your kids in a certain direction. (04BM-49/09-6/8U50)

> You can fully appreciate what the kids are going through and just help them. You know, be emphathetic, not judgmental; don't take things personally. You're there to help them grow. (13WM-62/28-6/8S60)

Virtually without exception, the respondents were future oriented and expressed hopes, dreams, and goals for the future of their school. They recognized that change sometimes must be incremental, and they expressed patience and a willingness to let important changes come about over time. Interestingly, when these principals talked about missing components of middle level education (i.e., advisories, transition programs, interdisciplinary teaching) and/or less-than-ideal district support, they characterized what could be considered negatives as opportunities for improvement rather than obstacles to success. For example, one first-year principal in an urban school said,

> If you look at parent involvement as having PTO meetings and how many people show up to sell candy at a fund-raiser, then [our school] is horrendous ... but we have a great degree of communication back and forth with parents. And we, for the most part, get nothing but full cooperation and full compliance with parents in regard to school and trying to get their kids squared away and be successful in school. So, in that respect, I think we have fantastic parent involvement. (05WM-48/01-6/8U45)

They talked with enthusiasm of the principal's role as provider of encouragement and motivator of teachers and students. When asked what makes leadership at the middle level distinctive, respondents cited the belief that they had made a difference for the school, students, and teachers. Many expressed their belief that a healthy sense of humor was a necessary ingredient in successful middle level leadership. In addition, their frequent choice of plural pronouns reflected a positive sense of connectedness with others in the school. Responses to questions were peppered with phrases such as "we decided," "our culture is," and "we are prepared to."

These principals were complimentary and supportive of their teaching staffs. As one principal said, "Good things are happening in the classroom" (09BF-50/05-6/880). Another principal (14WM-56/06-6/9S90), in explaining that "our teachers care about the kids," listed more than a dozen activities throughout the school year designed to heighten collegiality and foster positive relationships. Others demonstrated similar support by saying:

> ...maybe comfort teachers in knowing that the things they are doing aren't necessarily wrong but if you can apply them a little differently they can be effective. (12WM-41/05-7/9S75)

> If a teacher wants to come in and tell me what they think or what their concerns are, I'll take the time to listen to them. If I'm going down the hall and

somebody says, "I need to talk to you about this," I'll say, "do you have the time right now?" and we'll do it right there. (15WM-51/03-7/9S60)

There's a real human side to change, too. You have to be really respectful of the culture and the traditions. So, it's a balance of all that. I think the key to change is understanding the culture and working to create the culture that you want. (11WF-35/04-6/8S50)

In short, this group of principals shared a high degree of personal optimism. One individual actually espoused optimism as a personal leadership philosophy. "You've got to surround kids with optimism. It's the only way. Any person learns best when they are surrounded with optimism" (07WM-46/05-7/8S60). By far, the majority of these principals worked to generate optimism in others through celebrations and other forms of appreciation.

Teacher Orientation

Almost every principal in this study was oriented toward hiring student-centered teachers who are interested in both the young adolescents and the content areas they teach. Among the essential elements of a middle school, *This We Believe* (1995), the official position paper of the National Middle School Association, includes educators knowledgeable and committed to young adolescents and a curriculum based on the needs of young adolescents as two of the ten fundamentals of middle schools. The survey used in this study asked the principals to list university courses important for middle school teachers. Their top three responses were teaching methods for the middle school (54%), psychology of the middle level student (49%), and developmentally appropriate curriculum (42%). Whether based on research findings or on their tacit knowledge, principals clearly indicated a need for middle level teachers to understand the students they taught as well as to understand how to best approach curriculum in the middle level classroom.

The NASSP Middle Level Council, which published *An Agenda for Excellence* (1989), calls for student development, curriculum for middle level students, appropriate learning and instruction, client centeredness, and specifically trained teachers. In their own words, principals noted many of the tenets of the *Agenda*. For example, one principal responded that he

appreciates teachers who provide the best practices, allow kids to get up, to think, to use higher order thinking skills, to get away from rote memory activities, to get their hands dirty and to create an environment where youngsters can really flourish. (13WM-62/28-6/8S60)

These are the teachers who meet the students' needs and work well with young adolescent learners. Another principal similarly listed the characteristics important for middle school teachers as "high energy, to be able to sell the subject, to make it relevant, and to have a clear interest in youngsters" (16WM-54/20-6/9S55).

This We Believe (1995) additionally calls for cooperative planning among a team of middle level teachers. The common planning time allows teachers to plan interdisciplinary units and to discuss the ways to best meet the needs of the students. Principals addressed this issue by indicating that their schools were structured so teachers were able to meet every day with a common planning time. Listen to what they had to say:

> A common group of teachers with a common group of students is critical. Without that what you have is a mini-model of a high school. (01WM-50/17-6/8S80)

> They (teachers) have double planning. We arranged the schedule so the guidance counselors meet with them (the teachers) once a week. The administrators meet with the teams once a week, so we can talk about the kids and the curriculum. (09BF-50/05-6/8S80)

> That gives them the facility, the opportunity, for lots of conversation about what is happening in their classrooms. (08BF-47/01-6/8S60)

Another element of a good middle school according to *This We Believe* (1995) is advisement and counseling programs for young adolescents. Whether they were familiar with the research or had observed practices that work, principals commented on the need for advisory and counseling opportunities. A fairly new principal concluded, "They need to be caring, to be understanding, and empathetic; they need to have the skills to instruct in a classroom setting that makes the best use of students of this age group and their personality types" (12WM-41/05-7/9S75). Principals were concerned about their interactions with teachers and stressed the need to hire what they called "good," student-centered teachers.

> A good teacher—caring nurturing person—loves kids. I feel that is as important as content. If there's a question, always err on the side that it's the adult's responsibility, and when a kid is ready to accept, you'll know and they'll know. You won't have to dictate it to them, and you'll that they take it naturally. (07WM-46/05-7/8S60)

> You (the principal) have to be attuned to the needs of the students and the teachers because the teachers need to know how to address the middle school students. Teachers have to have knowledge of content, high vitality, be reflective, and reach beyond. They have high expectations for the kids.

> They're willing to reach beyond by constantly learning more so that they can better affect learning in the classroom. They're open to change. (17WF-44/03-6/8U55)

> We look at responses in their essays for their belief in a seamless curriculum for the kids, and the integration of subject matter, obviously that thematic approach. We are heterogeneously grouped; they have to address all the learners' needs in this setting. I am looking for people that have a work ethic for kids. I guess very child-centered is important. That's why we're here. (11WF-35/04-6/8S50)

> ...having a young human being in front of them ... that's the whole piece there. They understand what the kid is going through, especially in middle school terms of what they're going through in their growth and maturation right now. (15W-51/03-7/9S60)

Other principals discussed the need for caring teachers committed to young adolescents. "Caring; knowledge of their subject, and I'd love a teacher who'd say, 'kids are always first in my class'" (15WM-51/03-7/9S60). Another principal viewed successful teachers as, "Well, number one is they have to have a child-centered orientation. They have to care about kids. There's got be a real caring concern" (14WM-56/06-6/9S90). Other principals made very poignant comments regarding the teachers they saw as best suited for middle level learners. They used words like flexibility, creativity, sense of humor and a love of children to describe strong middle level teachers. Similarly, others stressed what they saw as important:

> I'd say the number one quality is to identify the individual differences of the kids, be able to modify your program to meet those individual needs. At the middle level you deal with extremes, and you need to adjust, accommodate, and accept those things. (05WM-48/01-6/8U45)

> Concern for students as people, concern for academic progress, openness to changing the plan. If it is not working and being able to take a risk to do something different with that kid, willingness to make accommodations and adaptations, to get out of the box so we're not teaching the same old way, and to really connect kids with the learning. (06WF-48/03-6/8U65)

> In addition, somebody who is organized, somebody who has strong subject skills, and I think somebody who really understands middle level. That is somebody who has a lot of patience. Somebody who can laugh at themselves as well at the children. Somebody who can really know when to set limits and hold to those limits (fair limits), and by the way, I think this is true for an administrator, too. (02WF-54/12-5/8R35)

> I look for the individual to have some type of magnetic personality, that's going to be able to ... that you can sense is going to bring some excitement to the kids and the classroom. I look for the sparkle in their eyes. You look for some ability to communicate both orally and verbally in terms of writing. Now you look for the ability to think with some creative intelligence. (10WM-58/18-7/8S60)

Overall, the principals in this study focused on teachers and their abilities to positively educate the "whole" student, not just the academic side. Principals stressed the need for middle level teachers to be strong in content areas and in the context of teaching the young adolescent. According to these principals, teachers with a commitment to excellence and a positive attitude toward young adolescents were the best teachers for middle schools.

Desire to Involve Parents and Community

The needs for enhanced and meaningful parental involvement and community connection seems to be among the least controversial areas in public education. One challenge facing middle schools is the decreasing parent involvement as students progress from the elementary grades to the middle grades (Epstein, 1992).

Middle level administrators appear to be in universal agreement that the involved parent leads to a more successful school-home relationship. Parent involvement increases clarity in communication and allows a first-hand exposure to the middle school culture. Middle level principals report that students of involved parents show evidence in varying ways of the value behind and beyond the connection:

> So when you bring the parents in, there is first of all ... you break down the miscommunication. And secondary, they get to see and experience what the school is all about and ... we have nothing to hide. (05 WM-48/01-6/8 U45)

> Our parents who are here on the formal and informal levels are, almost without exception, the parents of children who are in the top ten, the top twenty, or top thirty of our classes. (06 WF-48/03-6/8 U65)

> The parent who's involved in their child's education and who knows what's going on, that child generally will be doing better in school ... Their kids generally have a better connection to school..., are they always better in achievement? Not necessarily. But I think the parent who knows what is going on has a better understanding when they ... ask questions. (15WM-51/03-7/9 S60)

As the student enters early adolescence, the parent increasingly loses touch with the school, hence with their education. The solution seems to lie in giving new and creative definitions to school and community involvement. Reaching beyond the traditional PTO, school newsletter, open house, and parent conferences we find such techniques as a "help" solicitation form to be completed by parents; "if you want to help us out, here are the things you can do ... we get about three or four hundred of these back ... it gives us a database and that's how we get parents involved" (15WM-51/03-7/9 S60) and one that builds upon diversity for involvement, "...our team ... geography program ... built on multi-cultural ... ten or twelve parents a day ... with different things ... to share from their culture" (O6WF-48/03-6/8 U65).

A successful strategy mentioned in numerous surveys was to invite and include parents in the middle school teams:

> ...let parents know we're a team here ... it's not us and them. This is a community process, a community building. They are part of the team ... if your child is in the sixth grade, you can sit in a sixth grade level meeting and hear what's going on. (13WM-62/28-6/8 S60)

Even when a school endorses the notion of a PTO or a newsletter, the middle school program that speaks to parents can enhance broader participation:

> We got away from just having a business meeting ... started to theme ... had a guest speaker come in and talk about a subject specific to middle level needs, and that attracted parents. (07WM-46/05-7/8 S60)

While the need for parent and community involvement remains indisputable, the solution calls for new and creative solutions. Parents will stand for no less than meaningful involvement. Principals are increasingly sensitive to the value of parent involvement; "I suspect if we don't have broad family support, or (in turn) broad student accountability to their families, we lose" (10WM-58/18-7/8 S60).

Tolerance for Ambiguity and Uncertainty

Literature on leadership suggests that effective middle level principals exhibit a high tolerance for ambiguity and uncertainty (Goodman & Associates, 1986; Neufeld, 1997; Wheatley, 1992). Almost without exception the middle level principals interviewed for this study supported this finding-a high tolerance for ambiguity and uncertainty when working to effect change, addressing conflicting needs, and/or responding to conflicting priorities.

Veteran principals talked about comfort with uncertainty as a strategy for bringing about change. Other self-described risk-takers try to encourage teachers to take the power that is offered to them and work to provide a role model by taking chances with their supervisors. They believe that this helps teachers become more willing to take chances and build a risk-taking mentality. Several principals mentioned that in order to encourage teachers to engage in decision making, administrators must be willing to live with the results of their deliberations.

> You listen; you meet as a group, and then you make a decision and you take a risk as the principal. You implement, and if it doesn't work, you have to take it back to be willing to stand by your mistake and make the necessary changes. (02WF-54/12-5/8R35)

> ...trying to show teachers that I was willing to hang myself out there and make a commitment to things that had to get done. (07WM-6/05-7/8S60)

> We invite everyone into the conversations, and I'm willing to live with what that group or committee decides. (12WM-41/05-7/9S75)

The participants in this study had a high degree of agreement when describing flexibility as a quality of a middle level principal in the 21st century. "I think they have to be flexible. Flexibility is the name of the game ... It takes trying something different every day ... Anything can happen, any day, that makes you have to throw those plans to the wind and try something different" (09BF-50/05-6/8S80).

Others explained that flexibility extends to a variety of areas:

> It would help that people would see that the ability to be very flexible and to have some spontaneity in the school is a wonderful thing for the students. (02WF-54/12-5/8R35)

> You have to be flexible; you [as principal] have to have a schedule that provides an opportunity for the teachers to be flexible and do what they feel needs to be done at the time ... like a juggler; you have to juggle your activities and provide a nice balanced program for your youngsters. (14WM-56/06-6/9S90)

In addition, several participants mentioned the need to accept different ideas and acknowledge different (and sometimes conflicting) needs of student, parents, teachers, and/or governing boards. A third-year principal also shared the juggling metaphor:

> You juggle a lot of balls when you're an administrator. First of all, I think you have the trouble of finding out who your public really is. Is it the kid? Is it the parent? Is it the teacher? Is it the superintendent or the school board? You're trying to satisfy four or five different publics. You have to learn the balances; it's a balancing act. (15WM-51/03-7/9S60)

To Assemble, Develop, and Maintain a Dedicated Staff

What characterizes an effective middle school teacher? There seems to be little substantive research available related to characteristics of effective middle level educators. The paucity of teachers professionally prepared specifically for middle school is compounded by the reality that middle school emphasized teacher preparation programs and advanced degree programs for leadership are few (NMSA, 1997). Although there is apparent agreement as to the need for content-strengthened preparation programs for middle school teachers, principals still appear quite divided as to the desirability of secondary/content prepared candidates in contrast to those prepared as elementary teachers. When an administrator is fortunate enough to have involvement at the initial stages of assembling and staffing a quality middle school, it is important to identify their focus beyond the generalized agreement of content strength within the preparation of the candidate?

Personal qualities take a prominent role when principals identify a strong candidate among choices for a middle school staff. As noted by two principals:

> ...I look for the individual to have some type of magnetic personality ... that you sense is going to bring some excitement to the kids and the classroom ... I look for that sparkle ... sometimes it's the quite kind of motivation. (11WF-35/04-6/8 S50)

> High energy ... ability to sell the subject ... make it relevant ... you're in the classroom ... hallways ... at their events ... you understand that one day ... they may love you and they may dislike you the next for no apparent reason ... even though they (the prospective middle school teacher) may know the subject you hire them more on their personality as much as their subject ... Personality characteristic is very, very important for a middle school teacher. (16WM-54/20-6/9 S55)

Upon exploring the challenges of both developing and maintaining a dedicated staff we find a variety, but yet recurring, number of recommendations stated by principals. The organization that nurtures teacher empowerment and the teaming concept are approaches frequently mentioned:

> Team organization lends itself ... to empowerment because they're kind of self-led. So a team of four (teachers) function(s) ... they take care of their discipline ... of their kids ... decisions for their team ... so right there you have a different mind set. (11WF-35/04-6/8 555)

Teacher empowerment appears to take root in gradual steps that set the stage for even more professional growth:

> ...empower teachers as much as possible ... We have a school improvement planning groups now. Every teacher is on it ... get them to see that they do have the power to change their class, team, school, then go from there ... I don't think I've said "no" to a teacher (generated) project this year. (06WF-48/03-6/8U65)

The value of professional development, in various formats, is consistently endorsed by principals—so long as the focus is upon meaningful application and input by those involved:

> I think in-services are absolutely critical ... if it's a one shot deal, and there's no other follow-up, then it's going to be lost ... seek opportunities for all teachers to go out and experience as much as they can ... it's complicated we need time to interact around progress. When teachers see other teacher experiencing success in the same type of demographic arena, that is the best motivation for them to pursue it. ... I think a lot of the best professional development is for, to give teachers time to work together ... be able to think about what they are doing. (15WM-51/03-7/9S60)

Open communication and witnessing a principal as a team member goes far in establishing a bond of trust in the middle school environment. A skilled middle level leader has in balance the quantifiable preparation for success in combination with security in making judgement calls and initiative reactions.

MIDDLE LEVEL LEADERSHIP FOR THE 21ST CENTURY: THE WHEN, WHERE AND HOW OF PRINCIPAL PREPARATION

In addition to the essential skills necessary for leadership are the unanswered questions of "when, where, and how" these middle level leaders acquire the positive outlook, teacher orientation, community involvement, high tolerance for ambiguity, and inspiring dedication necessary in order to lead today's middle schools. The final section of this analysis documents what our sample of middle level principals said regarding their administration preparation programs and the role of professional organizations in support of their development as school administrators.

Educational Administration Preparation Programs

General Leadership Preparation

The purpose of most educational administration programs is to produce school leaders with the knowledge, skills, and commitment to assure student success while increasing the level of academic expectations and performance for all students. But the efficacy of graduate preparation in educational administration is relatively unstudied. In 1997 Haller, Brent, and McNamara noted that "overall, our reading of the limited literature on this subject suggests that there is little evidence that graduate training increases the effectiveness of school managers" (p. 224).

According to the remarks of the interviewees for this study, formal preparation did not influence their acquisition of essential skills. Even though two-thirds of the principals surveyed received their graduate training in educational administration, many described their programs as inadequate, impractical, and unrealistic. Several commented about the lack of reflective, personal preparation.

> Again, I don't think a whole lot of time or effort was spent on the personal side of understanding what's involved in being a principal and dealing with people. It was a lot of theory and not a whole lot of practical application. (03WM-45/13-7/8R25)

> Again, I'm not certain about certification. I don't know how much you really learn from courses, you'll forgive me ... I have two masters degrees in education, one's in curriculum and instruction and one is in instructional leadership, and I'm not really certain how much one learns from being in the classroom, reading all the research. (08BF-47/01-6/8S60)

> I think people need to get out and need the opportunity to see what the job's about, maybe a little more job shadowing ... Sit and talk about what I do and observe what I do in this building. When I was in training there wasn't any of that ... they need to get in and see what the job's all about. (15WM-51/03-7/9S60)

According to Scales (1992), preparation that enables prospective middle level educators to "understand early adolescent development but not to be responsive to it" (p. 65) is futile. Responsible leaders therefore need to engage in the process of self-reflection and discernment, to assess their strengths and weaknesses, to examine their experiences, and to determine if they are in the right place. They need to construct and/or reconstruct core ideas about their role and, therefore, how they should spend their time, set their priorities, seek new knowledge and skill, and situate themselves with respect to teachers and others in the educational community.

In their desire to become facilitators of students' learning, today's middle level principals need to rethink their conceptions of content, pedagogy, and assessment. As a result, Zehm (1999) believes that there is a critical need for education programs to emphasize the "personal-professional esteem and understanding of self necessary ... to build effective relationships with students, parents, and teachers" (p. 49). Hamachek (1999) agrees and speaks about helping educators to deepen their self-awareness and become effective in all phases of their work, "We must offer them opportunity, time, and guidance in the direction of becoming mentally healthy, self-aware persons" (pp. 217–218).

Specific Middle Level Preparation

Because practicing principals perceived a deficiency in their overall leadership training, we explored their feelings about the added dimension of working in a middle school. After all, encountering elements such as teaming, flexible block scheduling, advisories and integrated curricula adds to the uniqueness of the culture. Assuming that the mission of the middle school is to meet the developmental needs of young adolescents who are undergoing rapid and complex changes, it seems important that educators receive specific preparation in how to interact with this distinctive age. Presently, most university programs in educational leadership prepare prospective school leaders together, making no distinction between levels—elementary, middle, or secondary. The principals interviewed for this study would like to see that changed. They view middle level education as distinctive. "It pretty much is a whole different animal" (04BM-49/09-6/8U50). Despite their varied backgrounds, many felt similarly and echoed the following comment:

> Well, first of all, they (middle level principals) have to have their own program. Right now you can be a middle level principal with an elementary certificate or a secondary principal certificate and so especially tailored administrative training at the college/university level should be the number one priority. (01WM-50/17-6/8S80)

The results from a national survey conducted by DeMedio and Mazur-Stewart (1990) regarding educators' attitudes toward middle level certification "support the belief that those preparing to teach middle grade students need special middle grade preparation and appropriate middle grade certification" (p.70). While the middle level principals interviewed were not able to reach a consensus regarding this notion of certification/endorsement for administrators, they were able to voice a common concern surrounding their lack of practical middle level preparation.

The reform literature advocates that effective middle level principals support and promote the establishment of structures that address the developmental needs of young adolescents, such as advisory programs, exploratories, teaming of teachers, transition programs, interdisciplinary teaching/thematic units, and flexible/block scheduling. Although almost 80% of the principals polled are currently implementing at least five of the six structures mentioned, only 46% have had *some* training in *some* of the areas. The unfortunate reality, as one respondent so bluntly stated, is "you kind of learn by practice at this level" (05WM-48/01-6/8U45). Others concurred:

> Certainly the training I got did not really address or get into middle school issues at all. (04BM-49/09-6/8U50)

> The hardest thing I learned on the job was that I needed to learn more. I knew that when I got here and started to work with middle school kids that if I was going to be a success at all this, I needed to learn what the kids were all about, and it focused my learning better. I just needed to know what middle school kids were all about, and what techniques worked with them. So I began to focus my learning on that area. (07WM-46/05-7/8S60)

> But there's no specific training for the middle school principal. And a lot of it is on the job experience. So, therefore, I think if they had middle level certification with the appropriate courses and background, I think they (principals) would be stronger for this particular group of youngsters. (13WM-62/28-6/8S60)

> I don't know that being an administrator *per se* is good enough training to jump into middle school. There really needs to be pre-curricular activities or courses to let you understand the things you learn on the job. I think it's very difficult to learn unless you're immersed in it. So in some way you must see the model in action. I think to read a book or to take a course in it and not be involved in it is very difficult. (14WM-51/03-7/9S60)

Results of this study indicate that middle level principals are seeking better preparation and professional development specifically geared to effectively administering a middle school. They are requesting specific preparation dedicated to the concept of structuring educational programs to meet the unique developmental needs of early adolescents. They are searching for opportunities to learn about themselves and their particular leadership styles. In so doing, they offer two major pre-service suggestions for institutions of higher education: (1) train middle level leaders together in a supportive cohort style, and (2) provide real, meaningful middle school internships for prospective administrators and professors alike. Advocating for a cohort model, one principal commented, "I'd like to see middle level principals trained together ... to be able to relate the problems and look at what have been solutions in other schools, and one of the pieces that would be helpful for me would be to meet with principals in a similar sized district" (02WF-54/12-5/8R35). On the subject of internships, two principals noted:

> I think they should have to do an intern period ... in a middle school. I really think that you can't learn this job from a book, you have to be in the job, and nobody really understands that until they've spent some time seeing the job. (02WF-54/12-5/8R35)

> I think people need to get out and need the opportunity to see what the job's about, maybe a little more job shadowing ... spend time ... sit and talk ... observe. When I was in training there wasn't any of that. They need to have the time to observe what's going on in a school, to get a feel of what that principal does. Um, maybe have some kind of a program where the pre-service people can ask principals questions ... Uh, but they need to get in and see what the job's all about. (15WM-51/03-7/9S60)

Even fairly new principals see these two pre-service suggestions as important in that "many of the things needed to be effective cannot be taught in any course ... they're not something that anybody can teach you in an administrative course because every school is unique" (06WF-48/03-6/8U65). Then, once they are working as principals, the participants suggest that professional associations take a more active role in providing valuable professional growth opportunities.

Professional Organizational Involvement

Having addressed the "when, where, and how" dilemmas for future middle level principals, the questions regarding practicing administrators remain. Principals once trained to be managers are now expected to be leaders. Despite these role changes, many school districts and professional organizations provide little opportunity for principals to learn what they need to know to implement reform at the school and classroom level. As Neufeld (1997) points out, the work of school leaders is becoming "more ambitious and more ambiguous. What counts as good curriculum, pedagogy, and assessment is distinctly different than what counted as good 10 years ago" (p. 490). A principal with 12 years administrative experience verifies that "this job has changed tremendously in the last 15 to 20 years" (02WF-54/12-5/8R35). This is important, especially because 79% of the principals who participated in this research (not unlike their colleagues) were professionally prepared in the 1970s and/or 1980s. Since that time, roles and relationships between teachers and principals and between schools and central offices have changed tremendously with respect to power and authority (Gainey, 1994; Murphy, 1994; Smylie & Brownlee-Conyers, 1992).

Administrators want to understand leadership as an idea and as a set of practices, a process to develop and accomplish the tasks. Personal and professional updates are needed. Organizations and associations need to increase the frequency and accuracy of their training for administrators presently serving in middle schools. While 70% of the principals surveyed belong to NASSP and 60% to ASCD, only 37% are members of NMSA, the leading national organization for middle level educators. There seems to be a disconnect between principals and the organizations focused specifically to the middle level. Participants report that:

> And you have a wide range of students from "A to Z" with different abilities. And dealing with that. That's a difficult nut to crack. And you combine that with the fact that we're in an urban setting. A lot of schools that you go to when you're at the middle school conferences, the presenters, the ideal middle schools ... that's suburbia. That's the wealthy part of the cities, or that's suburbia. It's not even rural for the most part. ... they do not have the wide range of kids to deal with. (04BM-49/09-6/8U50)

> Again, we have been through lots of different stages here. The truth is that there is really nothing new in all of this. We happened to attend the National Middle School Conference in Colorado, and they were celebrating the 30th anniversary of middle school reform. It was interesting, because they were revisiting everything that we already do. And for me, it was a confirmation for what I have internalized in my professional life. It was reaffirming, but also, not disturbing—kind of interesting how we strayed away, and now we need to come back. (08BF-47/01-6/8S60)

In the same breath, many of the participants recognize the importance of the conferences, presentations, and association offerings and testify to this fact. They speak about needing further knowledge and skill in the meaning and practice of leadership, in creating a beneficial school culture, in understanding the newly proposed approaches to teaching and learning, and in assessing progress toward school improvement. They want to increase their understanding of themselves and their leadership styles.

They look to their professional organizations to help them develop a greater sense of efficacy, a sense that they are capable of learning, improving, and gaining insights. They would like to see national, regional and state middle level associations consider collaborative efforts in establishing approved programs that would meet administrative standards while simultaneously addressing relevant and practical learning opportunities.

> What I started to do as an administrator was I focused my in-service training on leadership. I took a lot of in-service training on leadership, and then almost everything I did was focused on middle school. Anything that was sponsored by the National Middle School Association, I attended. Anything sponsored by ASCD, specific to middle level education ... I bugged the living daylights out of the *Turning Points* people. They were a tremendous guide along the way. (07WM-46/05-7/8S60)

> Number one, I think the districts who do not let the principals out, neither one year or two years to attend National conferences, um, are not staying current. They're doing their principals a major disservice. I think conferences are very, very important. Um, certainly school districts should allow that to happen. (13WM-62/28-6/8S60)

> Um, I think, um, there should be a requirement to go to conferences. Like the state level middle school conference. And they should look at best practices and relate them to the models we use in our buildings. (14WM-56/06-6/9S90)

CONCLUDING DISCUSSION

If, indeed, educational excellence is inextricably linked with effective school leadership, there is much to be gained from studying the experiences of school leaders. More specifically, given the virtual absence of research specific to middle school leaders, this study and others like it provide us with the opportunity to learn from individuals as they live out their professional lives in schools. The administrators in this study shared with us their views, their hopes, and their frustrations; we believe that we learned much from them. Table 3 presents what we discovered in comparison to Bauck's (1987) reanalysis of the NASSP data on middle level principals.

Table 3. Principal's Identified Skills and Knowledge Necessary for Success: 1987 Compared to 2000

Variables Related to Success	*Bauck (1987)*	*Anfara et al. (2000)*
1. Formal education has no bearing on principal effectiveness	X	X
2. Participation in professional organizations unrelated to effectiveness	X	X

Table 3. Principal's Identified Skills and Knowledge Necessary for Success: 1987 Compared to 2000 (Cont.)

Variables Related to Success	*Bauck (1987)*	*Anfara et al. (2000)*
3. Positive outlook about their work: High job satisfaction	X	X
4. Teacher oriented	X	X
5. Encourage parent/community involvement	X	X
6. Tenure (years in principalship) directly related to effectiveness	X	
7. Uses time efficiently	X	
8. Ability to work with people and respond to multiple expectations	X	
9. Lead schools having larger enrollments located in larger communities with higher per pupil expenditures	X	
10. A variety of course offerings in the middle school	X	
11. Tolerance for ambiguity and uncertainty		X
12. Ability to assemble a dedicated and capable staff		X

Interestingly, participants in the current study exhibited a tolerance for ambiguity and uncertainty that was not noted in the meta-analysis conducted by Bauck (1987). Perhaps never before has the role of the principal been so ambiguous; early principal preparation programs prepared individuals to be THE leader in the school—to be decision-makers, to be "in charge" of their schools. For at least fifteen years, the teacher education literature has been replete with calls for teacher empowerment, site-based decision-making, and shared leadership. Perhaps the changing nature of teaching and teachers has influenced the nature of the effective principal; this certainly bears further study.

In addition, middle school reform calls for schools where administrators and teachers work as colleagues to create governance structures that allow them to share decision-making and provide opportunities for success to all middle level learners. As teachers have been encouraged to find their own voices, to exercise the authority that results from their knowledge of students, content, and pedagogy, have they challenged the authority of the principal? The principals in this study, working to assemble a dedicated and capable staff, expected to share responsibilities and successes with the teachers in their buildings. Future studies that address the ways in which principals and teachers negotiate and create processes for shared governance may prove helpful to principals and teachers engaged in the transformation called for in *Turning Points* and other school reform documents.

Despite their sense that they were not sufficiently nor effectively prepared for the complexities of their roles as middle level principals, the participants in this study seemed to be creating climates that allowed students and teachers to be successful. They were implementing practices called for in various middle level reform documents, and they were doing so with enthusiasm for the nature of their work and for the relationships they developed with teachers and students. They were, in fact, reaching out to parents and the community to enhance support for students, teachers, and school programs. It seems likely that systematic study of effective middle level principals could provide information that would be helpful in leadership preparation. In fact, we could (perhaps even should) use their experiences and views in shaping curriculum for educational leadership and principal preparation.

Clearly, advocates of middle level education are striving for a more compatible pairing and coordination of the professional preparation needs of their administrators and the organizations designed to support them. "If middle schools truly do address the needs of early adolescents, then our administrators have to be trained to deal with this age group ... to understand what those needs are and to tailor curriculum and instruction to their needs" (01WM-50/17-6/8S80). Principals cannot be expected to mold middle level education principles into meaningful programs and experiences without both the theoretically-based knowledge and the practical, performance-based skills deemed necessary to do so. Enhancing the social, emotional, physical, and educational growth of young adolescents while ensuring students a smooth transition from elementary school to high school requires distinctive preparation. The administrators interviewed during this study recognized this. "There need to be some areas of study that address the specific needs of a middle school ... there have to be areas where the uniqueness of a middle school is brought up and studied and discussed" (05WM-48/01-6/8U45).

Given this realization, educational administration preparation programs in general need to acknowledge the immense shift in the principal's role in recent years. Issues have become more multifaceted, and situations have become more complex. Leaders now need to be visionaries, constructivists, facilitators, participatory instructors, and advocates, among a host of other qualities not commonly described in traditional textbooks or readily taught in graduate courses. Practical, performance-based skills are vital. Reflective, self-analysis is imperative.

Principals who are serious about reforming their middle schools face a daunting task. They need to reconstruct core ideas about their role, and, therefore, how they spend their time, set their priorities, seek new knowledge and skills, and situate themselves with respect to teachers and others in the educational community. In many respects, the demands on principals are similar to those on teachers who are attempting to become facilitators of students' learning and are rethinking their conceptions of content, pedagogy, and assessment. The process is complicated, takes time, and requires models of good practice. With the widespread and serious efforts given to revising programs in educational administration there needs to be a recognition of the unique qualities of middle schools (see Table 4).

Table 4. The Evolution of Middle Level Principal Preparation Programs

Generalized Components of Current Preparation Programs 20th Century (From)	*Recommended Practices to Prepare Middle Level Leadership For The 21st Century (To)*
Generally no distinction among preparation for elementary, middle level and secondary principalship	Preparation programs with specific courses focused on the middle level and its uniqueness; extended middle level internships/ field experiences
Early adolescence as a developmental period viewed as not important to the development of programs, curriculum, or instruction	"Developmental appropriateness" used as a template in the development of all components and functioning of a middle school
Recognizes content as a need and curriculum as "what is"	Understands and applies the components of flexible/block scheduling, integrated curriculum, advisory programs, small learning communities, team teaching, etc.; Aware of the need to address both cognitive and affective domains of the learner
Uncoupling of administration from teaching and learning	Reconnecting administration to teaching and learning
Pre-service principals "trained" to be aware of trends in education and to respond to needs	Establishes the principal as a life-long learner; emphasizes the central role that inservices and professional organizations provide; emphasizes the importance of the principal as "risk-taker"
Trained to manage and efficiently administer a school	Prepares principal to be collaborative in one's approach to leading; to deal with ambiguity and uncertainty
Maintenance of organizational infrastructure	Development of human resources
Excellence is a "state of being"	Excellence is a "state of becoming"

The middle level principals participating in this study advocate for administrative preparation and personal/professional development that is thorough, challenging, and meaningful. They propose supportive middle level cohort structures and apprentice-like internships that are instructive, guided, and developmental. They are requesting numerous opportunities to delve deeply, to take risks, to explore new skills, to review impact, and to discuss possible refinements. Middle level principals are challenging their graduate preparation programs and professional organizations to provide such experiences and exposure that will support their quest to be viable, lifelong learners cognizant of their own thoughts, feelings and actions. In the end, they are grateful for the chance and the process to "seek interpretations and give voice to what they know [and still need to know] by virtue of their experience, combined with close and disciplined examination of their practice" (Freeman, 1996, p. 107).

APPENDIX A
INTERVIEWEES' IDENTIFICATION KEY

(8 character code used to identify the source of verbatim quotes)

1st character = PARTICIPANT'S NUMBER
Ranges from 01 to 17 total participants
2nd character = RACE W = White B = Black H = Hispanic A = Asian
3rd character = GENDER M = Male F = Female
4th character = AGE Ranges from 35 to 65 years old
5th character = ADMINISTRATIVE EXPERIENCE
Ranges from 01 to 30 years experience
6th character = GRADE LEVELS WITHIN THE MIDDLE SCHOOL
5 = Fifth 6 = Sixth 7 = Seventh 8 = Eighth 9 = Ninth
7th character = LOCATION OF SCHOOL
U = Urban S = Suburban R = Rural
8th character = NUMBER OF TEACHERS IN THE MIDDLE SCHOOL
Ranges from 20 to 100 teachers

(e.g., 07WM-46/05-7/8S60 = The seventh participant is a white male, 46 years of age with five years administrative experience. His middle school consists of seventh and eighth graders, it is located in the suburbs, and he has sixty teachers working for him.)

REFERENCES

Barth, R. (1985). The principalship. *Educational Leadership, 59*(3), 92–94.
Bauck, J. (1987). Characteristics of the effective middle school principal. *NASSP Bulletin, 71*(500), 90–92.

Carnegie Task Force on Education of Young Adolescents. (1989). *Turning points: Preparing American youth for the 21st century.* Washington, DC: Carnegie Council on Adolescent Development.

Clark, S., & Clark, D. (1994). *Restructuring the middle level school: Implications for school leaders.* Albany: State University of New York Press.

Crawford, J. (1998). Changes in administrative licensure: 1991–1996. *UCEA Review, 39*(3), 8–10.

Creswell, J. (1994). *Research design: Qualitative & quantitative approaches.* Thousand Oaks, CA: Sage.

DeMedio, D., & Mazur-Stewart, M. (1990). Attitudes toward middle grade certification: A national survey. *NASSP Bulletin, 4,* 64–70.

Eichhorn, D. (1966). *The middle school.* New York: The Center for Applied Research in Education, Inc.

Epstein, J. (1992). *School and family partnerships.* Center on Families, Communities, Schools and Children_s Learning. Baltimore, MD: Johns Hopkins University.

Freeman, D. (1996). Redefining the relationship between research and what teachers know. In K. Bailey & D. Numan (Eds.), *Voices from the language classroom: Qualitative research in second language education* (pp.102–117). New York: Cambridge University Press.

Gainey, D. (1994). The American high school and change: An unsettling process. *NASSP Bulletin, 78* (560), 26–35.

George, P. (1990). From junior high to middle school—principals' perspectives. *NASSPBulletin, 74,* 86–94.

George, P., & Grebing, W. (1992). Seven essential skills of middle level leadership. *Schools in the Middle, 1*(4), 3–11.

Goodman, P., & Associates. (1986). *Designing effective work groups.* San Francisco: Jossey-Bass.

Haller, E., Brent, B., & McNamara, J. (1997). Does graduate training in educational administration improve America_s schools? *Phi Delta Kappan, 79*(3), 222–227.

Hamachek, D. (1999). Effective teachers: What they do, how they do it, and the importance of self-knowledge. In R. Lipka & T. Brinthaupt (Eds.), *The role of self in teacher development* (pp. 189–224). Albany: State University of New York Press.

Hipp, K. (1997). The impact of principals in sustaining middle school change. *Middle School Journal, 28*(2), 42–45.

Keefe, J., Clark, D., Nickerson, N., & Valentine, J. (1983). *The middle level principalship: Volume II: The effective middle level principal.* Reston, VA: National Association of Secondary School Principals.

Kilcrease, A. (1995, November 8–10). *Principals' perceptions of the functions and characteristics of middle schools in Mississippi.* Paper presented at the Annual Meeting of the Mid-South Educational Research Association, Biloxi, MS.

Lightfoot, S. (1983). *The good high school: Portraits of character and culture.* New York: Basic Books.

Lincoln, Y., & Guba, E.(1985). *Naturalistic inquiry.* Beverly Hills, CA: Sage.

Merriam, S. (1988). *Case study research in education: A qualitative approach.* San Francisco: Jossey-Bass.

Montgomery, J. (1995). From K-3 to junior high: A principal_s challenge. *Principal, 74,* 51–53.

Murphy, J. (1994). Redefining the principalship in restructuring schools. *NASSP Bulletin, 78*(560), 94–99.

National Association of Elementary School Principals. (1997). *Elementary & middle school proficiencies for principals* (3rd edition). Alexandria, VA: Author.

National Middle School Association. (1995). *This we believe.* Columbus, OH: Author.

National Middle School Association. (1997). *A 21st century research agenda: Issues, topics and questions guiding inquiry into middle level theory and practice.* Columbus, OH: Author.

Neufeld, B. (1997). Responding to the expressed needs of urban middle school principals. *Urban Education, 31*(5), 490–510.

Olson, L. (2000). Policy focus converges on leadership: Several major new efforts under way. *Education Week, 19*(17), 1, 16–17.

Pollio, H. (1991, Fall). *Hermes in the classroom: Interpreting what expert teachers say about teaching* (Teaching-Learning Issues, No. 69). Learning Research Center, University of Tennessee.

Rubinstein, R. (1990). A teacher's view of the quality principal. *Educational Horizons, 66,* 151–152.

Scales, P. (1992). *Windows of opportunity: Improving middle grades teacher preparation.* Carrboro, NC: Center for Early Adolescence.

Schmidt, D. (1988). Do squirrely kids need squirrely administrators? *Principal, 68,* 48–53.

Smylie, M., & Brownlee-Conyers, J. (1992). Teacher leaders and their principals. Exploring the development of new working relationships. *Educational Administration Quarterly, 28*(2), 150–184.

Tarter, J. (1995). Middle school climate, faculty trust, and effectiveness: A path analysis. *Journal of Research and Development in Education, 29,* 41–49.

Valentine, J., Clark, D., Nickerson, N., Jr., & Keefe, J. (1981). *The middle level principalship; A survey of middle level principals and programs* (Vol. I). Reston, VA: National Association of Secondary School Principals.

Valentine, J., Maher, M.C., Quinne, D., & Irvin, J. (1999). The changing roles of effective middle level principals. *Middle School Journal, 30*(5), 54–56.

Wasser, J., & Bresler, L. (1996). Working in the interpretive zone: Conceptualizing collaboration in qualitative research teams. *Educational Researcher, 25*(5), 5–15.

Weller, L. (1999). *Quality middle school leadership: Eleven central skill areas.* Lancaster, PA: Technomic Publishing Co., Inc.

Wheatley, M. (1992). *Leadership and the new science: Learning about organization from an orderly universe.* San Francisco: Berrett-Koehler Publications.

Whittaker, T., & Valentine, J. (1993). How do you rate? *Schools in the Middle, 3,* 21–24.

Williamson, R. (1991). Leadership at the middle level. In J. Capelluti & D. Stokes (Ed.). *Middle level education: Programs, policies, and practices* (pp.36–41). Alexandria, VA: National Association of Secondary School Principals.

Zehm, S. (1999). Deciding to teach: Implications of a self-development perspective. In R. Lipka & T. Brinthaupt (Eds.), *The role of self in teacher development* (pp. 36–52). Albany: State University of New York Press.

CHAPTER 9

POINT TO POINT

Turning Points to Turning Points 2000

Gayle A. Davis

ABSTRACT

This chapter describes, analyzes, and compares two landmark books on middle level grades education. *Turning Points: Preparing American Youth for the 21st Century* (1989) and *Turning Points 2000: Educating Adolescents in the 21st Century* (2000). These two reports, both funded by Carnegie Corporation of New York, represent bookends on the middle school movement of the 1990s. This investigation of the two reports highlights the evolution in thinking about how best to improve middle grades schools during the 10+ years between the publication of the first report and the second report.

INTRODUCTION

In June 1989, Carnegie Corporation of New York released a new report, based on two years of work by the Task Force on the Education of Young Adolescents. The report, *Turning Points: Preparing American Youth for the 21st Century,* made eight recommendations for improving schooling for young adolescents, children aged 10–15, and made history. With the help of its spokesperson, then-Governor of Arkansas William Jefferson Clinton, the report garnered national media attention and gave a much-needed boost to long-running efforts to focus energy on improving middle grades schools.

In November 2000, Carnegie Corporation released a long-anticipated follow-up report on middle grades schools, *Turning Points 2000: Educating Adolescents in the 21st Century. Turning Points 2000* outlines seven recommendations for improving middle grades schools, recommendations which build on the original *Turning Points* report but take it several steps further and deeper. Anthony W. Jackson and I coauthored *Turning Points 2000.* Jackson was a program officer at Carnegie Corporation for ten years and is currently a director of the Disney Learning Partnership. I served as national director of the Middle Grade School State Policy Initiative (MGSSPI), Carnegie's program of grants to states to stimulate changes in policy and practice in line with the 1989 report's recommendations, and have just joined the Middle School Program faculty at the University of Georgia.

This chapter describes the big ideas in *Turning Points* and *Turning Points 2000*, including:

- A brief overview of their respective recommendations.
- An analysis of the vision that unifies the two reports.
- An analysis of the organizational framework for school improvement implied by one and explained in the other.
- A detailed review of their respective recommendations, analyzing how some things changed from point A to point B and some things remained the same.

POINT TO POINT: THE RECOMMENDATIONS, THE VISION, AND THE SYSTEMIC NATURE OF THE DESIGN

Overview of the Eight *Turning Points* Recommendations, Circa 1989

In one of the most oft-quoted lines from the report, *Turning Points* pointed out that:

> A volatile mismatch exists between the organization and curriculum of middle grades schools and the intellectual and emotional needs of young adolescents. (1989, pp. 8–9)

To eradicate the mismatch, the Task Force made eight recommendations intended to "vastly improve the educational experiences of all middle grade students" (p. 9). The Task Force called for middle grade schools that:

1. Create small communities for learning where stable, close, mutually respectful relationships with adults and peers are considered fundamental for intellectual development and personal growth. The key elements of these communities are schools-within-schools or houses, students and teachers grouped together as teams, and small group advisories that ensure that every student is known well by at least one adult.
2. Teach a core academic program that results in students who are literate, including in the sciences, and who know how to think critically, lead a healthy life, behave ethically, and assume the responsibilities of citizenship in a pluralistic society.
3. Ensure success for all students through elimination of tracking by achievement level and promotion of cooperative learning, flexibility in arranging instructional time, and adequate resources (time, space, equipment, and materials) for teachers.
4. Empower teachers and administrators to make decisions about the experiences of middle grades students through creative control by teachers over the instructional program linked to greater responsibilities for students' performance, governance committees that assist the principal in designing and coordinating school-wide programs, and autonomy and leadership within sub-schools or houses to create environments tailored to enhance the intellectual and emotional development of all youth.
5. Staff middle grades schools with teachers who are expert at teaching young adolescents and who have been specially prepared for assignment to the middle grades.
6. Improve academic performance through fostering the health and fitness of young adolescents, by providing a health coordinator in every middle grades school, access to health care and counseling services, and a health-promoting school environment.
7. Reengage families in the education of young adolescents by giving families meaningful roles in school governance, communicating with families about the school program and student's progress, and offering families opportunities to support the learning process at home and at the school.
8. Connect schools with communities, which together share responsibility for each middle grades student's success through identifying service opportunities in the community, establishing partnerships and collaborations to ensure students' access to health and social services and using community resources to enrich the instructional program and opportunities for constructive after-school activities. (pp. 9–10)

None of these eight recommendations represented revolutionary ideas about how best to educate young adolescents. In fact, many of the essential ideas undergirding the recommendations had been reflected in the literature about middle grades education for decades prior to the report's publication. So why has the report been seen as such a watershed for middle grades education?

First and foremost, in *Turning Points*, the Task Force on the Education of Young Adolescents brought the best thinking and research about educating young adolescents into one place, providing a framework of ideas that deeply resonated with practitioners and parents. Second, the Task Force's roster read like a who's who list from the fields of educational improvement, adolescent health, psychology, government, and community-based organizations. When these people talked, through the medium of the report itself, the education community listened. Finally, Carnegie Corporation itself provided both an imprimatur of integrity and a launching pad for drawing attention to an age group that Joan Lipsitz could still legitimately describe as "growing up forgotten" (1980).

Overview of the Turning Points 2000 Recommendations

Turning Points 2000 offers seven recommendations for improving middle grades schools (pp. 23–24).

1. Teach a curriculum grounded in rigorous, public academic standards for what students should know and be able to do, relevant to the concerns of young adolescents, and based on how students learn best. This recommendation is a more complicated vision than that described in the original report of *how* to decide *what* to teach.
2. Use instructional methods designed to prepare all students to achieve higher standards and become lifelong learners. Note that *Turning Points 2000* divides the original report's recommendation to "teach a core of common knowledge" into two recommendations: one focused on curriculum and assessment and the other on instruction.
3. Staff middle grades schools with teachers who are expert at teaching young adolescents, and engage teachers in ongoing, targeted professional development opportunities. This recommendation takes the notion of preparing teachers a logical step further by including advocacy for quality professional development for teachers already in the classroom.
4. Organize relationships for learning to create a climate of intellectual development and a caring community of shared educational

purpose. As the original report pointed out, relationships matter for adolescents' learning, so creating a climate of support is crucial.

5. Govern democratically, through direct or representative participation by all school staff members, the adults who know the students best. This recommendation goes the 1989 version one better by insisting that all decisions be focused relentlessly on ensuring success for every student.
6. Provide a safe and healthy environment as part of improving academic performance and developing caring and ethical citizens. This recommendation reinforces the original report's focus on the connection between health and learning and more fully explores the complexity of an environment that is both safe and healthy.
7. Involve parents and communities in supporting student learning and healthy development. *Turning Points 2000* combines the recommendations regarding parent and community involvement into one recommendation, recognizing that families and communities are inextricably intertwined in their impact on and support of young adolescents.

The Turning Points Vision

The Task Force that wrote the original *Turning Points* report agreed on a vision to guide their work and the document itself (1989, p. 15). The vision is of a 15-year-old who has been well served during the middle grades. That 15-year-old would be:

1. An intellectually reflective person.
2. A person en route to a lifetime of meaningful work.
3. A good citizen.
4. A caring and ethical individual.
5. A healthy person.

That same vision is central to *Turning Points 2000*, and success is defined in the book as achieving that vision. Ensuring success for *every* student is the overarching goal that drives the Turning Points approach to improving schooling for young adolescents.

The congruence between the visions that drive each book is apparent. What may not be so obvious are the important differences in thinking about how that vision plays out reflected in *Turning Points 2000*'s overarching goal: ensuring success for every student.

The original report included, as one of the eight recommendations, a call for ensuring the success of all students. The specifics tied to that recommendation, e.g., eliminating tracking and allowing for more flexible use of instructional time, would be crucial to fulfilling that objective but far from sufficient. In the decade since the first report's publication, states and schools across the country demonstrated that ensuring success is not a spoke on the wheel of improving middle grades schools; it is the wheel's hub.

Another critical change appears in a vocabulary choice. In *Turning Points 2000*, we include a small change in wording from the original book, a small change that speaks volumes about what we had learned since the original report was released. The phrase "ensuring success for *all* students" has been changed to "ensuring success for *every* student."

From "all" to "every" may not seem like much of a difference; don't they essentially mean the same thing? We learned, however, that the two words do not mean the same thing in theory or practice. "All" was, and is, too often interpreted as "most" or "the majority" or "all except those kids who are (take your pick) limited-English-proficient or in special education or from some particular type of family situation or community. When we say "every" in *Turning Points 2000*, we mean *every* student, not some or many or the majority but every single student. Every is a term used in special education, where the attention is most definitely on the individual student, not the aggregate (Margaret McLaughlin, personal communication, January 15, 2000). Every student counts, and every student should have the real opportunity and support to achieve the Turning Points vision.

The Systemic (or Ecological) Nature of Turning Points Implementation

In his recent book, *Reinventing Middle Schools* (2001), the book's editor Thomas S. Dickinson notes,

> The majority of middle schools are in some stage of arrested development—where the middle school concept has not been completely implemented, or where it was once implemented and has now grown static and unresponsive.... What misleads many middle level educators, seduces may be a better word, is the feeling that some is better than none. What they are not acknowledging, what the movement has not made a forceful argument over, is that the original [middle school] concept is a totally integrated ecology of schooling, the likes of which we have never seen before. (p. 4)

Dickinson makes a powerful case for the systemic, ecological nature of what is often called "the middle school concept," and points out the factors that have led to arrested development in middle grades schools across the country. His argument meshes well with the case we make in *Turning Points 2000* for the systemic, interactive nature of the book's recommendations.

We describe the seven recommendations in *Turning Points 2000* as design elements in a system, with each element having an impact on every other element and on ensuring every student's success (see Figure 1). To explain further, a system is:

> ...an interacting and interdependent group of practices that form a unified whole. Each recommendation, or element, within the system influences the expression and reinforces the impact of other elements.... [T]he design system we describe, composed of the seven *Turning Points 2000* recommendations for improving middle grades schools, must be dealt with holistically, systemically, to ensure success. (Jackson & Davis, 2000, p. 27)

In the years since the original *Turning Points* report's publication in 1989, educators, researchers, and consultants have devoted considerable resources—financial, human, etc.—to investigating, writing about, implementing, and providing training on *each* of the eight recommendations the report outlined. The interaction between those recommended practices and the impact those practices together have on achieving the Turning Points vision (read: fulfilling the middle school concept) have not, by and large, been investigated in any great depth.

The attention to the parts and not the whole may be partly attributable to the lack of discussion in the original report about how the recommendations interact, an omission that Tony Jackson began correcting in speeches

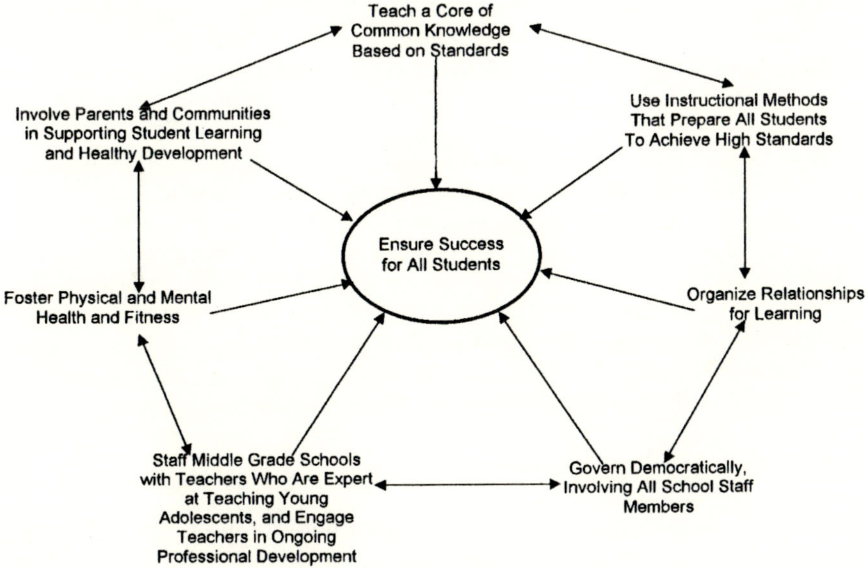

Figure 1. The *Turning Points 2000* design.

beginning in the early 1990s. At every opportunity, he pointed out that the original report's recommendations acted as a system in practice, though their systemic nature had not been explicitly described in *Turning Points.* It might also be due to the fragmented nature of American education, with the confusing overlaps, redundancies, and contradictions in policy and practice that have undermined other worthy efforts to improve schools (Tyack & Cuban, 1995). And, finally, perhaps the attention to the parts might be expected in a field where, despite the best efforts of thousands of people over the last century, the misunderstandings, prejudices, and biases about young adolescents and their educators have perennially made the middle grades the neglected stepchild of American education.

To pay attention to the whole would mean recognizing, planning for, and dealing with the interaction among the elements. Each element can either support, even accelerate, a move toward the goal of ensuring success for every student or serve as a drag on the ascent.

For example, as has been demonstrated repeatedly, when structural changes are put in place (e.g., establishing teams) but curriculum and instruction remain the same, student success is not even possible, much less attainable. The structural change is necessary to set the frame for other changes, but it is not sufficient without concomitant and complementary changes in everything else, including the seemingly toughest nut, what happens in the classroom. By the same token, parents and community members can reinforce and support changes in things like governance and access to health services or they can be a hindrance to those changes. In short, everything affects everything else.

In a speech on the day of the book's release, Tony Jackson and I acknowledged the difficulty in tackling everything at once:

> We have found over the past ten years that it is very difficult if not impossible to work to change all elements of the Turning Points design system at once. There needs to be a systematic approach to collecting data among the elements, setting priorities, and monitoring outcomes. So, rather than middle grades reform, which implies movement from bad to good, what actually happens in middle schools that are able to fundamentally improve student learning is a process of continuous improvement. (Jackson & Davis, November 3, 2000)

A Few Words about Depth and Detail

The first *Turning Points* report was a document totaling about 100 pages. Each of the eight recommendations appeared in a section, with each section consuming anywhere from two to seven pages. Though rich in vital information, detailed it was not. *Turning Points 2000* contains seven recommendations, each of which is fleshed out in a chapter. Each chapter ranges from 25 to 35 pages and delves much more deeply into what to do and, to the extent possible (short of a set of encyclopedias), how to do it. The first report served as a synopsis of vital ideas, meant to get everybody who cares about young adolescents, figuratively speaking at least, off the dime. The second report will hopefully serve as a more detailed guide to how to bring those vital ideas to life.

The next section of the chapter outlines the *Turning Points 2000* recommendations and contrasts those with the eight principles outlined in the 1989 report. A summary of the chapter titles (see Table 1) provides a quick synopsis of the differences and similarities between the structures of the two reports.

Table 1. Summary Comparison of *Turning Points* and *Turning Points 2000* Chapters

	Turning Points	*Turning Points 2000*
1.	Fateful Choices for Young Adolescents and the Nation	*Turning Points*: A Decade Later
2.	No equivalent chapter	*Turning Points 2000*: A Design for Improving Middle Grades Education
3.	Creating a Community for Learning	Curriculum and Assessment to Improve Teaching and Learning
4.	Empowering Teachers and Administrators	Designing Instruction to Improve Teaching and Learning
5.	Preparing Teachers for the Middle Grades	Expert Teachers for Middle Grades Schools: Pre-service Preparation and Professional Development
6.	Teaching a Core of Common Knowledge	Organizing Relationships for Learning
7.	Ensuring Success for All Students	Democratic Governance to Improve Student Learning
8.	Improving Academic Performance Through Better Health and Fitness	A Safe and Healthy School Environment
9.	Reengaging Families in the Education of Young Adolescents *and* Connecting Schools With Communities	Involving Parents and Communities
10.	Building a Future for Young Adolescents	Taking Action: Challenges and Opportunities

POINT TO POINT: *TURNING POINTS* AND *TURNING POINTS 2000* RECOMMENDATIONS

Curriculum, Assessment, and Instruction

Turning Points (1989) recommended that middle grades schools teach "a core of common knowledge," one that would prepare students to "think critically ... lead a healthy life, behave ethically and lawfully, and assume the responsibilities of citizenship in a pluralistic society" (p. 42). The original report's description of a "core," however, does not:

1. Reflect the ever-expanding nature of important knowledge.
2. Address the skills and habits of mind that young adolescents should acquire.
3. Account for the changing concerns of adolescents.
4. Incorporate the growing understanding of how students learn best. (Jackson & Davis, 2000, pp. 25–26)

In short, too often the interpretation of a "core" curriculum provided a loophole allowing for stasis and stagnation in the classroom. In trying to implement the Turning Points ideas, schools could profess their adherence to a core curriculum without ever significantly challenging or changing the content students were expected to learn.

Turning Points 2000 made several significant changes in its recommendation about curriculum. First, the book acknowledges the tremendous impact of the standards movement by calling for a curriculum grounded in agreed-upon standards for what students should know and be able to do. Standards were just beginning to gain attention when the first *Turning Points* was released. By the time *Turning Points 2000* was published, 49 of the 50 states had developed content standards in several subject areas (American Federation of Teachers, 1999).

Standards promote equity by setting the expectation that every student can meet or exceed high standards. To make that happen, students must have the support and the time required to take them from where they are individually to where the standards say they need to go. Ensuring that support means providing access to high-quality teaching, resources, and materials, in an atmosphere of high expectations for every student. Setting standards is not enough; students must have the real supports they need to reach those standards.

Second, *Turning Points 2000* recommends that curriculum be connected to young adolescents' concerns about themselves and the world. Without relevance, content is too often meaningless (and quickly forgotten) noise, to be memorized or ignored. With relevance, content helps create links,

links that students make from one key idea to another and links that students discern between what goes on inside the classroom and what is happening outside it. A curriculum relevant to the concerns of students also builds on their diversity rather than ignoring it.

Curriculum should reflect the latest research about how students learn best. The burgeoning arena of so-called "brain research" and a recent synthesis from the National Academy Press of significant research in several different fields focused on how people learn (Bransford, Brown, & Cocking, 1999) are just two of several information sources that should be influencing what is taught and how.

Finally, in an echo of the original report, *Turning Points 2000* calls for an integrated curriculum. An integrated curriculum crosses disciplines by using a broad-based concept, essential question, or theme, drawn from students' concerns, as its driving force. The integration should support and provide for deep and rich investigation of content, as described in the work of, for example, James Beane (1997), Pate, McGinnis, and Homestead (1997), and Stevenson and Carr (1993).

Turning Points touches briefly on using assessment as an instructional tool and alludes to instructional practices in the recommendation on ensuring success for all students (see pp. 48–50 and pp. 52–54). However, the 1989 report says little about the crucial connections between and among decisions about curriculum, assessment, and instruction. Just as in the overall ecological model of schooling for young adolescents described previously, these three elements of teaching and learning affect and are affected by one another in both theory and daily practice.

To confront this interaction, the notion of "backward design" provides a framework for the chapter in *Turning Points 2000* on curriculum and assessment and the chapter that follows on instruction. The elements of backward design include:

1. Deciding what to teach—the curriculum based on the foundations of standards, relevance, and research described above;
2. Deciding how to tell if the students have learned, in other words, what assessment strategies to use.
3. Deciding what instructional strategies will engage students deeply in learning and prepare them to demonstrate what they have learned.

This framework is called "backward" design as an acknowledgment that, traditionally, educators have often begun their planning with instruction, targeting favorite activities, then matched the activities to curriculum, often as defined by the textbook, before considering assessment. Backward design provides a frame for analyzing the connections among curriculum, assessment, and instruction and a tool for planning in anticipation of and in response to those connections.

In backward design, curriculum decisions are inextricably tied to decisions about assessment. As both Turning Points reports contend, assessment should be designed to provide ongoing, useful feedback, to both students and teachers, on what students have learned. This feedback should be used to improve teaching and learning, not just to audit performance. Effective assessment connects directly to curriculum and instruction, meshing perfectly with what students are intended to learn.

In *Turning Points 2000*, we recommend using a variety of assessment methods, ranging from formal to informal, in the same way a court of law accepts evidence ranging from circumstantial to tangible. Taken together the assessment methods should be sensitive to small gains, should consistently monitor learning—daily is best—and should lead to corrections in instruction as needed.

As alluded to above, the original *Turning Points* has little to say about how to improve instruction. In *Turning Points 2000*, instruction gets the attention due "the daily bread of classroom life" (p. 63), and is defined as the tools, strategies, lessons, and activities teachers and students use to learn. To be effective, instruction must mesh with three other aspects of teaching and learning:

1. The curriculum.
2. The assessments students will use to demonstrate their knowledge and skills.
3. The needs, interests, and concerns of students themselves.

Instruction is incredibly complex. The three connectors to instruction vary from classroom to classroom and even from day to day. No single model for organizing instruction has captured how to deal with that complexity. So, *Turning Points 2000* describes three useful models for organizing instruction, each of which draws on the current state-of-the-art knowledge about how people learn. Then, Jackson and I offer our own recommendations for organizing instruction, drawing on the key shared traits of the three models and adding a few ideas that appear either in only one model or not in any of them.

The first model, authentic instruction, focuses primarily on instruction's connection to curriculum, specifically the intellectual quality of what and how students learn (Newmann, Marks, & Gamoran, 1995; Newmann, Secada, & Wehlage, 1995; Newmann & Wehlage, 1995).

The second model, WHERE, is an instructional design tool developed by Grant Wiggins and Jay McTighe (1998). The acronym WHERE stands for:

1. Where are we headed.
2. Hook the students.
3. Explore the subject and equip the students.
4. Rethink our work and ideas.
5. Evaluate results.

This model, in keeping with the expertise of its creators, highlights instruction's connection to assessments.

Carol Ann Tomlinson describes differentiated instruction, the third model, as teachers becoming "students of their students" (1999, p. 2). Differentiated instruction provides students with many different avenues for learning based on:

1. Their diverse levels of readiness, their entry points to learning particular skills and ideas.
2. Their diverse interests, the things and ideas for which they have a built-in passion or curiosity.
3. Their diverse learning profiles—how they learn best, which can be shaped by their cultural background, past experiences, learning style, etc.

In a differentiated classroom teachers are, according to Tomlinson, "diagnosticians, prescribing the best possible instruction for their students" (1999, p. 2). This model is by far the most detailed of the three, and obviously concentrates most on instruction's connections to the students.

Our recommendations for instruction in *Turning Points 2000* reflect:

1. Themes apparent in all three models.
2. What we learned from the experiences of practitioners and the best research on how people learn/
3. Our recognition that we could not prescribe specific instructional strategies and still honor the complex nature of instruction. As Ruth Mitchell and her colleagues put it, "No single teaching strategy is good or bad as such—it is either useful or not useful." (1995, p. 89)

Expert Teachers for the Middle Grades

In its recommendation on staffing middle grades schools with teachers who are expert at teaching young adolescents, *Turning Points* (1989, pp. 58–60) got one major thing right and another wrong. The report absolutely was right about the need for middle grades teachers prepared specifically for teaching in middle grades classrooms. As Dickinson pointed out in his recent description of factors leading to the arrested development of middle schools:

> In essence, many middle schools have been operating outside their original purpose as schools for young adolescents, adding an unenviable burden of undergraduate education to their agenda, often at the expense of developing the school and its understanding of the complex concept of a middle school. This form of arrested development is played out in middle schools across the country every time a school year begins and new teachers—educated with either elementary or secondary preparation, but not middle level—are introduced. (Dickinson, 2001, p. 7; McEwin & Dickinson, 1996)

Pre-service programs designed specifically for prospective middle grades teachers would ensure that many more young adolescents are taught by those who understand them and the schools intended to serve them best.

Though it got it right regarding teacher preparation, *Turning Points* got it wrong in recommending endorsements as an effective tool for increasing the numbers and strength of middle grades teachers (p. 60). *Turning Points 2000* actually reverses position on endorsements, citing them as one of the least effective methods for ensuring specialized preparation for middle grades teachers. Most endorsements are not required, and many amount to little more than two or three courses that may or may not focus directly on middle grades teaching. Without the requirement to get an endorsement or worthwhile substance within the coursework required, few prospective teachers choose to obtain endorsements. After a few years, universities that did offer the coursework may drop it entirely, and state licensing agencies eventually drop the endorsement "because it's not being used." That history of pseudo failure for specialized middle grades preparation colors the landscape for any future efforts to move toward real, substantive programs and licenses.

Turning Points 2000 also goes the original report one better, so to speak, by calling for distinctive, not overlapping, licensor for the middle grades. Overlapping licenses—for example a state with a K-8, 6–9, and 7–12 set up—send the clear message that the middle grades license is relatively unimportant, since those trained in either elementary or secondary can also teach in the middle grades. However, expecting teachers educated to teach five-year-olds to teach young adolescents is akin to expecting history teachers to teach algebra.

The current nearly nationwide teacher shortage has been used as yet another excuse for not establishing middle grades licensor. Granted, emergencies may require districts and schools to allow teachers to temporarily teach outside their area of expertise, but emergency contingencies should not become permanent, acceptable policy for the teachers of young adolescents. As Kati Haycock recently argued, "Just like I don't want an emergency credentialed surgeon to operate on my child, I also don't want an emergency credentialed teacher to teach my child" (Education Development Center, 1999).

The new report goes beyond teacher preparation to describe the whole of a teacher's career as a seamless continuum of learning and development, always focused on improving student learning. Steps along the continuum include high-quality teacher preparation programs, initial certification and licensor, mentoring and induction programs within middle grades schools, and ongoing professional development, perhaps leading to certification by the National Board for Professional Teaching Standards.

The attention to professional development in *Turning Points 2000*, a topic virtually ignored in the 1989 report, marks the growing recognition that teachers, and by extension students, benefit from ongoing opportunities to build their knowledge and skills. To be effective, professional development must be:

1. Focused on improving results in relation to student learning.
2. Based on standards for what both students and teachers should know and be able to do.
3. Embedded in the daily work of teachers (Sparks, 1997).

Relationships for Learning

Perhaps the most frequently implemented recommendation from the original *Turning Points* was the first on the list, "creating small communities for learning" (p. 9). The attention to developing teams of teachers and students, as one piece of creating such communities, actually has been seen as a basic feature of middle schools for decades, long before the 1989 report or its successor.

In the twelve years since the first report was released, research and practice have confirmed that teams are an absolutely essential characteristic of high performance middle grades schools (e.g., Erb & Stevenson, 1999; Pounder, 1998; Guiton et al., 1995). What *Turning Points 2000* tries to do is understand why that is so, and what the critical characteristics of effective teams are.

The "why" appears to boil down to an essential truth about motivation to learn: relationships matter. Research demonstrates that students' relationships at school, both with teachers and with their peers, significantly impact the degree to which they are motivated and engaged (Eccles & Midgley, 1989; Lee & Smith, 1993). In like manner, teachers are more motivated to invest energy in their students when they know those students well (George & Alexander, 1993).

One of the characteristics of effective teams' appears to be related to size. Data from the Kellogg Foundation's Middle Start initiative show, for example, that teams of 4–5 teachers and from 90 to 125 students more often engage in the kind of educational practices that are linked to positive outcomes for students than larger teams (Flowers, Mertens, & Mulhall, 2000). Over the past decade, practitioners have increasingly recognized the value of even smaller "partner teams" of two or three teachers with 40 to 75 students.

Another crucial characteristic of effective teams is the availability of regular common planning time. The original report mentioned common planning time, and research and practice in the last decade have demonstrated its importance, providing yet another example of one element in a complex system impacting on all the others. Sufficient common planning time—totaling 3–4 hours a week—helps teachers more effectively integrate curriculum across disciplines, coordinate their instruction and assessments, involve parents, and communicate with health and other services (Erb & Stevenson, 1999, pp. 47–48).

Governance

Both *Turning Points* and *Turning Points 2000* call for empowering teachers and administrators to make decisions regarding the education of young adolescents, as the adults who know those students best. As the 1989 report argued:

> Deeply ingrained in our society is the belief that individuals can be trusted to make decisions for themselves and for the common good. This belief is the bedrock of the democratic political system. Increasingly it is being adapted in business and industry as a means of involving employees in decisions about their work. Business managers find that empowering workers to decide on a wide range of issues affecting them increases their productivity, improves the quality of their work, and heightens their morale. (p. 54)

The logic of more democratic decision making in business also applies to education. Practitioners know the idiosyncrasies of individuals and school cultures and can respond appropriately to those idiosyncrasies in ways that those further away from the daily reality of school life could not anticipate, much less make policy to dictate. More to the point, collaborative decision making among the adults who know students best is essential to improving teaching and learning.

Turning Points 2000 outlines the kinds of structures that need to be in place for middle grades schools to operate democratically, which include student and teacher teams feeding information into and implementing decisions made by leadership teams and other schoolwide working groups. The key point here is that these structures are not for the purpose of "school-based management" because managing a school, no matter how efficient, does not automatically lead to improvement of the organization. Instead, democratic school governance should be the system by which the adults and young people in the school proactively identify problems or opportunities that need to be addressed to enable every student to achieve success, and to design and evaluate solutions to those problems on an ongoing basis. In effect, it is a strategic mix of collaborative decision making and action research.

The structure and processes of democratic governance described in *Turning Points 2000* require, and, in turn, foster a high level of distributed leadership within the school. That said, as *Turning Points* noted, effective middle grade schools must have strong, competent principals. What has changed since the original report outlined the potential roles of a building administrator is our understanding of how a middle school principal successfully leads a school community toward improved student performance.

Just as democratic governance is not about school-based management, an effective principal is not a school manager in the traditional sense of a lone figure controlling virtually all aspects of the school. The most effective principals are those that take on the role of "principal change agent," individuals who set the intellectual and interpersonal tone of the school and shape the organizational conditions that promote distributed leadership.

A key part of that role is to keep the schools' eyes on the prize, to keep a relentless focus on improving the quality of teaching. An effective principal does that by being in close touch with teachers on a daily basis and making sure that teachers have the resources and professional development opportunities they need to keep getting better.

Finally, while *Turning Points 2000* makes the point that a middle grades school acts as a kind of system of interacting design elements, that system is itself embedded within larger systems that make a huge difference in what a school is able to do. The original *Turning Points* also made reference to the district and other macro systems within which a school must operate, e.g., communities, states, and the nation.

Turning Points 2000 goes into more detail about what districts can do to effectively support improvement efforts, e.g., providing schools with autonomy to make decisions crucial to teaching and learning including decisions related to personnel, budget, and curricular resources.

The local district is responsible for holding middle grades schools accountable for enabling every student to meet or exceed high academic standards. District, and state, accountability systems should be forces to drive improvement in instruction in middle grades schools in the same manner that teacher-developed assessments should drive instructional practice. To be clear, *Turning Points 2000* calls for standards-based accountability not narrowly construed test-based accountability. The difference between these two approaches can make an enormous difference in not only *what* young adolescents learn but *how* they learn. There is a great deal more work that needs to be done to make district and state accountability systems as supportive of middle grades students' learning as they must be to fulfill the Turning Points vision.

Safe and Healthy School Environment

In pointing out that students must be healthy to learn, *Turning Points* concluded that:

> Middle grades schools must accept significant responsibility, and be provided sufficient resources, to ensure that needed health services are accessible to young adolescents and that schools become health-promoting environments. (1989, p. 61)

Turning Points 2000 concurs with that conclusion, and goes into more detail about how to make middle grades schools health promoting. A safe and healthy school environment is actually yet another system composed of elements that interact with, and transform, each other. Critical components of a healthy learning environment include:

1. A challenging curriculum and supportive instruction that promote every student's learning, as described in the *Turning Points 2000* chapters on curriculum, assessment, and instruction.
2. Close, personal relationships between teachers and students and among students, as described in the chapter on organizing relationships for learning.
3. Students' feelings of connectedness to school, as described in the chapter on organizing relationships and the chapter on democratic governance.

All of these components are crucial to better health outcomes for students, though the book deals with them in chapters without the word "health" in the title. In the chapter on safe and healthy schools, *Turning Points 2000* highlights other important actions middle grades educators can take to strengthen the learning climate and support the healthy development of young adolescents.

For example, a healthy learning environment must be safe. The strength of relationships between teachers and students and among students can support safety, as can effective classroom management and discipline policies. What makes such policies effective? The policies are proactive, not reactive, and help students move toward intrinsic motivation for appropriate behavior. Effective policies rely on collaboration and on shared responsibility among everyone in the school for sustaining a climate for learning.

Young adolescents are deeply engaged in figuring out who they are in relation to others. The patterns of friendliness, or antipathy, they develop in these years will become the foundation for lifelong attitudes and behaviors, for good or ill. Middle grades schools can do a lot to affect those attitudes and behaviors, beginning with eliminating inequities for minority-group adolescents. Inequities take many forms in schools, but one of the most damaging, and unfortunately most pervasive, is tracking students by perceived ability level or past performance. Tracking is a manifestation of differing expectations, and, as research has shown repeatedly, leads to differing opportunities to learn and differing outcomes (e.g., Braddock, Dawkins, & Wilson, 1995; Oakes, 1985; Tucker & Codding, 1998). Like the 1989 report, *Turning Points 2000* calls for the elimination of tracking, and is joined in that call by the National Forum to Accelerate Middle Grades Reform's recent policy statement on student assignment (2001).

When conflicts do occur among students, peer mediation and conflict resolution programs can defuse those conflicts and teach anger management and communication skills. And, when students experience difficulties academically, socially, or otherwise, a student support team can generate ideas and a plan for helping overcome those difficulties.

Health education was not mentioned explicitly in the original Turning Points, though it was implied in the notion of creating a health-promoting environment. Health education can help prevent or at least minimize the onset of risky behaviors, and helps students make appropriate choices to safeguard their health more generally. Middle grades health education should reflect high standards for what students should know and be able to do, leading toward "health literacy," defined as having the capacity to obtain, interpret, understand, and use health information and services.

Regular exercise is critical to adolescents' immediate and future physical and mental health, yet nearly half of 12 to 21-year-olds are not vigorously active on a regular basis. And, in the push to strengthen academics, sometimes there's been an unfortunate trade off, swapping time in gym class and other organized opportunities for physical activity for more time in the "core" classes. That trade off poses a real danger which must be avoided to ensure young adolescents' develop healthy habits that will in turn support their healthy growth.

Access to appropriate health services is the major problem in adolescent health. As noted above, given the link between the health of young adolescents and their success in school, *Turning Points 2000* concurs with the original report in stating that middle grades schools should accept significant responsibility for ensuring that health services are accessible to students. How that is done can vary tremendously from school to school, depending on students' needs, the mix of available health-related resources, and community values regarding the appropriate way to meet the needs of young adolescents.

Involving Parents and Communities

Turning Points 2000 combines the two recommendations regarding parent and community involvement outlined in *Turning Points* into one recommendation, recognizing that families and communities are intertwined. A central theme here is that schools, families and communities must collaborate to establish a kind of "force-field" of high expectations and key resources to support young adolescents' success.

As Anne Henderson and Nancy Berla pointed out in 1994, "the evidence is now beyond dispute: When schools work together with families to support learning, children tend to succeed not just in school but throughout life. In fact, the most accurate predictor of a student's achievement in school is not income or social status, but the extent to which the student's family is able to:

1. Create a home environment that encourages learning,
2. Express high (but not unrealistic) expectations for their children's achievement and future careers, and
3. Become involved in their children's education at school and in the community. (p. 1)

Research also shows that when parent involvement is absent or declines, students are less engaged and successful in school, are less self-reliant, and have lower self-esteem and social competence (Steinberg, Brown, & Dornbusch, 1996).

Turning Points 2000 outlines four key aspects of effective parent-school relations. First, as James Comer has recommended for many years, we advocate establishing continuity between home and school. Children can avoid a sense of divided loyalty when they know that their parents and teachers understand and respect each other, share similarly high expectations for their achievement, and communicate on an ongoing basis.

Second, continually monitoring student work is one of the primary ways in which parents make the importance of school clear. A third important area for school-home collaboration is engaging students in out-of-school opportunities for learning. Such activities allow students to explore new ideas and social issues, develop strategies for solving problems and be exposed to a variety of role models. Research has shown that high-achieving students spend at least 20 hours a week outside school engaged in constructive formal and informal learning (Clark, 1990). Schools can help point out the opportunities, and parents can arrange for and supervise their children's participation.

Finally, parents can play a crucial role in assisting a school's effort to improve. Their input is essential in assessing needs, analyzing promising approaches, and developing and implementing a plan of action.

For all middle grades schools, the surrounding community is an enormous resource for educating young adolescents. The community potentially serves, as Anne Lewis and Anne Henderson pointed out, "as an extension of the classroom filled with skilled and knowledgeable residents with teaching and learning agendas and capacities of their own" (1998, p. 45).

Service learning is "curriculum-based community service that integrates classroom instruction with community service activities" (National Center for Education Statistics, 1999, p. 3). As did the original report, *Turning Points 2000* recommends that schools incorporate service learning into the academic program. *Turning Points* stated "early adolescence offers a superb opportunity to learn values, skills, and a sense of social responsibility important for citizenship in the United States" (p. 45).

Career education provides opportunities for students to see what their "lifetime of meaningful work" might look like, guiding their choices in school and giving them a clear sense of the level of effort and knowledge required for life in the 21st century world of work. Young people should be exposed to a variety of work roles through job shadowing, field trips, youth-run enterprises, and visits to work places, in addition to the more traditional books, journals, videos, and the Internet.

Parents of children in all socioeconomic brackets often are not home during the so-called "witching hours"—from 3:00–8:00 p.m.—to provide transportation or supervise activities at home. In recent research in Michigan, the Center for Prevention Research and Development at the University of Illinois found that students home alone each week for three or more consecutive hours, even if only on one to two days, had significantly worse results on all student outcomes than those students who were home alone less than three hours at a stretch (Mertens & Flowers, 1998).

After-school programs are increasingly seen as a way of preventing young people from engaging in unhealthy or dangerous behaviors during the witching hours, reinforcing and extending classroom learning, and providing rich opportunities for young people to explore their own creativity. *Turning Points* referenced the many supports that youth-serving and other community-based organizations can provide. In fact, community-based organizations can be key partners in developing and staffing after-school programs, joining forces with schools and parents to support the fulfillment of the Turning Points vision inside and outside of school walls.

CONCLUSION

Turning Points 2000 is an in-depth examination of how to improve middle grades education. *Turning Points* provided a very valuable framework for middle grade education that resonated deeply with practitioners. *Turning Points 2000* offers much more "flesh on the bone" to guide practitioners in efforts to implement the model, drawing on the latest research and the best practice, and tackling many issues and topics not dealt with in the original (e.g., curriculum standards, reading instruction, professional development, etc.).

With the exception of the endorsement, as noted above in reference to teacher certification, very little in *Turning Points 2000* directly contradicts the original report. That congruence is striking considering how much has changed in the field of education broadly, and in middle grades education more specifically since 1989. Sue Swaim, executive director of the National Middle School Association, has described middle grades education as being at a crossroads. In the face of the standards movement and accountability systems focused on high-stakes testing, middle grades schools are asked to make a false choice between academic excellence and developmental responsiveness (for further discussion, see Anfara & Waks, 2000). At the same time, piecemeal efforts to implement "the middle school concept" have failed, and are doomed to continue failing because such efforts ignore the ecological, systemic design essential to success.

Those failures have been highlighted in the popular press in the last 18 months, in which the middle grades have been described as "an intellectual wasteland" (Bradley & Manzo, October 4, 2000, p. 3) and "the weak link" (*USA Today*, December 4, 2000, p. 26A). The more optimistic metaphor that we use in *Turning Points 2000* to describe the state of middle grades education is that we are halfway up the mountain and still climbing. A quote from the final chapter of the book highlights the celebration of what has been accomplished and the drive to do more.

> This book should stand as an affirmation of the enormous progress in improving middle grades education that has been made not only in the past decade but also since the movement began many years earlier. It is also a statement—

not to the community of middle grades educators, but from that community—that we are not satisfied with the quality of middle grades education today and we know that there is a great deal of difficult work ahead. And that we accept and are capable of meeting the challenges we face. (p. 219)

REFERENCES

American Federation of Teachers. (1999). *Making standards matter, 1999: An annual fifty-state report on efforts to raise academic standards.* Washington, DC: Author.

Anfara, V.A., & Waks, L. (2000, November). Resolving the tension between academic rigor and developmental appropriateness. *Middle School Journal, 32*(2), 46–51.

Beane, J. (1997). *Curriculum integration: Designing the core of democratic education.* New York: Teachers College Press.

Braddock, J.H., II, Dawkins, M.P., & Wilson, G. (1995). Intercultural contact and race relations among American youth. In W.D. Hawley A.W. Jackson (Eds.), *Toward a common destiny: Improving race and ethnic relations in America,* pp. 237–256). San Francisco: Jossey Bass.

Bradley, A., & Manzo, K.K. (2000, October 4). The weak link: In today's standards-driven environment, the middle grades are under pressure to produce—and are ill-equipped to deliver. *Education Week,* p. 3.

Carnegie Council on Adolescent Development. (1989, June). *Turning points: Preparing American youth for the 21st century.* The Report of the Task Force on Education of Young Adolescents. New York: Carnegie Corporation of New York.

Clark, R.M. (Spring, 1990). Why disadvantaged students succeed: What happens outside school is critical. *Public Welfare,* 17–23.

Dickinson, T.S. (Ed.). (2001). *Reinventing the middle school.* New York: Routledge-Falmer.

Eccles, J. S., & Midgley, C. (1989). Stage—Environment fit: Developmentally appropriate classrooms for young adolescents. In R. Ames & C. Ames (Eds.), *Research on motivation in education. Volume 3: Goals and cognitions* (pp. 139–186). Orlando: Academic Press.

Education Development Center. (1999, October). *Improving teacher preparation programs: A briefing paper for funders.* Prepared for the W.K. Kellogg Foundation. Newton, MA: Author.

Erb, T.O., & Stevenson, C. (1999). From faith to facts: *Turning points* in action—What difference does teaming make? *Middle School Journal, 30*(3), 47–50.

Flowers, N. Mertens, S., & Mulhall, P. (2000). What makes interdisciplinary teams effective? *Middle School Journal, 31*(6), 53–56.

George, P.S., & Alexander, W.M. (1993). *The exemplary middle school* (2nd ed.). Orlando, FL: Harcourt Brace & Co.

Guiton, G., Oakes, J., Gong, J., Quartz, K.H., Lipton, M., & Balisok, J. (1995). Teaming: Creating small communities of learners in the middle grades. In J. Oakes & K.H. Quartz (Eds.), *Creating new educational communities. 94th yearbook of the*

National Society for the Study of Education (pp. 87–107). Chicago: University of Chicago Press.

Henderson, A.T., & Berla, N. (Eds.). (1994). *A new generation of evidence: The family is critical to student achievement.* Washington, DC: Center for Law and Education.

Jackson, A.W., & Davis, G.A. (2000). *Turning points 2000: Educating adolescents in the 21st century.* New York: Teachers College Press.

Jackson, A.W., & Davis, G.A. (2000, November 3). *Turning points 2000.* Keynote address, National Middle School Association annual conference, St. Louis, Missouri.

Lee, V.E., & Smith, J.B. (1993, July). Effects of school restructuring on the achievement and engagement of middle-grade students. *Sociology of Education, 66,* 164–187.

Lewis, A.C., & Henderson, A.T. (1998). *Building bridges—Across schools and communities: Across streams of funding.* Chicago: Cross City Campaign for Urban School Reform.

Lipsitz, J. (1980). *Growing up forgotten.* New Brunswick, NJ: Transaction Books.

McEwin, C.K., & Dickinson, T.S. (1996). *Forgotten youth, forgotten teachers: Transformation of professional preparation of teachers of young adolescents.* Background paper prepared for the Middle Grade School State Policy Initiative (MGSSPI), Carnegie Corporation of New York.

Mertens, S.B., & Flowers, N. (1998, November). *The effects of latchkey status on middle-grades students: New research findings.* Paper presented at the annual conference of the National Middle School Association, Denver, CO.

Mitchell, R. Willis, M., & the Chicago Teachers Union Quest Center. (1995). *Learning in overdrive: Designing curriculum, instruction, and assessment from standards.* Golden, CO: North American Press.

National Center for Education Statistics. (1999, September). *Service-learning and community service in K-12 public schools.* (NCES 1999-043). Washington, DC: US Department of Education.

National Forum to Accelerate Middle Grades Reform. (2001, February). *National Forum policy statement: Student assignment in the middle grades: Towards academic success for all students.* Newton, MA: Education Development Center.

Newmann, F.M., Marks, H., & Gamoran, A. (1995). Authentic pedagogy: Standards that boost student performance. *Issues in Restructuring Schools, 8,* 1–11.

Newmann, F.M., Secada, W.G., & Wehlage, G.G. (1995). *A guide to authentic instruction and assessment: Vision, standards, and scoring.* Madison: Wisconsin Center for Educational Research.

Newmann, F.M., & Wehlage, G.G. (1995). *Successful school restructuring: A report to the public and educators by the Center on Organization and Restructuring of Schools.* Madison: University of Wisconsin, Center on Organization and Restructuring of Schools, School of Education, Wisconsin Center for Education Research.

Oakes, J. (1985). *Keeping track: How schools structure inequality.* New Haven, CT: Yale University Press.

Pate, E., Homestead, E., & McGinnis, K. (1997). *Making integrated curriculum work: Teachers, students, and the quest for a coherent curriculum.* New York: Teachers College Press.

Pounder, D.G. (1998). *Restructuring schools for collaboration: Promises and pitfalls.* Albany: State University of New York Press.

Sparks, D. (1997, September). A new vision for staff development. *Principal,* 21–23.

Steinberg, L., Brown, B.B., & Dornbusch, S.M. (1996). *Beyond the classroom: Why school reform has failed and what parents need to do.* New York: Simon and Schuster.

Stevenson, C., & Carr, J.F. (Eds.). (1993). *Integrative studies in the middle grades: Dancing through walls.* New York: Teachers College Press.

Tomlinson, C.A. (1999). *The differentiated classroom: Responding to the needs of all learners.* Alexandria, VA: Association for Supervision and Curriculum Development.

Tucker, M.S., & Codding, J.B. (1998). *Standards for our schools: How to set them, measure them, and reach them.* San Francisco: Jossey Bass.

Tyack, D., & Cuban, L. (1995). *Tinkering toward utopia.* Cambridge, MA: Harvard University Press.

USA Today Editorial Board. (2000, December 4). Middle school fixes fall short. *USA Today,* p. 26A.

Wiggins, G., & McTighe, J. (1998). *Understanding by design.* Alexandria, VA: Association for Supervision and Curriculum Development.

ABOUT THE AUTHORS

Laura Van Zandt Allen is Associate Professor of Education at Trinity University in San Antonio, Texas. She completed her degree at the University of Arkansas with an emphasis in middle level education. Since that time she has published numerous articles and chapters related to middle level education. She now directs the middle level grades teacher education program at Trinity University.

Vincent A. Anfara, Jr. is Assistant Professor of Educational Leadership and Policy Studies at Temple University, Philadelphia. He received his Ph.D. in Educational Administration from the University of New Orleans in 1995. Before entering the professorate he taught for 23 years in both middle and high schools in Louisiana and New Mexico. He is the Coordinator of Temple University's Middle School Endorsement and has published widely on advisory programs, the middle level principalship, and middle school reform. He co-edited the book, *Voices from the Middle: Decrying What Is; Imploring What Could Be*, with Peggy Kirby (2000). Currently he serves as the Program Chair/President-elect of AERA's Research in Middle Level Education SIG and as a member of the National Middle School Association's Research Committee.

Dave F. Brown is Professor of Elementary Education at West Chester University in Pennsylvania. He co-authored a book titled, *What Every Middle School Teacher Should Know* (2000, with Knowles). He recently completed another book, *Becoming a Successful Urban Teacher* that is intended for preservice and inservice teachers.

Kathleen M. Brown is Assistant Professor of Educational Leadership at the University of North Carolina at Chapel Hill. She received her Ed.D. in Educational Administration from Temple University, Philadelphia, Pennsylvania in 1999. Her research interests include middle level education, effective instructional leadership that links theory and practice, establishing an ethic of care and community in school bureaucracies, and qualitative research methods. She brings to the university 15 years of teaching, administrative and research experience.

Gayle A. Davis is Assistant Professor at the University of Georgia. A graduate of the University of North Carolina at Chapel Hill, Davis served as National Director of Carnegie Corporation's Middle Grade School State Policy Initiative. Davis is co-author, with Anthony Jackson, of *Turning Points 2000: Educating Adolescents in the 21st Century.* She is also chair of the National Middle School Association's Research Committee, and serves on the National Forum to Accelerate Middle Grades Reform.

Kimberly J. Hartman is Assistant Professor at the University of North Carolina at Charlotte where she teaches graduate and undergraduate middle grade courses. She is a former middle grades interdisciplinary facilitator and teacher and has worked with middle schools in urban and suburban school districts.

Charlotte Kritzer is Distinguished Teacher in Residence at California State University, San Marcos. She taught language arts at martin Luther King, Jr. Middle School in Oceanside. She holds a M.A. in Literacy Education from CSU San Marcos. Her research interests include multicultural literature, democratic teaching, and middle level education.

Maureen Lorimer is a doctoral student at Claremont Graduate University and Adjunct Faculty Member in the College of Education at California State University, San Marcos, where she teaches learning and instruction and supervises student teachers. She has been a middle school educator for 15 years in the public schools of Southern California.

Janet E. McDaniel is Professor of Education at California State University, San Marcos, where she serves as Coordinator of the Middle Level teacher Education Program. She received her M.Ed. and Ph.D. from the University of Washington. Her research interests include middle school teaching and teacher education.

Robert J. Mahar is Associate Professor of Curriculum and Instruction at Temple University, Philadelphia. He received his Ed.D. in Elementary Education from Wayne State University, Detroit. His professional career began as a middle school teacher in Connecticut and has served as a consultant with schools in Boston, Detroit, Atlanta, Las Vegas and Philadelphia. Presently he is co-coordinator of Temple University's Middle School Endorsement.

Rebecca Mills is Professor of Secondary Education at the University of Nevada, Las Vegas where she currently serves as Vice President for Student Life. Her research focuses primarily on middle level teaming and its impact on the classroom teacher.

Juan Necochea is Associate Professor of Education at California State University, San Marcos. He received his Ph.D. from the University of California at Santa Barbara. Juan has conducted research in the areas of school reform, policy implementation, leadership, labor relations, character education, bilingual education, and diversity.

Richard Powell is Associate Professor of Education at the University of Colorado at Denver. He has experience at the middle school and high school levels. He received his Ph.D. from Indiana University at Bloomington and has experience teaching at UNLV and Texas Tech University. He has published three textbooks and his middle level publications have focused on integrative curriculum theory.

Kathleen Roney has recently completed her doctoral studies in Educational Administration at Temple University, Philadelphia. Currently she serves as a member of the Senior Administration at Rosemont College in Pennsylvania. Her career spans 25 years as a teacher and administrator in urban and suburban middle level, secondary, and graduate schools in Maryland, New York, and Pennsylvania.

Laurie Stowell is Professor of Education at California State University, San Marcos, where she teaches language and literacy courses in middle level and elementary teacher education programs. Her M.A. in reading and Ph.D. are from The Ohio State University. Research interests include children's literature, writing, critical pedagogy, middle level literacy and assessment.

Elizabeth Useem is Director of Research and Evaluation for the Philadelphia Education Fund. Prior to that, she served as Director of Teacher Education at Bryn Mawr College and Haverford College and as Associate Professor of Sociology at the University of Massachusetts at Boston.

INDEX

A

B

C

D

E

F

G

H

I

J

L

M

N

P

S

T

W

Printed in the United States
926900005B